A CHARLIE BROWN RELIGION

GREAT COMICS ARTISTS SERIES

M. Thomas Inge, General Editor

A CHARLIE BROWN RELIGION

EXPLORING THE SPIRITUAL LIFE AND WORK OF CHARLES M. SCHULZ

STEPHEN J. LIND

UNIVERSITY PRESS OF MISSISSIPPI / JACKSON

www.upress.state.ms.us

Designed by Peter D. Halverson

The University Press of Mississippi is a member of the Association of American University Presses.

Manufactured in the United States of America

First printing 2015
∞
Library of Congress Cataloging-in-Publication Data

Lind, Stephen J., author.
A Charlie Brown religion : exploring the spiritual life and work of Charles M. Schulz / Stephen J. Lind.
pages cm. — (Great comics artists series)
Includes bibliographical references and index.
ISBN 978-1-4968-0468-6 (hardback) — ISBN 978-1-4968-0469-3 (ebook) 1. Schulz, Charles M. (Charles Monroe), 1922–2000—Religion. 2. Schulz, Charles M. (Charles Monroe), 1922–2000. Peanuts. 3. Comic books, strips, etc.—United States—Religious aspects. I. Title.
PN6727.S3Z765 2015
741.5'6973—dc23

2015021087
British Library Cataloging-in-Publication Data available

Display font Frente H1 courtesy of www.frente.cc

THIS BOOK IS YOURS.

—SL

CONTENTS

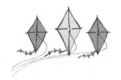

GOOD GRIEF.

AN INTRODUCTION AND AUTHOR'S NOTE

I WAS SITTING AT A HEAVY WOODEN TABLE SIFTING THROUGH BOXES OF OLD photos and letters at the Charles M. Schulz Museum and Research Center several years ago when the archive door's latch clicked open, signaling that someone was going to interrupt the silence of shuffled papers. While I was engrossed in reading notes that Charles Schulz had received over decades of work (the letter writers who knew him well called him "Sparky"; the ones who didn't misspelled his name as "Schultz"), I was always happy to have a new face come in, as it gave me another chance to learn about Sparky and his *Peanuts* properties. I must admit, though, that I was a little taken aback to see that Jeannie Schulz, Sparky's widow, was walking through the door. I was even more shocked when she said that she had come down to introduce herself to me!

It would not be long before I would know Jeannie and the five Schulz children to be wonderfully gracious supporters of my research, for which I am so deeply thankful. Soon after we first shared introductions and as I was still working to get my sea legs back, Jeannie started casually telling a story about one of the franchise operations. At one of the high points in her story, I involuntarily interjected "Good grief!" Now, it's entirely normal to audibly respond when someone is telling you a story, but my mind immediately started spinning. While I use the phrase quite often, I couldn't help but wonder, "Can I say 'Good grief!' to Charles Schulz's widow?! Is this allowed?!" I don't believe she noticed. If she did, it thankfully wasn't a deal breaker. After all, I am far from the first person to be influenced by the remarkable work of the late Charles Schulz.

Etching "Good grief!" and "security blanket" and the off-screen teacher's "wah wah wah wah" into the cultural vocabulary are merely the tips of the iceberg that is Schulzian success. Over his life, Schulz received the highest of awards, including Emmy, Peabody, and Congressional Gold Medal honors, along with two honorary doctorates and a Pulitzer Prize nomination. America's Apollo 10 lunar module was even named Snoopy. The command module was named Charlie Brown. With 17,897 *Peanuts* strips in newspapers, seventy-five (and counting) animated titles, and multi-million-dollar consumer product licensing (not including the countless unlicensed knockoffs and parodies), Charles Schulz clearly found a voice that engaged the American and global publics as he drew *Peanuts* for half of a century. Routinely ranking in the top five of *Forbes* magazine's "Top Earning Dead Celebrities" list (number three in 2013, only behind Elvis Presley and Michael Jackson), Charles Schulz and his massive *Peanuts* brand continue to make an impact in contemporary culture.

Many often wonder why Schulz's work has resonated so strongly and for so long. While there is no algorithm for such an impact, there are a few important elements that he mastered along the way. First, his work is simply funny. Sometimes it's complexly funny. Schulz sought to draw funny pictures for the newspapers to make readers chuckle, and he succeeded. His artwork is deftly crafted in such a way that with the smallest jot of India ink he could give Snoopy's face the most ridiculous of expressions, bringing a wide grin to the reader's face. Second, his work is authentic. Charles Schulz spoke from an original, often introspective voice, primarily addressing an adult readership in his comics (though the animated specials would turn slightly more toward family and child audiences). He took clever, even heavy and provocative thoughts from his own mind and put them on paper in a deceptively simple way that the cliffhanger strips of his childhood would never imagine. His was never the voice of factory output but rather one of sincerity. Readers could trust his voice. They could believe it.

Third, his work is open-ended. Not only did he have a lot of white space in his comics and often very little action (sometimes an entire strip would be comprised of a single leaf falling to the ground, something you would never find in a *Tarzan* comic), but he often asked readers to ponder deeper ideas, connecting their own understandings with those of Charlie Brown, Lucy, Peppermint Patty, and the rest. The individual is invited to view *Peanuts* through his or her own experience. Japanese culture, for instance, has gravitated toward Snoopy so strongly that Masuhiko Hirobuchi has written several Japanese texts trying to wrestle preconceived notions of *Peanuts* cuteness out of the grips of Japanese habits in order for the Japanese reader to see even more of Schulz's ideas.[1] Those ideas often rested on the universal human experiences of grief, joy, loss, and hope. Sometimes, he tapped into the social commentary of the day; Charlie Brown once even obliquely asking Lucy to consider what many 1960s readers may have seen as the threat of nuclear annihilation.[2] At other times, as will be the primary focus of this book, he invited readers not only to chuckle but also to think for a moment about diverse spiritual issues, including prayer, Scriptures, end-times theology, and church denominationalism.

Over the years, readers would pick up on these cues in simple and robust ways. While Clark Gesner would pen the most-ever performed Broadway musical *You're a Good Man, Charlie Brown* (taken up by almost every school and college troupe across the country at one time or another), in which Schroeder sings from Matthew 4:4 that "man does not live by bread alone," Bert V. Royal would write his own unauthorized and dark off-Broadway play entitled *Dog Sees God*, in which angsty teenage versions of the *Peanuts* cast movingly struggle to deal with issues of life and death.

Readers and viewers from diverse stations in life have been powerfully impacted by the franchise. When battling through a traumatic brain aneurysm as a small child, for instance, a Snoopy-hugging-Woodstock piggy bank the hospital staff gave young Scott Alan Blanchard became so meaningful that it inspired him later in life to donate to his local children's hospital and other research centers.[3] For Ann Elizabeth Downard, Snoopy was a respite from a traumatic childhood of foster care. "Having a Snoopy plush of my own meant everything to me," Downard described. "He hugged me, listened to me, and was my best friend. I could always count on him to be there for me."[4] As this book will demonstrate, such connections are not only the privilege of children, but countless adults as well, especially when related to the meaningful issues of religious faith that Schulz dared include in his work.

Peanuts is not just about a silly dog that can be discarded as mere pop culture. There is no such thing as "mere pop culture," and *Peanuts* is much more than silly . . . and about more than just a dog. Media research has routinely demonstrated that such properties can carve deep, lasting grooves in our society. In television research, for example, Gerbner, Gross, Morgan, and Signorielli have described television as a "centralized system of storytelling"[5] that is characterized by a comparatively restricted set of depictions. There simply does not tend to be a lot of diversity or complexity on television (which other researchers have demonstrated is quite true of religion). The more we watch these stereotypes of what it means to be poor or middle-class or white or Asian or a woman—or what it means to be religious—the more we get drawn in by the "gravitational process"[6] of cultivation and start to see these ideas as "mainstream"—as "normal." With the average American watching more than five hours of television a day,[7] it is worth noting when a franchise, even one featuring a funny little dog, bucks tradition and gives voice to ideas that studio executives think should not be broached. At one important moment on television, this included a child reciting from Scriptures the "real meaning of Christmas." These spiritual ideas are important to us. Giving voice to them impacts us.

Comics research has also demonstrated the otherwise obvious (but often overlooked) truth that the more you read a certain set of ideas, the more you are likely to think about them. A study by Berkowitz, Parker, and West demonstrates this, finding that school children who had read a comparatively aggressive comic book (*Adventures of the Green Berets*) were more likely to choose aggressive words in a posttest than their peers who read a neutral comic book (*Gidget*).[8] The exposure to an idea does not necessarily lead to direct imitation, of course, but we are primed to see it more and to consider it further. In a culture where we are often told not to talk about politics or religion in public, it matters that millions of readers pick up a beloved comic strip during their morning routine and find quotes from Scripture and questions about God. It is an important corrective to our culture of spirituality anxiety.

While I may be one of the few who chooses to adopt Schulz's double-period punctuation to give a slightly extended pause to a sentence,[9] I know I am not alone when I say that *Peanuts* has and likely always will be a personal favorite of mine. I also had the privilege of growing up in a loving Christian home, and my faith remains important to me today. For the writer of a biographic history, such connections should not supplant open-minded, well-studied approaches to complex subject matter, nor should they be wrongly eschewed as incongruous liability, but they should instead be leveraged for the insights and energies they can provide. Over the years of research, I had the pleasure of being able to chuckle out loud as I sifted through the archives, and I also had the opportunity to quietly reflect on deep questions of faith. One often led to the other. There is little more gift that a researcher could receive from his subject matter.

Biographic histories are stories as much as they are chronicles of fact, with all the benefits and challenges that come with each. This requires that the author exhibit proper care over the material that so many friends, family members, and dusty-but-lively archival boxes have entrusted him or her with. I trust that this examination of Sparky's life is a thought-provoking and enjoyable addition to the Schulzian literature, one that reflects the lived experiences of those who worked, laughed, sighed, and pondered alongside the cartoonist. That class, however, extends well beyond Charles Schulz's immediate family and coworkers, thanks to the massive global circulation of his *Peanuts* empire. In this book, I have endeavored to give historical space to the role of the millions of readers and viewers who made their own recursive impact on *Peanuts*. As you will see, their responses to Sparky's funny little pictures are a powerful force in the history of the franchise and will undoubtedly continue to be. In particular, readers from religious communities played a significant role in Schulz's work gaining momentum and in it eventually including sacred spiritual content.

This book concerns the thematic thread of religion in Sparky's life and work. It does not have much to say about his love for hockey, golf, or chocolate chip cookies (all of which were important in various ways to him), but the book has plenty to say about the importance of Charles Schulz's faith. The reader of this book should not see such a focus to be an indication that Schulz's life was entirely consumed and driven by religious thought. It wasn't. Yet such thought was deeply interesting and personally important to him, with a breadth and depth of context and performance that more than justifies a complete volume devoted to its history.

One might see this book as weaving together answers to two primary questions—"Was Charles Schulz a religious man?" and "Is there really much religion in *Peanuts*?" The simple answer to both of those questions is "Yes." But the simple answer is rarely the truest answer in history, and you may find that the questions themselves need challenging as we search for thicker answers. Schulz himself worried that simple explanations would not suffice in matters of spirituality, for there are too many "howevers" needed for such issues. This book will explore and explain much of Schulz's beliefs in the mysteries of faith, and those "howevers" will play an integral role (perhaps they should play more of a role in all of our contemporary discourse on religion).

Charles Schulz has been labeled a fundamentalist Christian and an atheist. Some have argued that both labels are correct and that Schulz simply suffered a crisis of faith somewhere along the way. Maybe he was just too depressed to have faith. Or perhaps he found secular enlightenment. Such explanations are not only incorrect, they are too simple. Charles Schulz's life was rich, and his faith in the mysteries of God was personal. He, like any artist (like any human), was a multifaceted, complex person. His spiritual beliefs were no different.

Charles Schulz and Charlie Brown both had a surprising amount to say on the topic of religion. Their voices were studied, open, and personal. They were often humorous, not seeking to grind any axes . . . but then again, maybe the difference in those options is a little too simple as well. Maybe what Charles Schulz and Charlie Brown have to say on religion is a little more interesting than that. As was the case with some of Sparky's most daring strips, you, the reader, will get to decide.

A CHARLIE BROWN RELIGION

Peanuts © Peanuts Worldwide LLC. Used with permission. July 9, 1969.

DO YOU EVER WONDER IF GOD IS PLEASED WITH YOU?
HE JUST HAS TO BE!
SCHULZ

Sparky's mother, Dena, and his father, Carl, stand with him. Mid-/late 1920s. Courtesy Pat Swanson.

1

CHURCH PILLARS

"I accepted Jesus Christ by gratitude."

—CHARLES M. SCHULZ

CHARLIE BROWN LEANED AGAINST THE TOP OF THE BRICK WALL. BY HIS SIDE, Lucy folded her arms on the steady surface as the two stared off, thoughts weighing heavy on their minds. "You know what I wonder?" Charlie Brown asked, resting his head in his hands. "Sometimes I wonder if God is pleased with me." Lucy listened, her expression unchanged, lost in the magnitude of Charlie Brown's concern. "Do you ever wonder if God is pleased with you?" he asked, turning to look at her with eyes that somehow knew such grief, failure, innocence, and hopefulness. Lucy paused to consider his question. It was no small matter. Was God pleased with her? Her eyes closed resolutely as she turned to Charlie Brown. With a wide grin she answered, "He just has to be!"[1]

Such questions were not commonplace for Charles Schulz growing up. As a small child, the boy known as "Sparky" to friends and family spent very little time interacting with any such weighty spiritual matters. He attended a few Sunday school classes with the neighborhood kids one summer, and a few of his mother's Norwegian kin had brought certain beliefs over from the old country, but Sparky's was not a theologically pondersome childhood. His mother enjoyed the hymns of the church, but his parents were not active in a local congregation. Carl, his father, was a civically popular barber in St. Paul, Minnesota, friendly with any local minister who happened to find himself in for a haircut. On Sundays, though, Carl did not make his way to a pew in a local

Dena stands with her young son, smiling and bundled for winter. Mid-/late 1920s. Courtesy Pat Swanson.

church. Instead, when time allowed, the hardworking man would find himself trolling for walleye in Mille Lacs. At other times, he would take his wife, Dena, and their son, Sparky, to visit the boy's extended maternal family at the Borgen farm over in Wisconsin. Almost always, Carl would study the Sunday comics with his son.

Sparky was a rather shy boy, an only child with an acute sense of aloneness, growing up in an era of strident church denominationalism. Carl and some of their extended family were from nominally Lutheran backgrounds. A few of his mother's Halverson kin maintained bits of their Scandinavian superstitious worries about visiting spirits and the dangers of good fortune. His great-uncle, Hallie Halverson (his mother's paternal uncle who would also occasionally host the family on Sundays at his farm in Wisconsin), was christened as a baby at the Rush River Lutheran

Church and confirmed as a teenager. Hallie donated much of his estate to the church; his name was commemorated on the back of church pews, and many Halversons were buried in the adjoining cemetery.

Sparky's Grandma Halverson had even given Sparky his own small copy of the Bible for Christmas. The book, printed by the Midwestern Whitman Publishers, a company specializing in children's books and greeting cards, was inscribed to "Charles Schulz." Though he enjoyed the company of his grandma, the sacredness of the book meant little to the young Sparky. Hockey, baseball, and the funny pages were more meaningful to him.

Born on November 26, 1922, as a child Sparky quickly became skilled with a pencil and paper, able to draw a respectable Popeye while still only a youngster at Richard Gordon Elementary School. "Someday, Charles, you're going to be an artist," his kindergarten teacher told him after seeing him deftly draw a creative Midwestern winter scene, complete with an unexpected palm tree (his mother had just read a letter from a relative in Needles, California, describing the tall trees).[2] With a father who studied the comics section as his primary literary endeavor, talking about his favorites with his young son as they walked home from the barbershop in the evenings, perhaps Charles Schulz just might fulfill the teacher's prophecy. The boy had, after all, been nicknamed "Sparky" at birth when an uncle said he looked like *Barney Google* comic strip character Spark Plug.

In high school, Sparky grew increasingly shy as he failed algebra, Latin, English, and junior-year physics. His parents were supportive, but found themselves to be of little help when it came to his studies. When he completed high school, his mother suggested he take a correspondence art course—the one with the "Draw Me" ads in the magazines. He took her up on the idea and enrolled. Sitting at the table, he began to learn what it meant to hone a craft, and he took the first steps toward his own career in drawing.

In 1943, he was drafted into a more dangerous calling—World War II. He would serve until 1945, and was deployed to the European theater to help defeat the Nazi terror. "I worry about almost all there is in life to worry about," he once said. "I place the source of many of my problems on those three years in the army. The lack of any timetable or any idea as to when any of us would get out was almost unbearable."[3] The most devastating part of the war, though, happened to Sparky before he could even leave Minnesota. His mother had been struggling for several years with a sometimes debilitating illness, later revealed to be terminal cervical cancer. "I used to wake up at night and hear her down the hall crying in pain," he remembered.[4] As Sparky reported for duty, Dena had little strength left in her.

While she was sick, Carl called upon a preacher friend who frequented his barbershop, the Reverend George Edes. Edes visited Dena, praying and sharing Scriptures. He was the pastor at the local Merriam Park Church of God, a small church only a mile from the Schulzes' home. Carl did not have a close relationship with any local Lutheran ministers, and had quickly come to trust Edes during Dena's last days. He tried to attend the pastor's services when possible. Knowing that Dena enjoyed hymns, Reverend Edes continued to visit and minister to her, once asking Bernetta Nelson from his congregation to join him, singing the music of the church in the apartment the Schulzes rented above Carl's barbershop.

On February 28, 1943, Sparky said goodbye to his mother, knowing it may be the last time he would do so. "Well, goodbye, Sparky," his mother said to him. "We'll probably never see each other again."[5] He had to report to the nearby Fort Snelling that evening. She died the next day. Reverend Edes conducted the funeral. Bernetta sang hymns.

While Sparky was away at war, Carl continued to occasionally attend the church. As a Church of God congregation, it was easy for Carl to visit, despite being new. The church was earnest and down to earth, not pompous or detached, and it was not interested in recreating the denominational borders that kept many other religious bodies from interacting with one another. "It's a non-denominational movement, and I think the message that it had," Sparky later explained, ". . . is that you did not have to join a denomination. By your belief you were already a follower of the Way. You were already a member of what the New Testament called the Church of God."[6] The Church of God characterized itself as a "movement," not a "denomination," seeking to unify believers in the most basic beliefs of Protestantism—the wisdom of Christ's teachings, the sacrifice of His death, and the miracle of His divine resurrection. The Holy Spirit would help guide one's study of the Bible, not denominational bylaws.

Many Midwestern ministers often spent only a small number of years with any given congregation, though, and Edes was soon succeeded by Frederick G. Shackleton, a young man the same age as Sparky. Visiting home briefly on furlough, Sparky met the new pastor and found someone with whom he could chat and play golf. "We became friends at once," Shackleton described.[7] Redeployed, Sparky kept in touch by letter, including drawings of his military life for his new pastor friend. His European tour escaped the worst horrors of World War II, though, so Ping-Pong games were the most exciting sketches Shackleton would receive. When he returned home in late 1945, after being spared an Asian Pacific tour by Japan's surrender, a grateful Sparky once again enjoyed spending time with Fred and his wife, Doris. "He was a regular at church," remembered the pastor, "although he had not yet received Christ as his Savior. We talked a lot about being a Christian."[8]

Like so many who returned from war, Sparky was striving to find a new normal. He had never had much attraction to formal theology, something largely absent in his childhood home, but he began to feel comfortable with the Merriam Park group, nestled in their small building at 330 North Prior, across from the community park. They were a friendly and modest group who enjoyed their Bible study and their fellowship. As a "holiness" group of Protestant believers, they did not smoke, drink, curse, or tell crude jokes—all things that Sparky had always naturally avoided. As he saw it, they were simply antithetical to his personality. "I like the niceties of language," he would say,[9] adding on another occasion, "We are creatures of habit. I never wanted to be in the habit of having to have a drink."[10] Though Sparky was not yet convinced by their spiritual beliefs, he grew increasingly comfortable with each service he made it to.

It was not long before Shackleton accepted a new post away from the Merriam Park group; in 1946, he took a teaching position at Anderson College,[11] a school founded by the Church of God in their headquarter city of Anderson, Indiana. He was soon replaced by Brother Marvin Forbes, an earnest, grounded, and middle-aged preacher in whom Sparky would soon find a trusted mentor and friend. When he first arrived, though, Sparky was busy trying to break into the cartooning business and was not yet ready to invest himself in the work of the church.

Sparky had recently landed a job teaching at Art Instruction, Inc.,[12] the correspondence school that taught Sparky himself how to draw through postal mail lessons and instructor feedback. While giving feedback to others, Sparky also worked twice a week to improve his own skills by taking night classes in life sketching at the Minneapolis School of Art. He was very skilled with a pen, able to create lines and letters quickly and fluidly, skills Art Instruction had imparted on him during his lessons years before.

With these skills, Sparky was able to taste a sample of the comic industry. In 1945, as his courtship to a Roman Catholic nurse named Virginia Howley[13] came to an end, Sparky was hired as a freelance letterer by Roman Baltes, the art director for the Roman Catholic comic book *Timeless Topix*, published by the Catechetical Guild Educational Society in St. Paul. "Catholics! They dog me. I can't get away from 'em," he joked with his army buddy Frank Dieffenwierth.[14] For over a year, he drew the narration and speech bubble letters for adventure stories of benevolent cardinals and fearless martyrs. That sort of religious story "doesn't really suit me," he told Dieffenwierth,[15] but he was happy to have the work. He not only lettered the balloons for the magazine's forty-eight-page English edition, but also its French and Spanish translations, despite not knowing the foreign words he was inking into the balloons. He often worked late into the night, taking an early street car to Baltes's office in the morning to drop off his work before heading back over to Minneapolis to work at Art Instruction. It could be exhausting, but he at least had his foot in the door.

Emotionally and socially, it was still a struggle being back from the war. "I know what it is to have to spend days, evenings, and weekends by myself," he admitted.[16] He shared a living space with his father, waited on job application responses from Disney and from Hearst without success, and got frustrated as local would-be employers could not tell a pen line from a brush stroke when he showed them his samples. Nightmares of the war plagued him some nights, causing him to wake up in a cold sweat.

On one Wednesday evening, shortly after Brother Forbes took his post at the Merriam Park church, Sparky was feeling particularly lonely. He decided to attend the midweek Bible study, walking the two-turn mile to church in the cool Minnesota air. The tiny church building had a tiny set of side rooms in which Marv, his wife, Ruth, and their three children lived. The church's basement was built partially above ground, and the congregation would climb a short flight of stairs opposite the ground floor's Sunday school area door in order to reach the sanctuary entrance. Turning from the sidewalk to begin up the steps, Sparky caught a glimpse of the lettering on the church's sign out front. It was fading. He did not yet know the Scriptures like the others, but he did know how to draw letters. He took a seat inside, and when the study and prayer service ended, Sparky approached Brother Forbes and offered to repaint the sign. Marv happily obliged the young artist, and as Sparky remembered decades later, "Thus began a friendship that has lasted over forty years."[17]

Sparky had begun building friendships with the several young adults near his age in the church group—Bernetta and Wally Nelson; Walt and Lois Ortman; Reverend Edes's son, William, and his wife, DoLores; and Harold and Elaine Ramsperger. Unlike what he may have expected of formal religion, Schulz never felt like an outsider. Comparatively, the Church of God was less formal, and he appreciated that. He was also forming new friendships across town at Art Instruction, but the two groups were different, never fully mixing for Schulz. At Art Instruction, he would socialize with a group that studied pen lines, listened to classical music, and played bridge. At church, he would build a community with a group that studied the Scriptures, sang hymns, and served the community. Through Art Instruction, he would establish the essentials of his art; through the Church of God, he would establish the essentials of his faith.

Sparky began borrowing book after book from Brother Forbes. The new friendships and the unexpectedly welcoming attitudes in the church had made it easier for his curiosities in theological thinking to be piqued. He became increasingly interested in what it might mean to study the character of God and what He may have done through this man called Jesus Christ. When Fred Shackleton had been his pastor, Sparky had seriously considered what his friend believed but had not yet embraced it as his own truth. Kneeling in prayer with Shackleton in the pastor's office, Sparky had stopped short. "I'm not ready for this," he said.

As Sparky became increasingly involved, Brother Forbes continued the friendship and support that Shackleton had shown, and Sparky enjoyed spending time in the basement parsonage, drinking root beer with the pastor and his family. "Our whole family welcomed him and we had many happy hours talking mostly about the Bible," Ruth remembered. "Sparky was eager to learn all he could about the Bible and the church." Their discussions rang true for Sparky. The hope of the Bible, especially as expressed in the open community of the Church of God, was a comfort and a guide with which he wanted to identify.

In 1948, Charles Schulz embraced the faith that his new Bible studies and his new church friends had exposed him to. "The more I thought about the matter during those studying times," Sparky later recalled, "the more I realized that I really loved God."[18] It was the Holy Spirit that would come and reveal the truth of God to a person, he once described, though he could not identify a moment of decision in his own experience, and it is likely that he was never baptized by the church.[19] "These convictions did not come upon me at any particular great moment of decision. I never went forward at a Sunday evening service. I cannot point to a specific time of dedication. I was just suddenly 'there,' and did not know when it happened that I arrived."[20]

He was grateful for what his pastors had shown him. "I'm convinced," Ruth remembered Sparky saying in one late night call to the Forbes home. "I see it, I see it! My conclusion is: the Church of God is it! No doubt about it."[21] To the Shackletons, Sparky wrote, "You two were instrumental in leading me to Christ, and I appreciate it. This makes us permanent friends, and I know I am getting the best part of the deal."[22] On July 17, 1948, Sparky wrote to Dieffenwierth, resolutely sharing with his friend the sincerity of his belief:

> Soon after we all got home, and were all busy getting reconverted I got a letter from [a mutual friend]. He told me then that among other things he was an 'agnostic.' That I am glad to say is not what I have turned out to be. I wasn't a steady church goer when you knew me, but I did believe in God. My lack of formal religion was do [*sic*] merely to not knowing better. Now, however, I am right where I belong. I am a firm believer in Jesus Christ.[23]

To a reporter Sparky said in 1955, "Sooner or later every person has to give an answer to this question: Who is Jesus? You have to face up to it;

you can't avoid it and kick it around. It is how you answer that question that determines the course of your life. 'No man cometh unto the Father but by me.'"[24]

Years later, Sparky would describe his faith as intimately tied up with his time in the war. It had given him the context through which the witness of Shackleton and Forbes could open his heart to the working of the Holy Spirit. "I felt that God protected me and helped me and gave me the strength to survive," he explained.[25] "I accepted Jesus Christ by gratitude. I have always been grateful for the things the Lord has provided me with: good health, education, family, and the experiences of World War II which have now passed into history."[26] For a twenty-five-year-old who had been raised as an only child, who had attended his mother's funeral much too early in life, and who had survived a worldwide war, the grace of God through Christ was a very real comfort and source of security.

In the late 1940s, Sparky was also holding to the hope that came with incremental achievements in his pursuit of a career in comics. In February 1947, Baltes printed a full-page cartoon Schulz had drawn as a filler for *Timeless Topix*. The page consisted of four panels of gag cartoons and was entitled *Just Keep Laughing*. Schulz would have one more printed in the Catholic comic, and then on May 29, 1948, the *Saturday Evening Post* printed artwork that would prove to be tellingly Schulzian. With a simple and sure pen line and with significant white space, as was the custom of magazine editorial cartoon panels, Sparky drew a small boy scooted to the very edge of a chaise lounge, only to have his feet propped up on a footstool. The *Saturday Evening Post* would run a total of seventeen of Schulz's cartoons; one was reprinted in Czechoslovakia, one in London, and one in Milwaukee. The local *St. Paul Pioneer Press* newspaper had also begun running a weekly series of a strip Sparky had developed, called *Li'l Folks*, and the artist began to eye the possibility of syndication.

The successes came with increased financial security. The Minnesotan, however, had little interest in vain luxuries, leaving little risk that he would squander his reasonable pay on extravagancies. Instead, a portion of Sparky's earnings went into the church offering plate as his tithe.[27] Sparky also took it upon himself to use his modest income to write and pay for a weekly series of mini-articles to run in the "Church News"

CHURCH OF GOD

"A United Church for a Divided World"

On the question of church membership the united testimony of the New Testament Scriptures is decisive and beyond all controversy. "But now hath God set the members every one of them in the body, as it hath pleased him" (I Cor. 12:18). This body is the church. That is what Paul is treating on in this chapter, the New Testament church. And how do we become members of this institution? Here is the answer: "But now hath God set the members every one of them in the body," the church. He didn't leave a single one to be taken in by a preacher. This modern process of ministers' taking members into the church is absolutely without scriptural authority. There is no example anywhere in the New Testament where any apostle or primitive minister attempted to take members into the church.

Merriam Park Church of God

330 N. Prior Ave.

Sunday School 10:00 A. M.

Morning Worship 11:00 A. M.

Evening Worship 8:00 P. M.

CHURCH OF GOD

"A United Church for a Divided World"

The present reformation identified by the scriptural name "Church of God," does not claim exclusive right to the use of this universal name, but sincerely seeks to assume and maintain a universal attitude refusing to set up human creed barriers, denominational standards of its own, or any other boundries to separate itself from other real Christians . . . It is the purpose of this reformation to emphasize only those principles that will be conductive to a scriptural gathering together of all God's people into one universal fellowship and communion, where all truly regenerated believers in the world are fully recognized as already being members of the church of God.

May the omnipotent power of the Holy Spirit hasten this great work.

Merriam Park Church of God

330 N. Prior Ave.

M. L. Forbes Pastor

Sunday School 10:00 A. M.

Morning Worship 11:00 A. M.

Evening Worship 8:00 P. M.

Written and paid for by Sparky, these short weekly articles shared Church of God doctrine and the Merriam Park group's meeting times in the Saturday paid advertisement "Church News" section of the *St. Paul Dispatch*. June 4, 1949; June 11, 1949.

section of the *St. Paul Dispatch*, in which he explained the basic tenets of the Church of God's doctrine. Sitting in his Merriam Park Sunday school class and borrowing books from Brother Forbes, Sparky had grown significantly in his wisdom and knowledge of the Scriptures. He

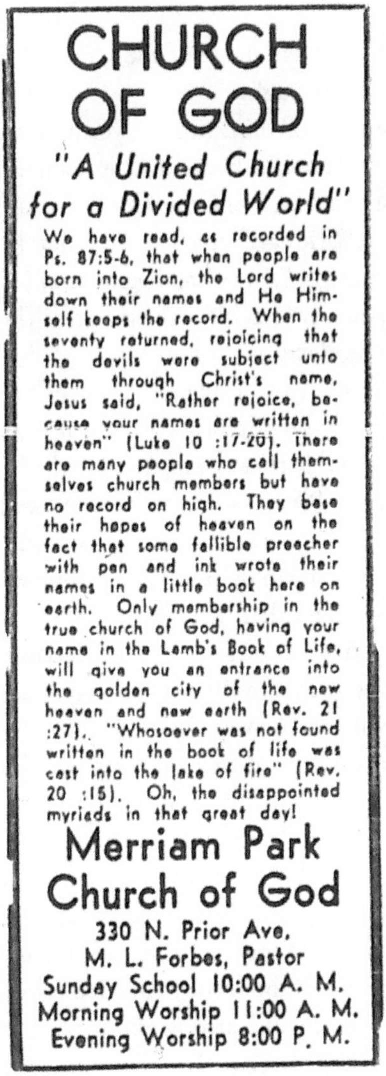

CHURCH OF GOD

"A United Church for a Divided World"

We have read, as recorded in Ps. 87:5-6, that when people are born into Zion, the Lord writes down their names and He Himself keeps the record. When the seventy returned, rejoicing that the devils were subject unto them through Christ's name, Jesus said, "Rather rejoice, because your names are written in heaven" (Luke 10 :17-20). There are many people who call themselves church members but have no record on high. They base their hopes of heaven on the fact that some fallible preacher with pen and ink wrote their names in a little book here on earth. Only membership in the true church of God, having your name in the Lamb's Book of Life, will give you an entrance into the golden city of the new heaven and new earth (Rev. 21 :27).. "Whosoever was not found written in the book of life was cast into the lake of fire" (Rev. 20 :15). Oh, the disappointed myriads in that great day!

Merriam Park Church of God

330 N. Prior Ave.
M. L. Forbes, Pastor
Sunday School 10:00 A. M.
Morning Worship 11:00 A. M.
Evening Worship 8:00 P. M.

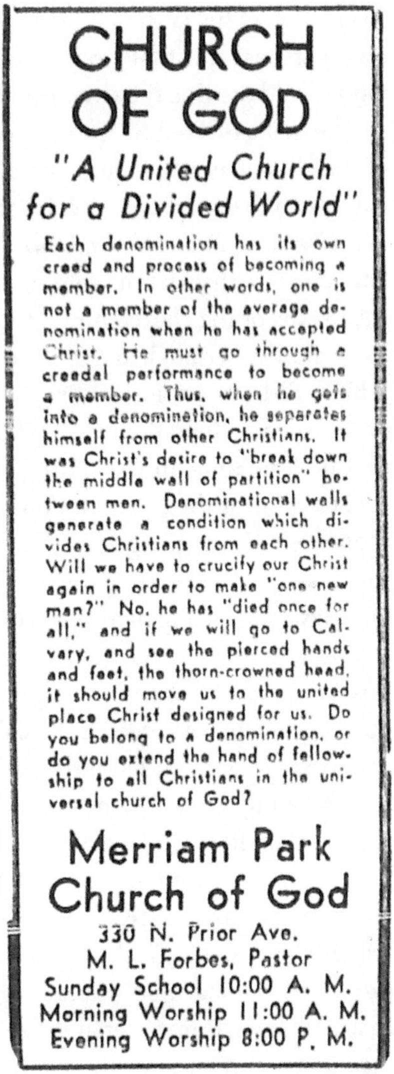

CHURCH OF GOD

"A United Church for a Divided World"

Each denomination has its own creed and process of becoming a member. In other words, one is not a member of the average denomination when he has accepted Christ. He must go through a creedal performance to become a member. Thus, when he gets into a denomination, he separates himself from other Christians. It was Christ's desire to "break down the middle wall of partition" between men. Denominational walls generate a condition which divides Christians from each other. Will we have to crucify our Christ again in order to make "one new man?" No, he has "died once for all," and if we will go to Calvary, and see the pierced hands and feet, the thorn-crowned head, it should move us to the united place Christ designed for us. Do you belong to a denomination, or do you extend the hand of fellowship to all Christians in the universal church of God?

Merriam Park Church of God

330 N. Prior Ave.
M. L. Forbes, Pastor
Sunday School 10:00 A. M.
Morning Worship 11:00 A. M.
Evening Worship 8:00 P. M.

Pleased with the outreach he was providing, Sparky even sent a clipping of his small articles to his former pastor, Fred Shackleton. June 25, 1949; July 5, 1949.

read Church of God leaders H. M. Riggle, F. G. Smith, and Charles E. Brown,[28] incorporating their wording liberally in his newspaper posts. He was fully committed to his spiritual beliefs, having developed what others in the church might describe as a "personal relationship" with

God through his faith in Christ, but Schulz had not yet developed his own personal spiritual voice. Instead, the language of the Church of God would provide the structure for his thought.

The voice of Fred Shackleton continued to inspire the young man of the church as well—quite literally. After Shackleton left St. Paul, he continued to lend his tenor voice to the Church of God radio program, *The Christian Brotherhood Hour*. "Sensational!" Sparky said when he heard one of Shackleton's solos over the air. Sparky had begun to enjoy the hymns of the church himself, especially Shackleton's originals. The Merriam Park group had a 1:30 p.m. Sunday time slot on Minneapolis's KBTR-FM 98.5 station and recruited pledges of one dollar a week in order to keep their airtime and regularly broadcast a Church of God production. Some in the church group felt that it was not worth the cost to sponsor the program on the air. "We are short on pledges, and sooner or later are going to be way behind," Sparky admitted to Shackleton in 1949. The church was actually growing in numbers and resources, but they were setting their sights on venues other than radio.

Soon, Sparky's career would enter a new venue as well—syndication. His *Li'l Folks* had been running for two years in the St. Paul paper, almost netting him a syndication deal with the Newspaper Enterprise Association. When that fell through, he continued to deliver his samples to publishing syndicates in person and by mail, taking the train to Chicago and sending packages off to New York. On one ride up to Chicago, he struck up a conversation with a man who introduced himself as a Methodist minister. "Yes, I sort of figured you were a minister," Sparky replied, immediately feeling as if he had said something possibly inappropriate, then having to explain what it was about the man's demeanor that had seemed ministerial.[29] Schulz was still learning about what it meant to overcome his own shyness and insecurities, a lesson from which he would never fully graduate.

It was one of his packages to New York that netted Schulz his life's big break. He had sent United Feature Syndicate two-tier combinations of his single-panel drawings, wanting to show the editors that they could get their money's worth from him. Jim Freeman, the editorial director in New York, thought there might be some potential in this hopeful artist and invited him to visit the city to talk. Sparky took the train to New York, arriving at the syndicate's office before anyone but the

Dena, holding a puppy, stands by her sister, Marion, and young son, Sparky. Mid-/late 1920s. Courtesy Pat Swanson.

receptionist. He left a new comic he had been working on at the desk and went out for breakfast. When he returned, the editors had already looked over his work and were ready to give him a contract for a comic strip.

They would call the strip *Peanuts*. Schulz himself hated the name, but he was clearly not in a position to negotiate. *Li'l Folks* was too close to Tack Knight's already-registered *Little Folks*, so Bill Anderson, the production manager, came up with a list of names which included "Peanuts," after the children's seating section called the "Peanut Gallery" on the then-popular *The Howdy Doody Show*. The executives liked it, figuring it was a good reference to the kids in the strip. Schulz believed it

Sparky's trusted dog, Spike, who had a vocabulary of nearly fifty words, including potato, shakes Sparky's hand. 1930s. Courtesy Pat Swanson.

lacked dignity and that readers would confuse it as one of the characters' names. The executives assured him it was a title that would attract the interest of newspaper editors who might subscribe to the comic. "So, who was I, an unknown kid from St. Paul, to argue with them?" conceded Sparky.[30]

On October 2, 1950, Sparky's first *Peanuts* strip ran in seven newspapers across the country. Sitting by the sidewalk with Patty, Shermy watched as a smiling boy walked down the street. "Well! Here comes ol' Charlie Brown!" Shermy declared. "Good ol' Charlie Brown. . . . Yes, sir!" As the boy walked by, Shermy concluded, "Good ol' Charlie Brown . . . How I hate him!" In the *Washington Post*, Sparky's first *Peanuts* strip ran across the page from the "Give-Aways" classifieds ads, including one ad for a "mixed beagle, male, good with children." Sparky's own comic strip beagle would appear in rudimentary form in the strip two days later and would have his own zany bond with the *Peanuts* children. He would certainly be good for the strips' success. By 1952, the strip had gained enough popularity to warrant Schulz writing extended Sunday strips and the syndicate licensing a paperback book anthology.

As immensely exciting as it was to be a syndicated cartoonist with a company that would actually honor his contract, working for the big Eastern syndicate was not actually Sparky's first choice for employment. Not only had he unsuccessfully applied for work as an artist with the Walt Disney company, he had also set his sights on doing work for the church. He had reached out to the president of the Gospel Trumpet Company, the publishing arm of the Church of God in Anderson. President Steele C. Smith and Harold L. Phillips, the editor, had to turn down the eager cartoonist. Like many religious groups, the Church of God was still trying to sort out how they might use the various and increasingly popular mass entertainment forms in their church publications. It would not be long before many churches embraced Schulz's work, but for the time, they simply had no place for his talents. "I would have been very happy to have accepted some sort of job with the Gospel Trumpet Company. I think it would be the greatest thing in the world to be able to associate daily with men like yourself," he wrote to a Church of God editor a few years later, adding, "but I guess we must labor in different fields."[31]

Sparky had finally achieved success in syndication. He had also achieved success in romance. He had been turned away by Virginia Howley and by the red-haired Donna Johnson, an Art Instruction accounting coworker and a very real inspiration for the little red-haired girl of later *Peanuts* comics. They had dated, mused about marriage, and Sparky had given her a Bible as a present. Donna, however, was ultimately more interested in her other suitor, Alan Wold, and the two were married.[32] Schulz had also fallen short in a brief courtship with a colleague in the Educational Department at Art Instruction, Judy Halverson (of her own unrelated Halverson clan), and Sparky's church friends were simply all married. It was with Judy's sister, Joyce, that Sparky found the promise of a family.

Joyce was a determined and keen counterpart to the often reserved but clever Schulz, and once the two began dating they progressed quickly toward marriage. Joyce had a one-year-old daughter, Meredith, whose New Mexico horse-wrangler father, Bill Lewis, had divorced Joyce after learning she was pregnant. Sparky quickly grew close to the young child, and on April 18, 1951, Joyce and Sparky married, making the three a family. They would later lie about their marriage timeline, citing 1949 as the year of their wedding in order to keep the secret of Meredith's birth and to protect their family from scandal. By the end of the decade, they would have four more children—Monte,[33] Craig, Amy, and Jill.

Brother Forbes was willingly on hand to officiate their small marriage ceremony at the home of Joyce's cousin. A church wedding may not only have been a point of contention for some in Joyce's family, given that it was her second wedding and that Joyce was not particularly religiously inclined, but Sparky's church circle was also on the verge of no longer having a building to call their home. Those he was closest with had chosen to leave their small Merriam Park location in St. Paul.

In pleasant weather, Bernetta and Wally Nelson—whose aunt, Ruth L. Rear, was the former minister at Merriam Park before Edes—would walk to church. Crossing over the Mississippi River on the wrought-iron Lake Street Bridge into St. Paul, the couple would walk another mile to the Merriam Park church to avoid being charged the driving toll both coming and going. Their own little building in St. Paul had housed the Olivet Congregational Church from 1888 to 1907 and, later, the Pentecostal Church of God in 1923 and 1924. The Merriam Park Church of God had begun there in 1926, and by 1930, members of the church were dreaming of expanding their movement to a second gathering place in Minneapolis. In 1942, a three-person committee led the church to purchase a lot at the corner of Thirty-eighth Avenue and Thirty-eighth Street in Minneapolis.[34] This would give them an outreach across the river, and would be a closer location for several in the group who longed for a shorter trek to the Sunday service.

In January 1951, serious talks about the split began, which the group called "Minneapolis Missions" meetings. On Thursday evenings, they would meet at the Barton and Nelson homes, even meeting for a time at the Howe School only ten blocks from their plot of land in Minneapolis. In July, they had laid enough plans to formalize their new endeavor.

Taking a measured step of faith, twenty-five people, including Reverend Marvin Forbes, gathered to officially incorporate the First Church of God in Minneapolis, according to the State of Minnesota, and left Merriam Park.[35] It was an exciting time for the small group, but Sparky was not present. He and Joyce had moved to Colorado.

They had married in April, and by May they were settled in Colorado Springs, a thousand miles from Sparky's dad and from his church. The young cartoonist was at home in Minnesota and likely did not want to repeat the beleaguered move to Needles, California, of his childhood, but Joyce did not have the Twin Cities ties he had. She had enjoyed the time around the ranch culture years earlier and both she and Sparky believed they would be better able to conceal the details of Meredith's birth from prying mid-century eyes if they made a fresh start elsewhere. Once they were in Colorado, though, Sparky and Joyce struggled to spread their roots. In less than a year, they had returned to Minnesota.

While they were away, the newly fledged body of Minneapolis believers met at the homes of several in their group—the Hagens, Bartons, Jorgensens, and others. When the weather permitted, they even met on the banks of the mighty Mississippi where they would sing hymns, pray, and listen to Brother Forbes preach from the Bible. As September rolled in and the Minnesota weather started to change, the group paid rent to the nearby Baptist Church located at Longfellow Avenue and Thirty-first Street for their Sunday evening service and Wednesday prayer meeting while Mrs. Hagen hosted the Sunday school and worship.

In Colorado, Sparky got the first taste of what life was like without his service to his church, and he rebounded strongly when they returned. They arrived just as the Minneapolis core was breaking ground for the new church, and Sparky quickly reconnected. He rejoined Art Instruction, and the young couple, now including baby Monte, moved to a small temporary home at 5521 Oliver Avenue South in Minneapolis. Though it was rather tiny, they opened it up to host the church group's Sunday school and worship services while the new building was going up seven miles away. Sparky was home.

In July 1952, the First Church of God in Minneapolis held a prayer meeting in their new building, and on the 13th, forty people were present to hear Reverend Forbes preach the first Sunday sermon. The new church was a modest one with two floors of little more than a thousand

The First Church of God in Minneapolis, Minnesota (as it appeared with updated exterior in 2014). Amicably departing from the St. Paul Merriam Park congregation, the Minneapolis congregation built this church and began holding services in it in 1952. Courtesy Jennifer Lind.

square feet each. Walking up four wide cement steps, and entering through the front door, visitors could swing left through the arm's-length foyer to enter the small sanctuary, or they could turn right and head downstairs to the small basement unit built for the pastor and his family. The sanctuary could hold forty people comfortably. It could hold twice that, but little more.

As winter set in, Brother Forbes accepted the call to serve in Goshen, Indiana, and was replaced four months later by J. Clifford Thor, a young man Sparky's age who had just finished seminary after spending two years as a missionary to China (his grandparents and father had served there as well, as would his sister and her husband). Reverend Thor and his wife, Jean, had been living with Cliff's parents in Minneapolis until he could find a pastorate. He was happy to fill in when a member of the local Church of God expressed their need. The church group was still a new group, so their process of finding a new pastor was somewhat informal. "Why is it that you don't want to be our pastor?" one of the older members asked Thor, who was still only serving as pulpit supply. The young minister had simply not been asked to candidate for the position, but once the question had been broached, it was not long before the congregation officially hired him as their first incoming full-time pastor.

Sparky got along well with the Thors. "One day Jean made a butterscotch pie and [Sparky] and I ate the whole thing in my office at the church," Cliff remembered.[36] On another occasion, the two drove to Iowa to pick up a Hammond organ that was donated to their church. When the Thors opened up the parsonage for an "understanding ourselves" series taught by another minister's wife, Sparky made sure to attend.

Soon, Sparky was a member of the church board, which was a loose role in such a small church; all of the church's core members wore various hats at various times. On more than one occasion in downtown St. Paul, Sparky joined Walt Ortman, Wally Nelson, and usually a fourth to preach the gospel. All of them took turns sharing the good news of Christ to the hungry and homeless outside of the Union Gospel Mission, though they often could not remember whose turn it was. Once, in an attempt to answer the question of who should speak as the streetcars went by, they flipped a coin. Casting lots had gone out of style millennia before. Seeing this, a man who was likely down on his luck approached them. "Are you folks into gambling?" he asked. The men of the church put their coin away, and would have to decide more deliberately whose turn it was to share.

Speaking out like this was not a natural choice for the anxious Sparky, but his faith allowed him to overcome. By their third meeting at the mission, Sparky had been elected president of the small group, and when it was his turn, he shared with those listening in as unobtrusive of a fashion as he could muster. "I stepped out on the sidewalk and managed some way to make my statement for the Lord," he recalled.[37] As he was standing there, two of his golfing friends who did not even know he attended church walked by, surprised to find the reserved Sparky speaking. "I remember standing there one evening and suddenly two of my golfing friends appeared on the curb," Sparky described. "They were astounded to discover me, and I was astounded that they would discover that I was standing there, but I managed to survive the experience."[38]

On Sunday mornings, Sparky led an adult Sunday school class. On Wednesday evenings, as a small group reconvened for their midweek service, he systematically led them through the entire Old Testament. "He was a very learned scholar of the Old Testament," remarked seminary graduate Thor.[39] He would be asked when needed to fill in for the Sunday morning service, once using a book Forbes had sent him as the guide for what he would share with the congregation. He even used his newfound appreciation for music in service of the church, taking the pulpit to chair a concert that Fred and Doris Shackleton gave during a return visit. Fred sang "Amazing Grace," and Doris sang "Just When I Need Him, Jesus is Near." Taking charge publicly, Sparky asked one of the women of the church to "lead us to the throne of grace" in prayer, and he instructed the ushers to return to collect "a special love offering" for their former pastor. "No One Ever Cared For Me Like Jesus," Doris sang to her former church family. The pianist closed with "Be Still My Soul."[40]

Joyce never fully fit in at the Church of God. She became friends with Harold Ramsperger's wife, Elaine, and the four took a long weekend's camping trip to the Canadian border, portaging from one water hole to the next. She graciously gave Elaine her washer and dryer (the first Elaine ever had) when the Schulzes were to get a new set, and she enjoyed bowling in a foursome with Sparky, along with Bill and DoLores Edes. But Joyce simply did not share the type of personal faith that drew the others to eager service in the church. On the Valentine's Day before they were married, Sparky had given Joyce a Bible, likely because she did not have her own, with a card reading, "To Joyce with all my love—Sparky." On the first page, he inscribed "Ephesians 5:25-33," the passage in which husbands are told to love their wives just as Christ also loved the church. Joyce did not take to spiritual study like her husband, though, and the sacred book remained unmarked with the un-mussed Valentine's note inside. Later in life, the owner and architect of her own botanical gardens and not affiliated with any religious body, Joyce would tell her own employees, "The rule in the Garden generally is that we do not discuss religion or politics."[41]

Joyce was uncomfortable with what she perceived as criticism of divorcees in the church, and she shared with Elaine her discomfort with rumblings she heard a few make about the unwashed children of some of the group's lesser fortunate members. "When people have a choice between food and soap to buy, they don't buy soap," she told Elaine.[42] Joyce nonetheless typically joined her husband at services and church functions, bringing their own increasing number of young children along (though Meredith was the only one to attend Sunday school with any regularity). She hosted social events at their home, occasionally including friends from church. "She was good at it; she was very good at it, and she was generous," recalled DoLores Edes.[43] Little Susan Julian, the daughter of Avis Kriebel, enjoyed an invitation to one of Meredith's birthday parties. As Avis remembered, "The car was so full of balloons for the party that the back wheels would hardly stay on the ground!"[44] One Thanksgiving, as Joyce prepared the feast for their family and friends gathered in a slightly larger house they had moved into on Wentworth Avenue, Sparky ran over to the church to pick up three elderly members of the congregation who had no place to celebrate the day of gratitude. Placing lumber on sawhorses to extend their table, Sparky and Joyce welcomed them into their home.

In 1955, they purchased a beautiful three-story home at 112 West Minnehaha Parkway in the upper-scale Tangletown neighborhood for their growing family. Sparky's contract with United Feature Syndicate had been renewed, his subscription rates were growing (he was in 355 domestic newspapers and forty foreign dailies by 1958), and the National Cartoonists Society awarded him the 1955 "Reuben Award," their highest honor for the cartoonist of the year. *Peanuts* was proving to be quite a success. His four-panel dailies and expanded Sunday strips were a hit on college campuses and office break rooms nationwide. Charlie Brown and the gang were evolving into the characters that would persist for decades, and Schulz's magazine-style aesthetic had sharpened into a visual brand that other artists would soon yearn to emulate. On November 28, 1955, while Schroeder sits at his miniaturized baby grand piano, Lucy slowly and silently makes her way up to him, first behind, then in front, and then on top of his piano, telling the musical genius, "You fascinate me!"

Sparky's rise to fame in the mid-1950s gave Warner Press's youth editor Kenneth Hall the leverage he needed to bring Sparky on board to draw for the Church of God, something Sparky had wanted years before. Ken was a friend of Cliff Thor from their days together as students at Anderson, and the two conspired to find a place for the cartoonist. Warner Press was producing a weekly magazine called *Youth* in which messages from the church were shared with a teenage audience. This time, though, the syndicate told Schulz no. "They didn't want their young cartoonist draining away his creativity or diluting his market with this 'side' project," explained Hall.[45]

The two stayed in touch, becoming casual friends through their church connection. As Sparky's contract with the syndicate was renewed, he informed Hall, "This time I'm not going to ask them. I'm going to tell them." United Feature complied, and Sparky began writing single-panel cartoons that would run every other week in *Youth*, which at the time had a circulation of about 25,000. The nearly 250 panels would eventually gain the name *Young Pillars* and would run until early 1965. In a visual style that reflected what the *Peanuts* characters' teenage counterparts might look like, even if stretched out a bit, Schulz drew on his own Midwestern congregational experience to make gentle insider jokes about the church. "It's a special songbook I designed. . . ." one character said to a friend. "The pages are blank so all the little kids can have something to write in during the morning service!" In another, a recurring lanky boy recites to a little kid while unfolding his hands, "Here's the church and here's the steeple. Open the door, and see how few people turned out for Wednesday night prayer meeting!"

At times, Sparky would even mention a church friend's name, such as in a panel where a teenage boy, hair standing on end, tells the girl he is walking with, "Brother Forbes' preaching on Sodom and Gomorrah never fails to thrill me!" In other panels, his personally lived theme of anxiety would show through. "What worries me," a boy says to a girl, "is that if I decide to go into the ministry, and if I get married, and if I have some children, will those children want to be the children of a minister?"

The panels were quite the success in their own right. Filtering through the recently established National Council of Churches, *Young Pillars* was seen by other church bodies who wanted to use them for their own organizations. With Sparky's blessing, Ken Hall facilitated the syndication of the panels to nearly fifty different church magazines for various denominations across the country. Sparky was working for the kingdom. He was not interested in financial gain from the endeavor, though, so he instructed Ken Hall to direct the small syndication fee other magazines would pay to a youth scholarship program through Warner Press and the Church of God in Anderson. In 1958, there was such demand for the panels that Warner Press published a mass-market

"WHAT WORRIES ME IS THAT IF I DECIDE TO GO INTO THE MINISTRY, AND IF I GET MARRIED, AND IF I HAVE SOME CHILDREN, WILL THOSE CHILDREN WANT TO BE THE CHILDREN OF A MINISTER?"

Young Pillars. September 9, 1956. © 1989 Warner Press, Inc., Anderson, Indiana. Used with permission.

collection of the cartoons under the title *Young Pillars.* Churches even did their own marketing work for Schulz, with one newsletter telling readers to "check with your Baptist Book Store about Mr. Schulz's hilarious new cartoon book, Young Pillars (Warner Press, $1.00), picturing teen-agers in church activities."[46] In 1964, *Young Pillars* would enjoy mainstream syndication on the pages of the *Chicago Tribune*,[47] and Warner Press would publish an additional collection as well, *What Was Bugging Ol' Pharoah?* to join 1961's *"Teen-ager" is Not a Disease.* Another collection, *I Take My Religion Seriously*, followed in 1989.

Even with the success of *Young Pillars,* though, Sparky had not yet gotten comfortable with using religion in his *Peanuts* strips, which were now syndicated across the country. By 1958, he had borrowed phrases from the Bible only twice, neither time identifying them as scriptural quotations. When Charlie Brown has to praise Schroeder's musical talents in order to get him out of the street on June 28, 1952, Charlie Brown laments via Solomon's words in Ecclesiastes 1:14, "All is vanity!" Then, on December 16, 1955, a freezing Snoopy is consoled with Jesus's words from John 16:33, "Be of good cheer, Snoopy . . Yes, be of good cheer." Two days later, Charlie Brown avoids a dispute between Lucy and Schroeder about the existence of Santa Claus by telling them "I refuse to get involved in a theological discussion!"; and, on May 17, 1957, Charlie Brown tells Linus, "I don't pretend to be a student of prophetic literature!" when asked about the details of the nursery rhyme "Hey Diddle Diddle."

When *Young Pillars* hit the bookstore shelves in 1958, it was the first mass publication of Schulzian cartoons that engaged the Bible. "In my cartooning I draw for two kinds of editors: secular editors and church editors," he would explain. "I work for the secular press through a newspaper syndicate, and naturally I must exercise care in the way I go about expressing things. I have a message that I want to present, but I would rather bend a little to put over a point than to have the whole strip dropped because it is too obvious."[48] His *Peanuts* strips had mainstream strings attached to them, and he had the legitimate fear that including overt religious content could lose him subscribers, perhaps even his contract. Other comic strips simply did not broach religious matters. Then again, his was not like other comic strips.

Near the end of 1958, Schulz finally saw an opportunity to bridge the religious-mainstream gap. His endeavor would involve the warm sentiment of the Christmas season. It would also involve a little love and affection from the housewives who read *Better Homes & Gardens*.

A staff member of the journal asked Sparky to share his reasons for believing in immortality for a piece they were preparing. Sparky obliged, writing a short description of his thoughts. In his answer, he quoted Jesus, who had told the crowd around the rich young ruler, "Truly, I say to you, there is no man who has left house or wife or brothers or parents or children, for the sake of the kingdom of God, who will not receive manifold more in this time, and in the age to come eternal life."[49] The piece was too short, and perhaps too biblically based, though, so the writer for the journal added to the description an example of a dying fire and a quotation from Longfellow and sent it back to Schulz for review. "Either run it my way or forget the whole thing," Schulz told him.[50] In

August, the journal ran an article entitled "Why Can't We Live Forever?" written by a medical doctor. Schulz's piece was not included.

The magazine, which had a circulation of over 4 million, was still interested in the voice of the wildly popular Minnesota artist, though, and commissioned their own *Peanuts* strip for their December Christmas issue. Schulz and the syndicate agreed, sending the magazine a twelve-panel strip about a biblically based Christmas pageant. Perhaps drawing from his own childhood memory of belting out his line in the Christmas pageant as his classmates in turn quietly spelled out M-E-R-R-Y C-H-R-I-S-T-M-A-S, Schulz drew a twelve-panel set for the magazine called "The Christmas Recital." In what the magazine described as "one of childhood's classic holiday scenes," Lucy rehearses with Linus the younger Van Pelt's line in the play—"The star that shone at Bethlehem still shines for us today." He can't help but mix up the words ("The shining star at Bethlehem . ." "The star of Bethlehem . . ."), frustrating Lucy to no end. "Do you want to be in the Christmas program or don't you?" she asks. "I don't know . . . nobody ever asked me . . they just told me . . ." Linus admits. "Well," she hollers back, "you're going to be in it and you're going to say this piece, and you're going to say it right!! Now try it again . ." Stretching his arms out wide, Linus tries again—"It came upon a midnight clear . . ." It then dawns on him: "Why don't we start working on my Easter piece?"

Committing to the idea, Schulz decided that the story could be used in more than just the magazine. Writing a full eight-panel strip for the newspaper's last Sunday edition before Christmas, he finished the story. In turn, each of his characters recites their lines while Linus fears he has forgotten his line after all:

VIOLET AND SCHROEDER: "We are here to tell you of a wondrous light"
LINUS: (I'm sunk!)
SHERMY: "A wondrous light that was a star"
LINUS: (I wonder if there's any way I could get out of here . . .)
LUCY: "The wise men saw the star, and followed it from afar . ."
LINUS: Psst . . . Lucy . .
CHARLIE BROWN: "They found the stable in the night beneath the star so big and bright . ."
LUCY: What's the matter?

LINUS: I can't remember my piece!

PATTY: "The wise-men left the presents there . . . gifts so precious and so rare . ."

LUCY: Waddya mean, you can't remember it?

LINUS: I can't remember it!

PIG-PEN: "Look up, look up, the star still stands, seen by millions in many lands . ."

LUCY: You better remember it right now you blockhead, or when we get home, I'll slug you a good one!

LINUS: "THE STAR THAT SHONE AT BETHLEHEM STILL SHINES FOR US TODAY!"

LUCY: Merry Christmas

LINUS: Thank you . .

For the first time, Schulz made an explicit reference to biblical content. A humorous Christmas pageant scene where Jesus is not mentioned by name was certainly not the most daring of references he could have made, but it stood out nonetheless. As the *Chicago Tribune* readers thumbed back to the comics section that Sunday before Christmas, the only other reference to the hallowed meaning of the holiday was in the *Dick Tracy* comic in which the words to sacred carols came from an outdoor radio, stopping a crime from being committed through the sheer sentiment of the season. In the twenty other comics running in the paper on that day, no reference to Christmas was made at all, save for a few cheeky references to Santa, gifts, and a Christmas tree trimmed with real popcorn. Exploring or embracing religious ideas simply was not done in the funnies, which were the home of adventures, soap dramas, and sight gags. In his introspective and now religious content, Schulz was truly embarking on something new.

Meanwhile, as the success of *Peanuts* continued to grow exponentially, as his *Young Pillar* panels captivated more church audiences, Sparky was taking on yet another challenge—relocation to California. In 1958, Sparky and Joyce packed up their five kids and moved to the city of Sebastopol, north of San Francisco. It would be a very different lifestyle for them all, and for Sparky it meant losing the community of the First Church of God in Minneapolis. From his initial postwar days at Merriam Park, the group had given him a place to belong. They had

Peanuts strip commissioned by and printed in *Better Homes & Gardens*, December, 1958. *Peanuts* © Peanuts Worldwide LLC. Used with permission.

helped him find a faith in Christ. Now, with a wife restless for a warm climate she could call her own and the sheer possibilities of what their new location might hold, Sparky said goodbye to the little building they had built on the corner of Thirty-eighth and Thirty-eighth.

Arriving in Sebastopol, he would find a new church and would even embark on a more ambitious Sunday school endeavor. He would, of course, continue to challenge his friends with provocative theological

Peanuts © Peanuts Worldwide LLC. Used with permission. December 21, 1958.

inquiries throughout the rest of his life, but he would no longer have the late-night conversations at the parsonage or pie-eating sessions in the pastor's office that Minnesota had afforded. What he would have, though, was his strip, in which he could begin to ponder religious questions. In his strips, he could share with a global community his troubled or witty insights into a recently read passage of Scripture. In his strips, he could question "How long, O Lord?!" and "Do you ever wonder if God is pleased with you?"

He had now given license to his characters to have a biblical, even spiritual voice, and with them he would make lasting impacts in ways he could never have imagined. So much would be accomplished with a clever cast of diminutive characters now able to talk about religion. The stumblesome little character at the front of the pack would be none other than good ol' Charlie Brown.

2

LAND OF PROMISE

"People don't need me, they need to 'see Jesus only.'"

—CHARLES M. SCHULZ

CRAIG SCHULZ SAT IN THE PEW OF SEBASTOPOL UNITED METHODIST CHURCH as the brass offering plate made its way down the aisle toward him. The church was much larger than the one his father and mother had taken him to as an infant. This one even had a bell tower, sometimes hand rung by the children of the church. He looked on as the plate got closer and closer, passing from one hand to another as the church's faithful dropped in their Sunday's tithe. When the plate neared, Craig could see an innocent little girl peering into its depths. With disbelief he looked on as his own sister, little more than four or five years old, took a moment to consider the change that had been dropped in, and then apparently figuring she had some coming to her, took out her fair share.

In 1958, Sparky, Joyce, and their five children moved to Sebastopol, California. Located an hour's drive north of San Francisco, the inviting city offered the incoming Midwesterners its own towering redwoods, historic apple orchards, and budding vineyards. There was, however, no Church of God, leaving Sparky with added uncertainty after his move away from the body of believers he had served with for ten years. Not long after Sparky and Joyce had moved into their new home at 2162 Coffee Lane, though, a local doctor paid them a visit. He brought them apples, one of the region's prized fruits. Through the course of conversation, the doctor mentioned the nearby Methodist church and invited Sparky to attend. Without a Church of God

Sebastopol United Methodist Church (as it appeared with its original details in 2014). Photo by author.

congregation close by, Sparky decided to take the doctor up on his offer to visit for Sunday school at Sebastopol United Methodist Church.

The church building was beautiful—much more beautiful than the Merriam Park group could have ever afforded to build, and in a style they would have never considered. Perched above the intersection of North Main Street and Healdsburg Avenue, thanks to a railroad endeavor that had chopped away its sloping hill, the church bore the impressive aesthetic of the Spanish Colonial Revival movement. Flanked by palm trees, the church stood with high plaster walls topped with the crests and curves of a Spanish mission, large arched windows, and a domed bell tower housing a 42-inch Blymyer bell. The style had spread through California in the 1910s, popularizing the congregation's choice of architect W. J. Whyte's design for a new church building completed in 1915.

Methodist believers had been meeting in the area for two decades before their first church was built in 1867 on land donated by Dr. Plunkett, who ran her nearby home for wayward girls. In 1896, the little church burned, and was rebuilt a year later. Prohibition brought with it more dangers for local churches, especially the Methodist church whose Reverend Rankin, a man remembered as "humble, fervent in spirit, zealous against evil and for the right,"[1] spoke out strongly in favor of dry laws. On October 22, 1914, kerosene-soaked rags ignited a raging fire that burned the church to the ground. The "wets" were credited for the blaze, and the Methodist church members met in their singed youth building, Epworthian Hall, while their new Spanish-inspired sanctuary was completed.

Such history was different from that of the small Church of God group who had only recently built their own modest, white, four-wall building in Minneapolis when Sparky left amidst rumblings that his tithes had kept the church afloat.[2] In fact, the Methodist group had built their third sanctuary before the Merriam Park group had even inherited their first. The Minnesota group had reached nearly seventy-five in attendance each Sunday, but now in California, Sparky found the Methodist church's membership near 500, with upwards of 200 regularly attending each week.

Inside the church's large vaulted sanctuary, Sparky found more liturgy than he was used to, the Methodist church having carried some of its formality over from its Anglican origins. Its doctrine, however, had its roots in the Anglican theologian John Wesley, just like the Church of God, and he would find few differences in the churches' central theologies. Both believed that individuals could be saved from their sin through God's grace, thanks to the sacrificial death and resurrection of Jesus. Both groups taught the value of holy living and enjoyed sacred hymns. Both valued the personal study of the Scriptures and service to those in need.

Of course, Methodism was still a distinct denomination, a classification that the Church of God had resisted since *Gospel Trumpet* editor D. S. Warner had spoken against sectarianism in the 1880s. Sparky believed quite strongly in the Church of God's emphasis on unity over division, and in 1959 joked with Ken Hall by letter, "Because there is no Church of God in Sebastopol, I have been attending a Methodist

Sunday School. Am I excommunicated?"[3] While this mid-century California Methodist church valued its history, its structure, and its traditions, it too was less interested in division and tended not to deride the teachings of other groups from the pulpit, focusing more on showing love and service to the local community than any order of disapproval. Even explicit salvation messages were rather rare.

Sparky had come to prefer small, more organic gatherings of believers that he and others would refer to as the "primitive church," but he found that the large Methodist church's Sunday school still had something of that quality, with no more than a couple dozen in a given age group gathering in one of the church's many rooms to study and discuss the Scriptures. He had also enjoyed the open-minded nature of the Church of God's theology—"There must be constant striving for more knowledge and new insights," the church's National Historian had once written.[4] Believing that he could find some semblance of this again at the Methodist church, the reserved cartoonist from Minnesota decided to continue visiting the church, bringing his family along. Soon, he was a regular.

Around the same time as he was visiting the Methodist church in Sebastopol, the General Board of Education of the Methodist Church wrote Sparky, telling him, "Last week's magnificent Peanuts cartoon of Lucy and Snoopy in ecstasy over dancing seems to us to be delightfully appropriate for our book."[5] The book was the Methodist Church's rewritten *World of Fun* dance manual that would accompany their vinyl music album in 1959, and the minister writing for the board was seeking permission to include the comic strip in its opening pages. He assured Sparky that permission would "delight the hearts of dozens of Peanuts fans and perhaps recruit a few more to this increasing list." Not one to disappoint the two-steppers across an entire denomination, Sparky approved, and the strip of Snoopy and Lucy dancing[6] appeared across from the 1959 manual's Table of Contents. The dance kit was a hit and went into reprints well beyond 1959.

A dance set from a mid-century Protestant church may have been too scandalous for some religious bodies across the country, but including *Peanuts* in a church publication was becoming more and more common. Churches and religious student groups began writing in regularly to request reprints for their own assorted products. In 1958, the Wesley

Fellowship of Emory University requested the use of individual character drawings for their organization's informative leaflet, entitled, "Is Life Just Peanuts for You?" Next to pictures of the *Peanuts* gang, the pamphlet asked such questions as: "What do you have to have?"; "Who decides this for you?"; and "What if you don't get it?" The pamphlet promised that their organization gives members the "opportunity to discover the total relevance of the Christian faith to these questions." In 1960, the Board of Christian Education for the Presbyterian Church in the United States wanted to reprint three strips in an issue of their *Presbyterian Youth* quarterly, including a strip in which Linus utters a Schulzian take on a classic line, "I love mankind . . . It's people I can't stand!!"[7] In 1961, the United Jewish Appeal of Greater New York requested permission to reprint in their newsletter a strip in which Linus declares that when he grows up he wants "to be a great philanthropist with someone else's money!"[8]

Having recently launched their new publication in 1960, the *Decision* newsletter, the Billy Graham Evangelistic Association, one of the most prominent Christian organizations of the mid-twentieth century, also wanted to use a strip. Sparky had seen the power of the organization in the fall of 1957 when he attended one of Graham's crusades in New York City. He made his way to Madison Square Garden, taking a seat at no charge. No one was charged. Schulz was among the throngs of inquirers, an average of 17,000 nightly, who were moved by what the cartoonist described as "real Gospel singing and preaching"[9] brought by the likes of George Beverly Shea and, of course, Reverend Graham, for whom Sparky had "nothing but admiration."[10] The night Sparky attended, hundreds went forward, as they had every night, to receive Christ and reconfirm their commitment to Him. According to Sparky, the powerful response he witnessed must have been "the result of earnest prayer, and the working of the Holy Spirit and the building up of love."[11]

Now in his studio at Coffee Grounds, the name the previous owner had given their home on Coffee Lane, Sparky received a personal phone call from the crusading organization. *Decision* editor Sherwood E. Wirt was on the line from Minneapolis, the organization's headquarters. Wirt told Sparky about their newsletter, describing which strips they had particularly enjoyed. Giving his blessing to the influential organization, Sparky directed Wirt to the syndicate's office so that they could process the formal approval letter and get the editor good copies of the strips for reprinting. In the January 1961 edition, then, under an update about a musical crusade undertaken by Cliff Barrows, George Beverly Shea, and Tedd Smith, Charlie Brown hangs his head, lamenting, "Nobody likes me . . Nobody . . Nobody . . Nobody . ." Seeing him, Patty asks, "What's the matter, Charlie Brown?" Sighing, he tells her, "I've never been so discouraged in all my life . . . I think my soul needs a 'Band-Aid'!"[12]

Requests came in from across denominations and organizations—the Lutheran Student Association of America; the University Christian Association at Brown University; and the Episcopalian magazine of New York, which wanted to run a sequence of *Peanuts* strips along with an article on affection by Anglican apologist and author of the *Narnia* series, C. S. Lewis. The Westminster Presbyterian Church in Buffalo, New York, would later even want to include Schroeder in a stained-glass window honoring the beauty of music, below a large image of theologian and organist Albert Schweitzer at the keys.[13] Each of these requests and many more were routinely granted at no cost,[14] save for the requirement that the local paper that carried *Peanuts* be credited.

As strips were reprinted in various contexts, word spread across congregations and the circulatory effects multiplied. Seeing the strip in *Decision*, the editorial secretary of the *Brotherhood Journal*, a Christian men's magazine produced by the Southern Baptist Convention, requested reprint permission so that their 110,000 readers could enjoy a *Peanuts* strip "from time to time." United Feature Syndicate business manager James Hennessy responded with cordial approval to the broad request, as he and Schulz were accustomed to doing. The social circulation of *Peanuts*, even in the pre-smart-technology age of mimeograph, had developed its own sustaining momentum, and all Schulz and the syndicate had to do was continue approving to continue reaping the rewards of expansion.

Sparky and the syndicate did more than just approve the reprinting of *Peanuts* comics during this era, though. They also gave away, free of charge, Sparky's original drawings once the syndicate had sent off the proofs to their subscribing newspapers. Many readers who happened upon a favored strip in their local paper or in one of the massively popular books of reprints by Rinehart & Company simply wrote to Schulz or the syndicate, requesting that Schulz's original of that strip, drawn and lettered by his unique hand on the large paper stock comic artists use,[15] be sent to them as a gift. Schulz and his team at the syndicate granted each and every request without fail. When a strip had already been claimed by another adoring fan, the syndicate agent would write back, asking if there was another favorite strip—sometimes two—that the reader might want instead. The gifting stopped in the mid-'60s as the franchise grew exponentially, in part because the logistics of approving requests simply became unmanageable.

Sparky's liberality filled many domestic hallways and corporate waiting rooms with original strip drawings, adding witty insight to more than one pastor's office as well. Many personal requests came in from individuals associated with various Christian churches, from an assistant minister in a Presbyterian church whose mother had sent him *Peanuts* clippings all through his time in seminary, to an apostolic administrator in the bishop's residence at Infanta, Quezon. One Methodist pastor from New Mexico wrote to Schulz, letting him know that a strip in which Lucy is oblivious to what Charlie Brown was trying to share with her "is what every minister must feel time after time." Not having the artwork in his own studio, Sparky forwarded this request to the syndicate, and production manager William Anderson happily forwarded the original to the pastor.

Proving just how popular he was becoming with church communities, and the degree to which this amplified Sparky's reach, a number of requests even came from or on behalf of ministers who had actually incorporated *Peanuts* strips into their sermons. Requesting the original as a surprise for her Lutheran pastor, one churchgoer wrote in 1958 that her pastor had called attention to one of Sparky's strips in their Bible study; the pastor said that he was "an avid *Peanuts* fan and believed the artist possessed of a remarkably keen insight of human nature." Clergy of various ilk across the country were understanding Schulz's mainstream work to be consistent with their own worldviews, and many, like this Lutheran pastor who eventually received the strip as a surprise via his parishioner, contributed to Schulz's growing popularity through the power of their pulpits.

A number of national write-ups made it even easier for church communities to identify with the cartoonist by declaring Sparky to be one of their own—a man of faith. Hugh Morrow had broken the news to millions of readers in a 1956 *Saturday Evening Post* biographic piece in which he described Schulz as "deeply religious. A member of a fundamentalist congregation in Minneapolis in which everyone tithes, Schulz teaches Sunday school, is president of the board of trustees, serves on the board of Christian education, and sometimes preaches the Sunday sermon."[16] Ken Hall likewise published a biographic sketch in 1959 for *Youth*, telling readers the basic plot line of Schulz's religious faith, writing that "it was shortly after Schulz came home from army service in World War II that his own life was turned around, and he became a committed Christian." The religious biography, several short paragraphs in length, included a note about Sparky not drinking or smoking as well as listing several service roles Sparky fulfilled in the church, though Hall added that "Sparky would not like to be known as a pious snob about his religion," insisting that "Schulz's religion is an intensely personal thing." The piece was reprinted in dozens of church magazines. Such broad descriptions let readers know that Schulz shared some of their beliefs, and more localized church publications gave church readers the opportunity to personally embrace Sparky as one of their own—after all, his little strip was in their newsletter and an original was hanging on their pastor's wall.

As pastors, faith-based organizations, and religious readers across the country reached out to him, Sparky became increasingly confident in his use of spiritual references in his strips. "Just the mere fact of quoting from the Bible, of course, for a long while was forbidden in comic strips because somehow they just didn't want you to go near these areas," he described in 1966, "but I think over a long period of time, I established a climate where I built up a good audience among various members of all the clergy, and then they knew when I did mention these things that I was on their side, and I think I was ready to go into this sort of thing."[17] After his 1958 Christmas strips, Sparky continued to introduce a variety of deliberate references to religious topics. In March 1959, Linus builds a sandcastle, which the rain washes away. Linus says, "There's a lesson to be learned here somewhere, but I don't know what it is . . ."[18] Schulz later explained that to be a purposeful religious reference,[19] though only those familiar with the passage from Matthew 7 would notice. A more explicit reference to a scriptural passage came that December as Linus insists that he will not forget his lines, reciting from Luke chapter two, "And the angel said unto them, fear not: For behold, I bring you good tidings of great joy which shall be to all people."[20] In this strip, Schulz began his standard practice of putting quotation marks around biblical passages, signaling to readers that these words were not his own. He would eventually begin explicitly mentioning the book and verse as well.

Schulz's early religious references ranged from Linus praying that his beloved teacher Miss Othmar would not crack up[21] to Charlie Brown noting, after having gotten hit with a snowball that Linus had flung with his trusted blanket, that "for the first time in my life I have a slight idea of how Goliath must have felt!"[22] Linus even brought copies of the Dead Sea scrolls that he had been working on to school for show-and-tell, complete with a drawing of the ancient biblical manuscripts appearing in the strip's title panel.[23]

In 1963, as his momentum had taken him to nearly 700 newspapers printing *Peanuts*, Sparky drew rather dramatic attention to his religious references with a particularly timely strip. On September 11, he poked fun at the murky waters of religion in public school, having Sally recite the pledge of allegiance from her classroom desk, only to add what sounded to her to be the natural concluding word, "Amen!"[24] The topic was on the country's mind as the U.S. Supreme Court had ruled in 1962's *Engel v. Vitale* that school-initiated prayer, even if nondenominational, was a violation of the First Amendment's protection against governmental establishment of religion. In 1963, the Supreme Court affirmed the directionality of that case in *Abington School District v. Schempp*, finding that a Pennsylvania school district violated the Free Exercise and Establishment Clauses by performing daily Bible readings over the loudspeaker.

On October 20, Sparky spoke directly to this historical context in a Sunday strip. Returning home, Sally finds Charlie Brown sitting in front of the television. "Guess what?" she says. "What?" he answers. Looking around, she motions her big brother to follow her, peering around the door, tiptoeing down the hall, and sneaking by the window. Finally, crouched behind the davenport, Sally confides in her big brother, "We prayed in school today!"

Schulz was taking a risk with such a pointed reference. His medium was "a very strongly 'censored' form of entertainment" he told an interviewer at the time.[25] Across the spectrum, comic artists knew these

Peanuts © Peanuts Worldwide LLC. Used with permission. October 20, 1963.

limits. "Religion has *always been* a bit of a taboo subject [in comics], because you're writing a strip for the largest mass audience," explained comic artist Brian Walker of *Hi and Lois*.[26] Likewise, *Blondie* creator Chic Young would reportedly tell mid-century cartoonists to avoid mentioning controversial subjects like cigarettes, divorce, liquor, race, and religion.[27] With increasing pressure on comic artists to account for their influences on society, propelled by the release of Fredric Wertham's 1954 book, *The Seduction of the Innocent: The Influence of Comic Books on Today's Youth*, which resulted in the overlapping comic book industry adopting stricter codes of conduct,[28] those editors in the business of newspaper comic strips were not likely to gamble with backlash from readers or governmental agencies. According to *Time* magazine, the world of comic strip publishing was wrestling with a "breathtaking"[29] level of censorship.

Sparky's representative at the syndicate, vice president and general manager Larry Rutman, was naturally wary of pushback from readers, political leaders, and especially newspaper editors. As letters poured in about the school-prayer strip, Sparky and Rutman found themselves in a unique position of zealous displays of both support and criticism. "I have letters from people who told me that this was one of the most disgusting things they had seen in a comic strip, that they did not think it was funny and indeed thought it was extremely sacrilegious," reported Schulz.[30] "Your 'PEANUTS' strip of Sunday October 20th is a very sad performance for a cartoonist of your talent," wrote one reader, suggesting, "You must have been suffering from a truly desperate shortage of ideas to select the topic of prayer in schools." Explaining that he believed that prayer and Bible-reading were appropriate for the home but not public school, the reader added that "religion is also no fit subject for a cartoon. Especially since yours was neither funny, clever nor cute."

Many other letters expressed ardent approval of the strip, though, assuring Schulz that all was not lost. "Sir, you have displayed a master stroke of genius!" a Church of Christ pastor wrote. "These eight words in the settings which your genius provided for them are the most eloquent, forceful and to the point I have seen." According to another writer, Sparky may "have often been much 'funnier' but never better," and another suggested that Schulz might be "far more effective on our Supreme Court than a few of the incumbents," letting him know that "at least one citizen appreciates your well-placed, courageous sense of humor." Cartoon gag writer Al Morrison also wrote to Schulz, telling him of his distaste for editors avoiding such matters as they hit artists with the "'taboo' jab when you present it to them." Morrison perceived that Schulz's prayer strip "reflects to me a promising inroad to humor that many of us fellas have attempted to sell over the years."[31] Even William J. Butler, the attorney who had argued the petitioner's case against the school in *Engel v. Vitale* wrote to Schulz requesting the original art.

Such diverse reactions stemmed not just from the subject's controversial nature, but also from the open-ended way in which Schulz approached the subject. It was simply not clear from the strip what Schulz's position was, though many readers found it to be abundantly clear . . . in sundry ways. The strategy became one that Sparky would return to many times over the years, though in this case it was an approach that caused much grief for Rutman. Sparky would describe Rutman as a kind of father figure, and in this scenario it was perhaps the son who had brought home something of a mess. The syndicate was swamped with eager requests to use the strip. The problem was that these requests were coming from politically charged groups on both sides of the controversy, each side believing that the strip supported their perspective. It was a scenario that "disturbed" Rutman, Sparky admitted. Approval meant increased exposure, but also declaring a wide swath of readers to be mistaken about the strip's meaning. "So we talked about it," Schulz said, "and he decided that we wouldn't let anybody reprint them."[32]

Years later, Schulz would explain that from a practical perspective, school-sponsored prayer was "total nonsense."[33] Prayer was not only too personal, but it was untenable as an officiated activity. "Is the teacher going to be Catholic or Mormon or Episcopalian or what?" he asked. "It just causes all sorts of problems. And what are kids praying about anyway?"[34] Sparky had attempted to substantively comment on the issue concurrent with his strip's release by way of a letter to the editor of *Vital Christianity*, a Church of God publication, but it did not find its way into a published issue.

> October 6 [1963]
> To the Editor,
> The fears that Chief Justice Achor and others who have written in our weekly magazine concerning Supreme Court rulings against school prayers show a profound lack of faith. The success of our Lord's teaching and the survival of the early church was due to its holiness. It needed no government approval. If our spiritual lives need the support of governmental laws, then we are already doomed. The basic teachings of the Book of Revelations is the triumph of God's true church in spite of all that goes on around it. Our faith must lie in the ability of the Gospel to save the individual. The Gospel does not need the law on its side. "If God be with us, who can be against us?"
> Sincerely,
> Charles M. Schulz[35]

Attending the Methodist church gave Sparky new opportunities to discuss such contemporary issues with other open-minded believers. John Wesley, the denomination's eighteenth-century progenitor, had highly valued educated study, writing extensively[36] and encouraging the mass circulation of inexpensive educational books and pamphlets so as to nourish the flame of reason's candle. Sparky was an avid studier himself, enjoying sitting in his leather chair reading his Bible with a scriptural commentary book at hand on the side table. "I really enjoy sitting up late at night and going through the Scriptures and trying to find out new truths," he said in a 1960s television appearance. "Just the other night, going through some books, I discovered this little bit about the third letter that Paul had written to the Corinthians—the letter that the scholars call the 'stern letter.' Isn't this what they call it? Not having the educational background for this sort of thing, it's always exciting for me when I do come across something like this."[37] Though he never became a member of the Methodist church, believing that one did not need a membership card to be part of the Kingdom of God, a belief that the Methodist church shared,[38] the church's tradition of study and reasoned discussion was a welcomed discovery.

Soon after he began attending, Sparky was leading his own study at the church. He had visited the church's Sunday school upon the doctor's invitation, and "like I always do," he explained, "I speak up too much in those classes, and the next thing I know they invited me to teach a class."[39] Each Sunday, except when the business of being a cartoonist called him away, Sparky met with a group of between ten and twenty adults, most in their thirties and forties, often in the church's Epworthian Hall, a large fellowship hall that had survived the 1914 burning. At times they explored various topical matters like those he brought up in his strips. They discussed the value of the Apocrypha and the death of Martin Luther King, Jr., but Sparky had a strong desire for the class to know the Scriptures for themselves and not to be satisfied with uncited conjecture in their spiritual conversations. "I want them to be able to know where it says it and why it says it," he said.[40] As they sat around in a circle under the decoratively trimmed open rafters of Epworthian Hall each week, he thus had them read through the Bible, verse by verse, each person taking a turn giving voice to a short passage before the next person would pick up where the other left off.

Before getting to church, Sparky would study the upcoming passage, consulting his various Bible commentaries for insights. He had purchased a beautiful multi-volume set of commentaries by Abingdon Press called *The Interpreter's Bible*. Over twelve books and 12,000 pages, the work offered the accumulated insights of venerated theologians from across denominations and station, including professors

Young Pillars. April 6, 1958. © 1989 Warner Press, Inc., Anderson, Indiana. Used with permission.

from Emory University's Candler School of Theology, Princeton's Theological Seminary, Harvard's Divinity School, Southern Methodist University, Lutheran Theological Seminary, and ministers from Old St. Andrew's Church in Toronto, Hyde Park Baptist Church in Chicago, and the Broad Street Presbyterian Church in Columbus, Ohio. "*The Interpreter's Bible* is a guidebook to the city of the Bible," it described.[41] Within its pages, it contained King James Version and Revised Standard Version translations of the Scriptures as well as maps, indexes, topical articles, and in-depth verse- and word-level commentaries, all to help the reader better understand Scriptures.

With his favored *Interpreter's Bible*, a slightly more compact 1,400-page *Abingdon Bible Commentary* that he would occasionally bring to class, and the array of other theological works he was amassing in his personal library, Sparky would make notes and mark up his own Revised Standard Version of the Scriptures which his Aunt Marion Swanson and her second husband, Wesley "Bus" Reid, a kind trumpet player, had given Sparky for his birthday in 1953. She was like a second mother for Sparky after his own mother died, according to Marion's daughter, Patty,[42] and daughter-in-law, Ramona.[43] Marion had cared for her sister, Dena, with the help of Patty when Dena was dying of cancer and had been a constant comfort to Sparky after Dena's death. A woman of faith, Marion had been active in the Twin Cities congregations. "She was quite well acquainted with the people that came to the church," said Avis Kriebel about Marion, remembering that at one point Sparky's aunt may have attended in total more than Sparky or Carl.[44] When Sparky and Joyce moved to California, Marion and Bus joined them, but Marion could not be active in a church. She had fallen ill, suffering a stroke in 1959 and soon finding herself battling a tormenting colon cancer while living in the guesthouse at Coffee Grounds. Sparky's mother-in-law, Dorothy Halverson, would be able to attend Sparky's class often, though, having likewise joined the family in California. She could be deliberate and cool, not one to compliment Sparky's talent. He grinned while telling an interviewer, "In 17 years, I don't recall her once saying that she liked this particular strip or that one."[45] With his father and Aunt Marion not able to join him, Dorothy would fill the role of family elder in his Sunday routine.

Over the years, Sparky would mark nearly every page of his Bible with a pencil or pen, underlining meaningful passages, transcribing timelines, and circling key words, so much that he would naturally forget what had inspired him to do so for certain passages. He filled the margins with explanations drawn from his commentaries and scrawled out personal insights in the blank space left at the end of an Old or New Testament book. Across from the title page, he made notes on passages of love—"God's generous love" could be found in Matthew 20; "Family love gone wrong" could be found in Genesis 25 and 37. Inside the back cover, he taped a black and white picture of Jesus solemnly looking down to the side.

"We believe that discussion of the great fundamental Christian doctrines carried on in the sweet, reasonable spirit . . . ," Church of God theologian Charles E. Brown had written, "tends to the increase in

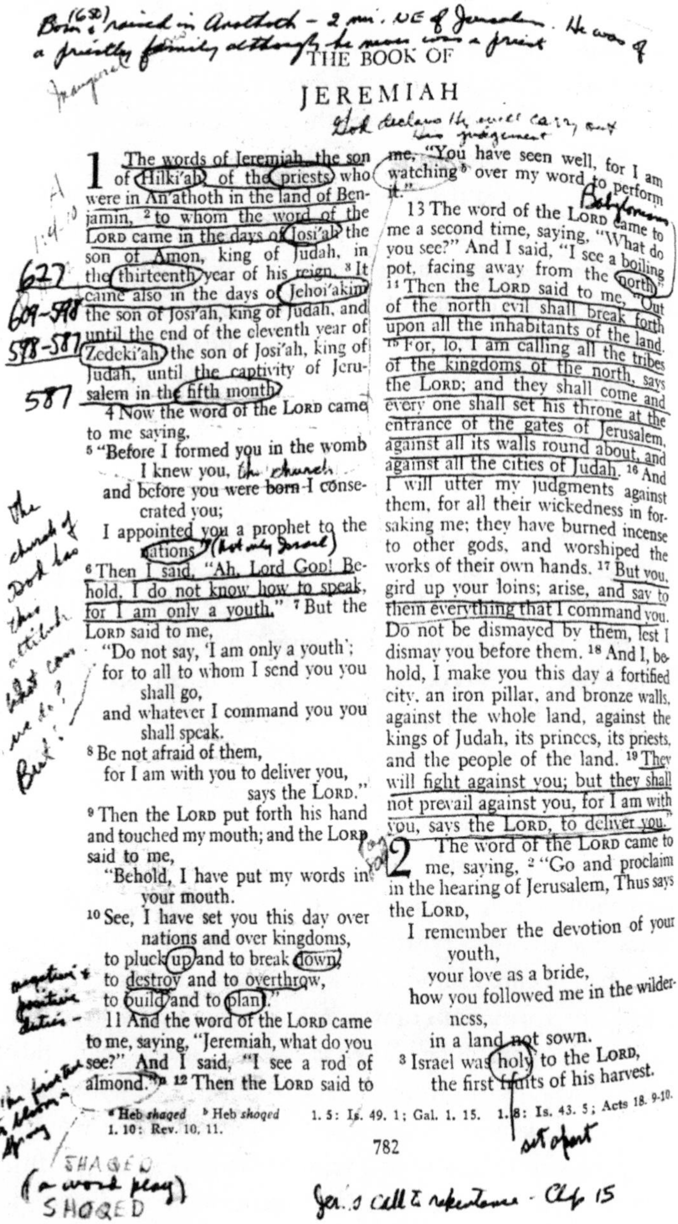

THE BOOK OF

JEREMIAH

1 The words of Jeremiah, the son of Hilki'ah, of the priests who were in An'athoth in the land of Benjamin, 2 to whom the word of the LORD came in the days of Josi'ah the son of Amon, king of Judah, in the thirteenth year of his reign. 3 It came also in the days of Jehoi'akim the son of Josi'ah, king of Judah, and until the end of the eleventh year of Zedeki'ah, the son of Josi'ah, king of Judah, until the captivity of Jerusalem in the fifth month.

4 Now the word of the LORD came to me saying,

5 "Before I formed you in the womb
I knew you,
and before you were born I consecrated you;
I appointed you a prophet to the nations."

6 Then I said, "Ah, Lord GOD! Behold, I do not know how to speak, for I am only a youth." 7 But the LORD said to me,

"Do not say, 'I am only a youth';
for to all to whom I send you you shall go,
and whatever I command you you shall speak.
8 Be not afraid of them,
for I am with you to deliver you,
says the LORD."

9 Then the LORD put forth his hand and touched my mouth; and the LORD said to me,

"Behold, I have put my words in your mouth.
10 See, I have set you this day over nations and over kingdoms,
to pluck up and to break down,
to destroy and to overthrow,
to build and to plant."

11 And the word of the LORD came to me, saying, "Jeremiah, what do you see?" And I said, "I see a rod of almond."[a] 12 Then the LORD said to me, "You have seen well, for I am watching[b] over my word to perform it."

13 The word of the LORD came to me a second time, saying, "What do you see?" And I said, "I see a boiling pot, facing away from the north." 14 Then the LORD said to me, "Out of the north evil shall break forth upon all the inhabitants of the land. 15 For, lo, I am calling all the tribes of the kingdoms of the north, says the LORD; and they shall come and every one shall set his throne at the entrance of the gates of Jerusalem, against all its walls round about, and against all the cities of Judah. 16 And I will utter my judgments against them, for all their wickedness in forsaking me; they have burned incense to other gods, and worshiped the works of their own hands. 17 But you, gird up your loins; arise, and say to them everything that I command you. Do not be dismayed by them, lest I dismay you before them. 18 And I, behold, I make you this day a fortified city, an iron pillar, and bronze walls, against the whole land, against the kings of Judah, its princes, its priests, and the people of the land. 19 They will fight against you; but they shall not prevail against you, for I am with you, says the LORD, to deliver you."

2 The word of the LORD came to me, saying, 2 "Go and proclaim in the hearing of Jerusalem, Thus says the LORD,

I remember the devotion of your youth,
your love as a bride,
how you followed me in the wilderness,
in a land not sown.
3 Israel was holy to the LORD,
the first fruits of his harvest.

[a] Heb *shaqed* [b] Heb *shoqed* 1. 5: Is. 49. 1; Gal. 1. 15. 1. 8: Is. 43. 5; Acts 18. 9-10. 1. 10: Rev. 10. 11.

782

Sparky filled his Bible with underlines, questions, and insights. In this opening of the Old Testament book of Jeremiah, for example, he recorded key dates, highlighted Hebrew wordplay, and noted that while some in his young Church of God denomination were still finding their voice, it was the Lord God who would give them words to say. Revised Standard Version translation. Courtesy Amy Johnson.

Scriptural knowledge among Christian people and arouses a fresh interest in religious matters among worldly people."[46] As Sparky's Sunday school group read through each of the Bible's verses, Sparky would stop the reader when they reached an interesting or challenging portion and would ask the group what the passage meant and what about it resonated with them personally. "Sometimes he could put you on the spot," remembered Paul Schoch, a class member who would lead the study from Sparky's notes when the cartoonist traveled for business, but Sparky was "never confrontational."[47] With his low-key demeanor, complete with its own paradoxical charisma, Sparky created an environment in which the other class members gradually felt comfortable engaging the material. Sparky would raise interesting questions, but he did not dictate what the right answer to a given question had to be. Instead, he would offer insights from the Abingdon texts, occasionally offering his own Schulzian perspective as well, but ultimately leaving it to each of the class members to decide what they personally believed. "It was just a nice class where everybody could get in the discussion if they wished. It was not a lecture class in any sense of the word," described Pete Coleman, a woodworker who had made the church's altar rail and who was a core member of the class. "It was a discussion class, and we read the Bible and we talked about it. It was as simple as that."[48] Over the course of a decade, the group would read through the entire Bible together four times.

Sparky's activities at Sebastopol United Methodist did not extend much beyond his Sunday school group, and he only stayed for the main service on select occasions over the years, once to hear a visiting college choir perform, giving his children very few opportunities to peruse the contents of the offering plates. He had made drawings to be mimeographed in a church fund drive publication, and had worked out the logistics for Frank Perry's 1962 film *David and Lisa* to be played in Epworthian Hall, but the Sunday worship services were more formalized and rigid than Sparky preferred, and he did not attend. The Minnesota services had been a little more flexible, and the preacher certainly was not expected to wear the formal regalia of the Methodist clergy. Sparky discussed this with Reverend Lewis Whitehead, telling the minister that he thought a preacher should have more freedom on a given Sunday. He should be able to tell the congregation that he needs more time for a sermon he's been burdened with and that they should only sing one song. "If, on the other hand, he does not feel that a definite message has been given him," Sparky said, "why not admit it from the pulpit and say, 'This morning, I'm not going to try to make up something to fill the time. We'll sing a few extra hymns and go home!'"[49] Sparky enjoyed his Bible study there, but the formalities and traditions were trappings he could not own.

The 1960s were a time of great activity and growth for Sebastopol United Methodist. They remodeled portions of the sanctuary, enjoyed the traveling ministry of their spirit-filled Methodist Men's group, and began holding church family camps, with Sparky meeting to lead the class on Sunday morning at the camp before returning to his own bustling home at Coffee Grounds. The church also added on an education wing, requiring that Epworthian Hall be moved from next to the church to behind it, after which Sparky's class could begin regularly meeting there. For a short period of time, the class had met in the balcony and then in the minister's living room. The environment was familiar to Sparky, having spent time in church family homes back in Minnesota, and the class found it to be rather cozy. As they began discussing one Sunday, Reverend Lewis Whitehead's wife, Edythe, made her way through the group and set a *Peanuts* display on her piano. It was a friendly gesture, acknowledging and celebrating Sparky's work, even if in only a small way. Though they were not awestruck by the presence of a semi-celebrity, the church members enjoyed Sparky's comics, and those who knew him in the church appreciated interacting with such a creative mind. But while Sparky had found something of a footing integrating some of his religious insights into his comic strip, he was not comfortable integrating his cartooning into his personal Bible study group for fear that it would focus the attention on him instead of their text. "He did not bring into the class personal things that were going on in his life or the cartoon," remembered Paul Schoch. "He was not the kind of guy who was trying to self-aggrandize." Sparky was not comfortable having his cartoon characters on display in the class, and as Edythe left the room to return to her church duties, Sparky got up from his seat. As he stepped over to the piano, he said graciously to the others, "This class is not about Charlie Brown," and he turned the display face down.

Balancing the relationships among his art, his personal faith, and his public statements could at times be a challenge, sometimes even producing something of a contradiction for the shy but confident artist. Schulz enjoyed the space he had carved for himself to discuss religion at church and in his strips, but he would resist claims that he was trying to instruct or preach in any of his work, even though that is what readers would find him doing in a 1963 piece he wrote for Billy Graham's *Decision* newsletter.[50] "If you are a Christian, you are the church. You are one of the 'called-out ones,' who have been called out to serve God. How, then, can you just sit there? But so many do," he wrote, adding, "I cannot fail to be thrilled every time I read the things that Jesus said, and I am more and more convinced of the necessity of following him."[51]

Sparky received letters from all over expressing their delight in reading his thoughts in the *Decision* article. They were an encouragement to many, which pleased him, but he was simultaneously wary about his role in the matter with the responsibility and perhaps misdirected attention it would bring. "I will never get over the feelings of guilt over being lauded publicly when so many others who appear to be 'least in the Kingdom' are really the 'greatest in the Kingdom,'" he wrote to Ken Hall after receiving some of these letters. Ken wanted to reprint Sparky's article, but Sparky was reluctant. He wrote to Ken, "If you think it will do any good, then you may, but please know that I tremble with fear for being built up too much. People don't need me, they need to 'see Jesus only.' I know you understand, and I trust your judgment."[52]

Billy Graham's was not the only organization wishing to hear Sparky's thoughts. As Sparky's popularity grew, he was called on by a variety of religious organizations to speak at their events, sharing with a gathered body of believers about not just *Peanuts*, but presumably the *Peanuts* artist's faith as well. Sparky did not particularly enjoy traveling, and over the course of his career he would occasionally hesitate to accept an invitation if it had even moderate travel requirements. On many occasions, though, he accepted the opportunity to give chalk-talks for various groups at churches and schools, sketching out characters and scenes for a live audience who would marvel at the speed and clarity of his drawings, chuckling at the humor in the episodes he described. He even welcomed a group of theology students once to Coffee Grounds.

In May 1958, Sparky had spoken in downtown Minneapolis at a conference for church magazine editors at Ken Hall's request. The church leaders were excited to have him, despite the fact that Sparky had recently begun his second short-lived newspaper comic, *It's Only a Game,* featuring humorous rounds of the non-conservative games bridge and pool which were tolerated by conservatives because of their great love for *Peanuts* and *Young Pillars*. Hall and Sparky met at lunch the day before the conference, and Ken interviewed the reluctant cartoonist for the bio in *Youth*. The day after the conference, they were surprised to find that they were both to board the Pennsylvania train line heading back to Anderson, Indiana. Sparky was on his way to speak to Anderson's Camarada Club, a request by his minister friend R. Eugene Sterner whose daughter was in the service-based women's student club and who he had met years before when the minster was a speaker at the Church of God's state convention in Minnesota. Sparky even invited him to stay at their house when Sterner was back in town for another series of unity meetings, and Sterner returned the favor as Sparky visited Anderson.

Sparky had worried about the trip, muttering to himself as the train pulled in that going to speak to a group of strangers seemed like a stupid idea. But Anderson had been meaningful for him in the past, Sparky having taken the train down to the 1949 Church of God camp meeting, singing hymns and listening to inspiring preaching. "One of the great memories of my life is standing next to my friend Harold Ramsperger in camp meeting singing 'Blessed Assurance,'" he reminisced decades later.[53] Back in Anderson for his presentation, he reconnected with friends and had a pleasant stay, giving an entertaining performance for the club, and then another chalk-talk at Ken's request for the College Youth Fellowship in the large Park Place Church of God sanctuary adjoining the campus. Nearly 800 people packed into the expansive sanctuary, under its tray ceiling and tall windows, to hear Sparky speak. Bob Reardon, the president of the University, was there with his daughter, Becky, and Bob made sure to give Sparky a tour of the campus when the cartoonist was free.

It was in 1963, though, that Sparky's relationship with Anderson hit a new high note. He was to be awarded an honorary doctorate for his contributions to the arts and the church. Sparky was honored, but he was concerned about the travel from his new home in California. Uncomfortable with flying, Sparky decided to drive across the country with Joyce to receive the special award. Joyce had been busy transforming

Sparky and Joyce stand with their dogs and their children: (left to right) Monte, Amy, Jill, Craig, and Meredith. Early 1960s. Courtesy Amy Johnson.

the rural landscape of Coffee Grounds for their family, complete with a baseball diamond, swimming pool, tennis court, and riding stables. "It's like a state park—only it's nicer," described Sparky's secretary,[54] and Sparky enjoyed many, many hours of carefree fun with his children across their rolling amenities. Telling the children not to ride the horses while they were away, Joyce and Sparky made their way to Anderson.

They drove the 2,000 miles to the school, and on June 17, Sparky took the stage with Reardon, both dressed in their academic gowns. As the 7,500 in attendance for the university's commencement looked on, Reardon placed an academic hood over Schulz's head, conferring upon him the honorary degree of Doctor of Humane Letters from Anderson College and Theological Seminary. Two others would receive honorary degrees as well—Harold W. Boyer, Doctor of Divinity, and Izler Solomon, Doctor of Music. Marvin and Ruth Forbes looked on from the audience as Reardon adjusted the collar of Sparky's hood. Visiting with the Forbes couple that trip meant "more to us than we can ever tell you," Sparky said to them.[55] Sparky had never attended a formal college,

Dr. Robert Reardon confers upon Sparky an honorary Doctor of Humane Letters degree from Anderson College with the symbolic regalia of the academic hood. 1963. Courtesy of Anderson University & Church of God Archives.

and had only barely made it through high school. Now, with a successful cartooning career and his dear friends in the audience, he had been awarded an honorary doctorate for his innovative work.

The warm feelings would end rather abruptly for Sparky, though. Calling home to check in, his secretary simply said, "All is fine; the ambulance just left." Unbeknownst to Sparky and Joyce, their daughter Meredith had suggested that the kids take the horses and go fishing. Meredith placed some buckets and jars on her ten-year-old brother Craig's horse for the expedition, and the young boy hopped in the saddle with a friend on the back. Riding down one of their trails, Craig's horse rubbed against a tree which rattled the jars and spooked the horse. "She took off at full pace," Craig remembered. "I couldn't get off

Sparky readies himself to leave for church while daughters Jill and Amy sit atop their horses, staying home for a morning ride. Mid-1960s. Courtesy Amy Johnson.

due to my buddy on the back. When he finally fell off, I jumped but my foot was stuck in the saddle and I was drug through the forest." A ranch worker cared for Craig while the ambulance arrived. The boy had broken his femur. When he tried to stand, the bone went through his leg. Sparky and Joyce readied to leave Anderson immediately. Before they did, Marv and Ruth prayed with them in their motel room, a memory that Sparky told Marv "will always be with me." Craig was in traction for a month, wore a cast up to his waist for five weeks, and then had to undergo physical therapy to return to normal walking. While Craig was recovering, the cancer in Aunt Marion took its final toll, and she died.

Upon returning, the contrasts between his visits back to the Midwest and his new life in California were apparent to Sparky. In Minnesota, he had attended church with his father, his aunt, his wife and kids, and a group of friends who would travel with him to visit mentors at the church headquarters. He had developed casual friendships with some members of his Sunday school class in Sebastopol, but it was not the same. "Our two days in Anderson was a treat for us. Joyce was especially taken with you and your wife. I wish we lived closer. Sometimes I think God purposely denies me this 'land of promise' of close Christian companionship," Sparky wrote to Ken Hall, adding, "but maybe I am meant to dwell alone behind a drawing board."[56]

Back in California, Sparky would find himself driving the five miles to church with only his mother-in-law. Joyce had stopped attending not long after their move. Their lives had become increasingly busy with five growing children and she did not share the same personal drive toward spiritual studies that her husband had. More and more, she wanted to pursue her own interests. Monte would later describe his parents as simply being like parallel lines that would not converge. "It's hard to be an individual with a famous person in the house," Joyce told an interviewer. "I know that I wanted to do things that were mine alone, and as the children get older, they begin to feel the same."[57]

With Joyce no longer attending, the children stopped attending Sunday school as well. "My children won't go to Sunday school. But my mother-in-law goes with me," Sparky said. "The children say that it's boring, but I really can't believe that. I think they don't like to get up in the morning, and they hate to get dressed up. I think that once they attended a few classes, they would have to admit that they enjoyed it."[58] They had attended for a short time, but preferred instead to enjoy their own childhood interests on the weekends, playing ball and riding horses at Coffee Grounds. Sparky tried enticing them with doughnuts, but they were children, disinterested in another type of school. They had seen their father sitting in his leather chair reading his Bible, but he almost never discussed his spiritual ideas with them at home, and they had not developed their own curiosities about the Bible.

In his Sunday school class, he had struck a fruitful balance of raising questions and provoking ideas without ever lecturing. He had even found a way to make religion humorous in the context of preschoolers through a new book project with Ken Hall. Hall visited Coffee Grounds with his wife, Arlene, and stayed for a week, collaborating with Sparky on *Two by Fours*, a "sort of serious book about children." The cartoonist drew endearing images of pint-sized Schulzian characters while Hall wrote the text for the short book that would explain to adults and church workers how to relate to a small child at church. "The Two-by-Four needs to be reminded constantly that he is loved,"

"GOD LOVES ME....
GOD LOVES ME NOT....
GOD LOVES ME....
GOD LOVES ME NOT...."

Two by Fours. 1965. © 1989 Warner Press, Inc., Anderson, Indiana. Used with permission.

penned Hall. "If he feels that another person loves him, he will readily accept that person into his own life. Happy is the child who feels that his parents love him, that the young people he meets love him, that the neighbors love him, that all the people down at the church love him. Happy is that child, for in this way he also can begin to know something of God's love for him." Across the page, Sparky drew a small boy in a striped shirt, picking petals off a flower, working out its meaning, "God loves me. . . . God loves me not. . . . God loves me. . . . God loves me not. . . ."[59] At home, though, Sparky did not strike the same balance through humor or study with his own children, choosing to remain rather silent on spiritual topics for fear he would sound too authoritarian. When they stopped attending church, Amy and Jill were too young to really remember any of the services. If they would develop spiritual interests, they would develop them on their own.

Parted from the comfort and support of Aunt Marion, his father, and the Church of God, Sparky could of course still pursue his faith, and he would, for none of these were necessary to make him personally a part of the Kingdom of God. By the mid-1960s, as his empire grew in the sunny land of California, Sparky had established strong new ties with churches across the nation and had proven that he could do what many other cartoonists had not been able to do. He had taken a risk and found that most audiences actually appreciated the way he provoked religious thoughts, his *Peanuts* subscriptions totaling more than 700 newspapers. Soon, Sparky would find that he could do this in more than a chalk-talk, an article, or a four-panel comic strip. Soon, he would find the opportunities afforded by the screen.

3

THE CHRISTMAS SPECIAL

"If we don't do it, who will?"

—CHARLES M. SCHULZ

"PIG-PEN," YOU'RE THE ONLY PERSON I KNOW WHO CAN RAISE A CLOUD of dust in a snow storm," Charlie Brown said to his dirt-ridden friend. "What's the paper?" he continued.

"That's my 'Git List,'" replied "Pig-Pen."

"What's your 'Git List?'"

"This is what I figure to git for Christmas from my mom and dad, and my two grandmas, and two grandpa[s], and my cousins, and my . . ." explained "Pig-Pen."

"Where's your give list?"

"My what?"

"I knew it!" exclaimed Charlie Brown, finding yet another compatriot felled by the commercialism of the season.

This scene, scene 8B, was originally to appear in the beloved classic *A Charlie Brown Christmas*, to occur in between Charlie Brown's spat with Violet over not sending him a Christmas card and Patty's suggestion to "try to catch snowflakes on your tongue" (it's fun). The snowflakes, however, needed sugar, and the scenes needed to be trimmed to fit the show's time allotment. 8B did not make the cut. And it was not the only content at risk in this original *Peanuts* animated special. One of the most iconic scenes in all of Christmas programming, Linus's recitation of the Gospel of Luke, was also called up for sacrifice. The voice of Charles Schulz, however, stayed the hand of any would-be editors, saving one of the few vocal religious references audiences would find on their television sets that season—or that decade, for that matter.

The 1960s saw significant reordering of the status quo. Racial and political hierarchies were challenged, with previous assumptions brought into the light for dissection. Religious orders were likewise called into question. It was not an era of wholesale secularization or abandonment of religion, but institutional authority of all kinds was examined, and that included the church. While for decades it had seemed like religion was a required social fixture, legal battles contributed to the strengthening perception that discussing one's religion was no longer appropriate for social settings.

Major court cases established new legal limitations on religious practice in public—i.e., *Engel v. Vitale*'s 1962 barring of school-initiated prayer and *Abington School District v. Schempp*'s 1963 ruling against a public school's daily Bible readings over the loudspeaker. In the wake of these cases, the American public was faced with perceptual tensions among their traditional practices, legal precedence, and developing notions of social pluralism. Some feared that the court's decisions were an attack on religion, even if legal scholars would explain that the intent was in favor of religious freedom. The perception of the court's involvement in religious affairs was compounded when the 1964 Civil Rights Act brought the state into questions of workplace discrimination of religion through Title VII claims.[1] Though the legal implications and technicalities of these events would continue to be debated, these cases propelled and codified the social restructuring of religious normativity that the demoralizations of war and the federal government's sponsorship of professionalized science had ushered in during the previous decades.[2]

Religious organizations were forced to muddle[3] through their new role in society. While Christianity would remain an embedded part of much of American life, explicit acknowledgments of such had become more marginalized, and a variety of social questions would become controversial issues for churches to broach anew. In 1961, the National Council of Churches, for instance, formally approved of birth control while the independent journals *Christianity and Crisis* and *Century* recommended in 1964 and 1965 editorials that homosexuality, even though sinful, should be decriminalized. Even the monolithic Catholic Church undertook massive introspective consideration during the era through the activities of the Second Vatican Council (Vatican II), which was held from 1962 to 1965. This event paralleled the 1960s broader rejection of tradition as inherently valuable, resulting in significant articulated changes to the Catholic Church. While the percentage of Americans who were formal church members actually rose slightly across the diverse Protestant and Catholic congregations—57.38 percent in 1950, 63.82 percent in 1960, and 64.46 percent in 1970[4]—many Protestant congregations likewise grew concerned that they could be losing capital in an uncertain social sphere, and many retreated to the church as a sanctuary from the world. There were not fewer religious individuals, but those individuals were no longer confident that it was appropriate for their religious interests to be voiced in public.

On the relatively young mass medium of television, the cultural hesitance about overt public spirituality was manifested in the predominantly secularized entertainment programming. Religious content in mainstream programming was infrequent, typically portraying limited versions of Catholic clergy and the "professed religious" (i.e., Catholic nuns) when including the church at all. Even shows that seemed to be overtly religious, like Sally Field's *The Flying Nun*, tended to trade in typical situation comedy writing instead of content that dealt in sincere matters of spirituality. Entertainment television was simply not seen as a space in which such matters could be broached. Many church organizations thus condemned the medium for its secularity in this pre-televangelism era,[5] echoing the FCC chairman Newton Minow's 1961 condemnation of television as a "vast wasteland."[6] When Schulz was then offered the challenge of producing a full *Peanuts* special for television at Christmastime, he was not being offered a pulpit from which to preach. Religious groups were reluctant to engage the medium, and network executives had bought into the cultural model of keeping religion mostly to oneself and off the airwaves.

In 1964, Schulz had worked with San Francisco producer Lee Mendelson to produce a documentary on the cartoonist's work. Mendelson, a Stanford grad and former Air Force lieutenant, had written and produced Peabody Award-winning documentaries for San Francisco station KPIX's *San Francisco Pageant* series, and had successfully sold his documentary on one of the world's great baseball players, Willie Mays, to NBC through Ed Friendly, vice president of special programs. Mendelson followed this documentary, *A Man Named Mays*, by producing *A Boy Named Charlie Brown*—a documentary about the world's worst baseball player. Schulz had been reluctant to get in too quickly with television opportunities, and had turned down many Hollywood pitches over the years. When Mendelson reached out, Sparky was sold by this local producer's idea of simply creating a documentary about his work with "pilot" animation sequences of the *Peanuts* characters. These would be created by Sparky's collaborating artist Bill Melendez, the former Disney animator who had animated the *Peanuts* characters for Ford motor commercials and welcome spots for *The Tennessee Ernie Ford Show* variety program a few years earlier. With the three—Sparky, Bill, and Lee—now working together, the documentary project was completed and ready for sale.

As the producer, Mendelson's primary role was to see to the business aspects of the program. Borrowing money to finance the project, he was eager to sell their finalized documentary either directly to a television network or to an advertising agency with a client interested in purchasing the project as a "sponsor" to then have it broadcast by a network. Much to their disappointment, though, Mendelson's visits to Ed Friendly at NBC, executives at CBS and ABC, and nearly twenty top ad agencies failed to garner a purchase of their completed special. Some enjoyed the product, but none could envision it generating a large enough audience to produce a significant profit in ad revenue. According to CBS News president Fred Friendly (no relation to Ed Friendly at NBC), "the schedule was so out of control that one of [CBS's] top executives publicly stated that most of what was broadcast no longer reflected what he himself would watch or could enjoy, but what would win the rating game."[7] Without the prospect of high ratings, the finalized *Peanuts* documentary piece was shelved.

A year later, on an afternoon in May 1965, Lee Mendelson was surprised by a phone call from one of the agencies he had visited. John Allen, vice president in charge of television at the prominent McCann-Erickson ad agency, was still not interested in the documentary, but he had a new opportunity, catalyzed by a *Peanuts* cover story that *Time* magazine had run in April. "Our client Coca-Cola is looking for a special," John said to Lee. "By any chance do you have a format for an animated *Peanuts* show that could be connected with Christmas?" "Absolutely," said Mendelson, having no such format.

When the call with John Allen ended, Mendelson called Sparky and pitched the idea. Sparky agreed quickly, undaunted by the task of writing a new program. McCann-Erickson, though, needed the outline by the end of the weekend in order to pitch it to the Coca-Cola executives. Sparky and Lee called Bill Melendez, and the three quickly set out to write an outline. Turning the four-panel *Peanuts* gags into a thirty-minute television special had never been done before, but Sparky took to it with appropriate command. He had always been the singular voice of *Peanuts*, and while he would remain so during the thirty-eight years he would work with Bill and Lee, the television special opened a new opportunity for Sparky to engage recommendations from others with expertise in the broadcast field. As they drafted the special, Sparky drove the storyline, while his two partners offered suggestions and feedback along the way.

Lee had been reading *The Fir Tree* by fairytale forefather Hans Christian Anderson, in which a forest's small fir tree feels unimportant and angry as all of the other trees—older and more magnificent—are used for great endeavors. Only when the small fir is cut down and decorated with splendid ornaments as a Christmas tree does the little fir become somewhat happy. Mendelson suggested the nineteenth-century story to Sparky as they brainstormed their Charlie Brown Christmas special. Anderson's tale ends with the little tree discarded in the days after Christmas, ultimately burned as firewood, and Schulz began to imagine what a Charlie Brown Christmas tree might look like.

Sparky was in good broadcast company as he put together a Christmas tree storyline for the special. The Victorian Christmas tree had remained an icon of the holiday into the 1960s, becoming a conventional part of television episodes, specials, and variety shows during the holiday season. Mr. Wilson, Mr. Mitchell, and young Dennis of CBS's *Dennis the Menace* had spent their entire 1961 Christmas episode trying to acquire just the right tree for the season.[8] The iconicity of the tree had become part of the standardization of Christmas on television, one of five conventions for the Christmas genre that would persist beyond the classic period of 1960s Christmas specials (the conventions include: emphasis on a universal non-religious "spirit of Christmas," inclusion of a "Scrooge" character, use of carols as an aesthetic device, centrality of the Christmas tree, and the ubiquitous presence of Santa Claus).[9]

In the late 1950s, the Victorian ideal of the natural tree had been revised in American culture as the artificial tree industry boomed. Artificial goose feather trees had been used since the late 1800s, quelling some of the concerns about deforestation from poor tree harvesting practices, but the Addis Brush Company revolutionized the market. The company used its toilet brush patterns to fashion a new breed of artificial Christmas trees that would last longer and could hold ornaments better. In 1950, Addis received a patent for their "silver pine" brush-based tree,[10] and in 1958 a Chicago company also began producing aluminum trees.[11] The artificial tree business became quite popular, with colored aluminum trees advertised and sold by major department stores, drugstores carrying artificial tabletop trees for less than $5, and natural trees painted in various in-vogue colors at local tree farms trying to stay relevant.

By the mid-60s, though, the cultural attitude was shifting back against this Christmas revisionism, re-emphasizing "real" Christmas trees. Schulz keyed in on this cultural trend, developing the story of Charlie Brown's little Christmas tree set in opposition to the artificial icons of the season—the shiny ones painted pink. He had already struck on the anti-commercialism angle in his strips, and the two stories folded in together nicely. The story of Charlie Brown's Christmas tree, a sad little tree that only needed a little love, was thus born. And it wasn't so bad after all.

Colloquial histories would later blame Schulz's story for a late 1960s decline in the artificial tree industry, but in truth Schulz was merely following the industry curve. Many episodes from the era made similar jabs, emphasizing the need for a "real tree" in order to enjoy the season. In *Green Acres*, Oliver insists on cutting down his own tree (which his neighbors allege must be illegal given the sale of artificial trees);[12] Lucy's 1965 tree salesman in *The Lucy Show* says he can paint the trees any color she wants, to which she responds, "Well, could you spray one green so it'd look like a Christmas tree?";[13] and in *Dennis the Menace*, Mr. Wilson insists on taking Dennis out to chop down their own real tree to replace the inferior white-painted tree Dennis's father had purchased. Additionally, in 1966 the National Christmas Tree Association began a tradition of presenting the First Lady with that year's champion tree to put on display in the White House, likely increasing the prominence of real trees in the eyes of many American housewives dressing their homes for the holidays.[14] To credit Schulz's *A Charlie Brown Christmas* alone with the mid-century downturn of the artificial tree industry would thus be an overstatement. His special, however, would become emblematic of the shift.

But Sparky would not ride every industry or cultural trend. If he was going to write an entire program to be televised as a Christmas special, he would have to make the program about the biblical foundation of the holiday. Any other option would be a betrayal to his personal convictions. "We're going to have to have Linus read from the Bible," he told Bill and Lee. "Gee, I don't know if you can animate from the Bible," Lee Mendelson said. "You know, it's never been done before." The unprecedented nature of the content was anything but a deterrent for Sparky. "If we're doing this show and it's going to be on at night, I'm going to add some meaning to it," he told them. "I don't want it just to be funny. If we're going to do it, I think we should talk about the true meaning of Christmas—at least what it means to me."

Bill Melendez, the eventual voice of Snoopy, would say years later that "I thought it was a very dangerous place to go into, especially as I didn't know anything about it, and I didn't like being involved." But Sparky was very well-read in the Scriptures, and was confident that incorporating an explicit statement about the birth of Christ was necessary in his program. He had done so successfully in his strips. "We can't do this; it's too religious," Bill told Sparky.[15] Sparky responded with a simple statement, speaking to the culture's inward reversion, the industry's secularity, and his own convictions. He told Bill and Lee, "If we don't do it, who will?" And that was it.

They sent a short, half-page outline for what would be a thirty-minute special to John Allen. "The core of the program had been established in the outline which had gone to our sponsor," Melendez remembered. "The show would include winter scenes, a school play, a scene to be read from the Bible, and a sound track combining jazz and traditional music." Allen took the proposal to Coca-Cola, adding his own spin to sell an otherwise thin description of the project. "[Allen was] one of the few guys left who will take a chance with prestigious programming,"

Mendelson had said at the time.[16] The soft drink giant bought Allen's pitch for the "visibility special" that would complement their regional bottlers' spot advertising, believing in the promise of an exciting Christmas program by a beloved American franchise—a promise that would net them even further dominance in the mid-century drink market. Viewers would love the *Peanuts* Christmas special, the Coke executives gambled, and they would know it was Coca-Cola who brought it to them. Sparky and Mendelson received the following telegram, officially confirming the start to a new future for the franchise:

> CONFIRM SALE OF CHARLIE BROWN FOR CHRISTMAS TO COCA-COLA FOR DECEMBER BROADCAST AT YOUR TERMS WITH OPTION ON SECOND SHOW FOR NEXT SPRING. GOOD GRIEF!

Allen then successfully sold the idea to CBS, who would televise the show that Christmas season; the network's financial risk had been sufficiently diminished by the involvement of a corporate sponsor.

With mere months to complete the program before its December airing, Sparky and Bill set out to finalize the script and give the team of animators their marching orders. Except for its rejection of a solely secular theme of goodwill, the program kept with the typical conventions of the genre—carols would provide a backdrop, the Christmas tree would be prominent, Charlie Brown would stand in as a pseudo-Scrooge, and characters would write letters to Santa Claus. Aesthetically, though, the team made a series of small choices that had a cumulative effect of appearing revolutionary, if not simply risky. The production would be in "limited animation" (sparse character movement filmed with few frames per second), actual children (most not being professional actors) would provide the voices, no laugh track would be included (an insistence of Schulz's, though Mendelson had tried to convince him otherwise), and a fresh jazz score would provide the musical backdrop to elevate the program to a more sophisticated level (which Mendelson commissioned, calling on local jazz celebrity Vince Guaraldi, who had written and performed the soundtrack for the unaired Charlie Brown documentary).

The combination of these features and Schulz's distilled approach to plot and dialogue resulted in a comparatively slow feature—one much slower than the vaudevillian variety shows of the era. Even Bill and Lee were worried that they had killed it. An agent from McCann-Erickson checked in on the work and was likewise taken aback by just how slow the program was. The adman was former CBS employee Neil "Moon" Reagan, who visited the Charlie Brown operation before a political campaign he worked on ramped up—the California governorship campaign[17] of his younger brother, Ronald Reagan. If the client saw this, Neil told the team, they would most certainly pull the funding. An ever-jovial fellow, though, Neil could connect with Sparky's enterprise. This whimsical brother of a future president, after all, had likewise been nicknamed from youth after a comic strip character—Frank Willard's popular Moon Mullins. Experienced in broadcast himself, he agreed to keep quiet about the progress he had seen, allowing the team to finalize their product and present it to the studio without interference from the agency or the sponsor.

At Fantasy Records in San Francisco, Vince Guaraldi began recording the special's musical score and lyrical song numbers. He asked a handful of talented members of the children's choir at St. Paul's Episcopal Church in San Rafael, California, near where he lived, to lend their voices to the project. He had worked with the choir on a jazz mass he was preparing, and they had enjoyed working with him. During what they thought would be a regular practice session, the children were whisked away with their choir director Barry Mineah (unbeknownst to some of the parents) to the city to record the numbers late into the evening. At the studio, they recorded "Christmastime is Here," which Vince had written the tune for and for which Lee came up with the words in the moment. The choir children even recorded a cheerful shout of "Merry, Christmas, Charlie Brown!" that would take the place of the child actors' voices just before the other song they recorded, the sacred carol "Hark! The Herald Angels Sing." A well-trained choir, they were asked to "untrain" themselves so that the closing song would sound more like a group of regular children from the neighborhood, matching the voice actors' sound. Many of the children would cringe in good humor about this unpolished approach many years later. "To be involved

"I CAN NEVER GET IT THROUGH MY HEAD.... WAS JESUS A GROWN MAN OR WAS HE A LITTLE BABY?"

Two by Fours. 1965. © 1989 Warner Press, Inc., Anderson, Indiana. Used with permission.

in a project that at the time was kind of a lark but turned into something that is so loved, so treasured . . . to be a part of that was just a very, very special feeling," reminisced David Willat, one of the choir members.[18] It took only a few evenings to finish the recordings,[19] after which the children were treated to ice cream and paid a flat fee of $5 per session for what would become an iconic sound of the season. (The young choir members, uncredited for their work for many years, included: David Willat, Dan Bernhard, Kristin Mineah, Mark Jordan, Debbie Presco, Marcia Goodrich, Nancy Goodrich, Steve Kendall, Ted King, David Hertzel, Toni Elizabeth Mehochich, and Cary Cedarblade.)[20]

Slow and unpolished as many parts may have been, the musical and visual style of *A Charlie Brown Christmas* fit the innocently unencumbered, openly introspective nature of Schulz's work. Moon's predictions proved apt, though, and Mendelson was greeted with anything but a pleased response from the studio executives. Melendez had finished his "answer print" (a polished draft used for final editing/approval before producing the "release print") just one week before it was to go to air. Mendelson took this finalized copy with him to New York City to show the executives at CBS, and they let him know just how displeased they were with everything—the slow pacing, the lack of a laugh track, the unprofessional-sounding child actors, and the religious content. "The Bible thing scares us," they told Mendelson. After all, none of their other properties were even close to as religiously explicit, even during the Christmas season. None of their competitors' were either.

Throughout the 1960s, less than 9 percent of Christmas episodes and specials would contain any substantive references to religion.[21] ABC's *The Brady Bunch* and NBC's *Bonanza* would have characters singing sacred Christmas carols, but the songs would go without commentary or theological extrapolation. The most viewers would typically see during the 1960s (and beyond) would be exemplified in 1965's Christmas episode of Lucille Ball's *The Lucy Show* on CBS. In the episode,[22] Mr. Mooney, Lucy's (Mrs. Carmichael) boss, says that Lucy's young boys' choir is not able to sing carols at the bank. Lucy contends that they used to do it back in Danfield. "We're in a big city now," demands Mr. Mooney, "Danfield was a little town." "Yeah, well so was Bethlehem," retorts Lucy. A defensive Mr. Mooney responds, "What does Bethlehem got to do with Christmas carols and the spiri . . . spir . . . ?!" An incredulous look from Lucy stumps Mr. Mooney, who says, "You baffle me, Mrs. Carmichael. I know I'm smarter than you are, but I can never win an argument!" The comedic turn that Lucy's expressive pause provides serves the humor of the joke well, giving the audience the opportunity to fill in the missing gap for themselves (Bethlehem has everything to do with Christmas, contends the joke). The structure of this moment, though, exemplified the general dynamics of religion on television—if it was referenced, it was only in passing. It was not typically explained or affirmed with any depth, nuance, or noticeable importance.

Television had more captivatingly realized the promise of radio programming, with families from all across the country sitting in their individual homes collectively transfixed by the entertainment program broadcast on one of the three highly competitive national networks.

To say anything that might offend their viewers, especially something so sensitive as public religion in the 1960s, was seen as much too large of a risk. Schulz, however, had developed a different vantage point surrounding his content, often saying that "there will always be a market for innocence,"[23] and that Christmas was the sort of season that needed the innocence of the nativity. In his study Bible, across from the Gospel of Matthew's recounting of Christ's birth, he had written:

> Christmas is primarily a children's day, for it takes the innocent faith of a child to appreciate it.
> The Christmas story is filled with characters who have the same perfect faith.
> Joseph and Mary, the 3 wise men.
> The Christmas story is a story of purity and can be appreciated only by the pure mind.
> Our Lord is a Holy God and if we are to approach Him, we must be holy and pure, and filled with the same faith as the wise men.

Though Christmas celebrations in the Schulz home were large, joyful, and rather non-religious affairs, with a nativity set on the mantle being a mostly unexplained adornment, Sparky embraced his *Peanuts* special as an opportunity to approach the innocence and spiritual faith that lay at the heart of the season.

The studio executives, who did not have the same philosophical approach to the season, worried about their market share. It was reasonable of them to do so, but their concerns were products of an industry that would routinely underestimate the collective interest the country would have in spiritual faith. In the broadcast business, entertainment had not only become commercial, it had become too dangerous for sustained religious reference, and network executives were not usually keen on embracing danger.

Leaving the screening with the executives, Mendelson felt dejected, kicking around the streets of New York in a fog, worried that they had ruined it all. Mendelson's role as producer was to sell the creative work that Schulz and Melendez had produced, and it was devastating personally and professionally to have a client on such a big sale disappointed. "For a few hours," he said, "I felt lower than Charlie Brown's batting average."[24] Thankfully, though, the studio would not pull *A Charlie Brown Christmas* from its lineup. It could not. The airing was barely a week away, newspapers around the country were already building up the buzz, and CBS and Coca-Cola had already taken out advertising for the special.

Around an image of Charlie Brown on television, an expensive half-page *TV Guide* ad read, "Happiness is watching 'A Charlie Brown Christmas.' See them all—the whole Peanuts gang—in their first television show. Brought to life from the pages of your favorite newspaper and presented to you by the people in your town who bottle Coca-Cola." That one advertisement alone cost $11,300 in 1965 (roughly the equivalent of $85,300 in 2013), and there were others across newspapers and trade magazines. If the studio pulled the special without time to re-advertise, viewers tuning in expecting to see Snoopy and the gang would be disappointed, feeling let down by not only the TV station, but also the client sponsor—Coca-Cola (which in October had already signed off on a second *Peanuts* program, a baseball special, for the following summer)[25] and its local bottlers. This would mean that CBS would lose even more money in ad revenue than if they simply went forward with a flop. The timing meant that *A Charlie Brown Christmas* was headed for the airwaves, even if it lacked a network cheering section. Whether or not the enterprise survived would be left to the American public—a public that the studio executives, like most in their industry, feared would reject the explicit religious message.

The final product was true to the original plans, including a pronounced scriptural recitation by Linus. In the special, Charlie Brown, feeling depressed before Christmas, laments the commercialism around him—Snoopy has entered a lights and display contest, Lucy yearns for real estate, and Sally asks Santa for cash. At Lucy's 5¢ psychiatric suggestion, Charlie Brown agrees to become the director of the school play in order to find for himself the season's meaning. What he needs is involvement, she tells him. Play rehearsals, however, go awry. Lucy assumes she'll be the "Christmas Queen," Frieda complains about the dust in the Bethlehem inn ruining her naturally curly hair, and Schroeder plays a lively jazz tune (Guaraldi's "Linus and Lucy," which would become the *Peanuts* theme music) instead of a thematically appropriate soundtrack for the scene at the inn.

To restore their endeavor, Charlie Brown and Linus set off to find a Christmas tree. Returning with a sad natural tree, instead of a flashy aluminum one, he suffers more ridicule, sinking him further into confused depression and causing him to desperately shout, "Isn't there anyone who knows what Christmas is all about?!" "Sure, Charlie Brown," says Linus. "I can tell you what Christmas is all about." Taking to the center of the stage with his trusted blue blanket, Linus calls for "Lights, please," and humbly yet earnestly recites from Scripture:

> And there were in the same country, shepherds, abiding in the fields, keeping watch over their flock by night. And lo, the angel of the Lord came upon them, and the glory of the Lord shown round about them, and they were sore afraid. And the angel said unto them, "Fear not, for behold I bring you good tidings of great joy, which shall be to all people. For unto you is born this day in the city of David, a Savior, which is Christ the Lord. And this shall be a sign unto you—ye shall find the babe wrapped in swaddling clothes, lying in a manger. And suddenly there was with the angel a multitude of the heavenly host praising God, and saying, "Glory to God in the highest, and on Earth peace, good will toward men."[26]

"That's what Christmas is all about, Charlie Brown," Linus concludes. As Vince Guaraldi's slow and jazzy "O Christmas Tree" begins playing in the background, Charlie Brown walks home under the twinkling stars with Linus's words echoing in his mind. "Linus is right," he says out loud to himself. "I won't let all this commercialism ruin my Christmas." Taking one red bulb off of Snoopy's prize-winning doghouse, Charlie Brown adorns his small tree with the simplest of decorations, but it falls over under the weight, and so does Charlie Brown's hope. All is not lost, though, as the again-defeated Charlie Brown has his spirits lifted by the gang who comes and restores the tree to beauty with a flash of waving hands and arms. "Merry Christmas, Charlie Brown!" they yell in unison, singing the sacred carol "Hark! The Herald Angels Sing" as the credits roll.

When it aired at 7:30 p.m. on December 9, 1965, complete with the passage from the King James Bible, *A Charlie Brown Christmas* dominated. The buzz around the beloved comic strip coming to television was enough to generate a massive viewing. Nearly half of all American televisions turned on were tuned to watch the *Peanuts* special, generating a 45 percent share with 15,490,000 viewers. The show was given a valuable timeslot after the evening news with Walter Cronkite, replacing that week's episode of *The Munsters*, and leading in for *Gilligan's Island*. Competition was not fierce, as NBC ran a new episode of *Daniel Boone* and ABC ran the U.S. Driving Championship competition *Road America 500*. Viewers would also have a few local independent stations in their reception radius, which ran programs like *Growing Up Today—In the Arts*, a multi-part leader training film for Girl Scouts; *The Devil's Partner*, a 1961 movie about a Texas goat breeder suspected of being a conjurer; and a rerun of the police drama *Naked City*.

It also helped that Schulz's Christmas special was listed as being in color (which was still something of a novelty in 1965) with a half-page advertisement and full-spread color comic feature in *TV Guide*, one of the few sources for viewers to see broadcast schedules. Some newspapers even included special promotional features in their own television digest booklets. They had been provided a synopsis in advance (some incorrectly including the Git List scene in their description), and Sparky had done telephone interviews with journalists from these newspapers and sent along panel drawings and production cels to help drive up the anticipation. *A Charlie Brown Christmas* had thus been in a prime position to sweep the viewership ratings, and it did, proving a huge success for CBS and sponsor Coca-Cola.

The days following the special's airing were even more telling of the program's success. "All heaven broke loose," described adman John Allen, as letters and phone calls flooded in. Reviews in the newspapers were largely positive. *Time* magazine had called the show special, unpretentious, and unprolonged.[27] The reviewer for the *Washington Post* praised the writing, animation, music, and voice acting: "[Schulz] took no chances with the happenstance of Hollywood," wrote reviewer Lawrence Laurent, noting that "good old Charlie Brown, a natural born loser . . . finally turned up a winner."[28] A few observers were tepid or sour; a columnist from the *Kentucky New Era* wrote that the characters "lost most of their special, piquant charm" and "fell on their little round faces as TV stars,"[29] because the special spelled out too much for viewers, but the overall reaction from critics was supportive of the special.

Perhaps more striking than the comments of formal media reviewers, though, were the earnest and personal connections that viewers felt. The pastor of Atlanta's prominent Northwest Presbyterian Church, Dr. Chilton "Chick" Frazier Thorington, was so taken by the special that he shared his praise with his congregation the following Sunday. "I hope that you had a chance last Thursday night to see the Coca-Cola Company's delightful half-hour show," he said from the pulpit, vividly recounting the show's plot and Linus's Christmas biblical recitation from the stage. "Christmas bursts upon our dark night of doubt and despair and announces: EMMANUEL has come. EMMANUEL! 'God with us,'" the pastor proclaimed in conclusion. Along with a handwritten note, Thorington gave a copy of his sermon to a member of his congregation that he thought might appreciate the vote of confidence—Charlie Adams, a vice president at Coca-Cola, and one of three vice presidents, along with Luke Smith and Cliff Hodgson, who attended the church. "The Christmas program was great!" the pastor wrote on his note to his soda executive parishioner. "Thanks to the Coca Cola Co.!"[30]

Scores of letters poured in to Coca-Cola from diverse viewers who wished to praise the company for its role in the production. Advertisements at the start had indicated that it was the local bottling company that had brought the show to the air, and Sparky appeared on television at the end of the broadcast, thanking Coca-Cola for their sponsorship. Singing their own personal praises to the soda company, many of the letter writers made note of the show's religious content, a noticeably unique part of the program in the minds of much of the American viewing public.

Aware of the routine secularizing decisions that studio executives made, one viewer from South Miami wrote, "At the point where the little character said: 'Can't anyone tell me what Christmas is all about?' I said, 'Don't tell me they're going to mention Jesus,' and I was so gratified and heartened at the next scene when he began to relate the Christmas story." The sisters of St. Sebastian Convent in Belle Vernon, Pennsylvania, thanked Coke for their portrayal of the "real spirit of Christmas which is so often obliterated by a false one," adding, "It is our hope that 'Peanuts' may find a permanent place in the T.V. realm." The praise for the religious content was often even coupled with praise for Coca-Cola's popular soft drink. "We were happy to see a company such as yours sponsoring a program that helps to lead us all back to the type of holy day spirit needed so badly in these days," wrote one viewer. "Thank you for a delightful half hour. It was as refreshing as one of your 'Cokes.'"

Mrs. Betty J. Knorr of Miami Shores, Florida, wrote to the president of the company with an appreciative and deft hand that laid bare the cultural context in which Schulz's characters spoke:

> December 14, 1965
> President,
> Coca Cola Bottling Company
> Dear Sir:
> Congratulations on your presentation of "Charlie Brown's Christmas" last Friday [*sic*] evening. It was a charming program well presented and at a time when the children could really appreciate it. Both of my children (ages 8 and 11) enjoyed every minute of it—even the Coca Cola advertisements!
>
> I particularly salute you for sponsoring a program stressing the true meaning of the Christmas season. In this dark day of everyone being afraid to mention Jesus and the Church for fear of some group boycotting their product or getting a Court Order handed down, of prayer being banned from schools and public meetings and the mention of God in general being hush hushed, I really commend you for this timely presentation.
>
> Thank you very much.
>
> I feel sure that I echo the gratitude and sentiments of most concerned parents. Unfortunately, we are more prone to criticize than compliment. As a result, most of the good things that are done daily go unheralded while all the evil and vile things receive banner headlines.
>
> Best wishes for the holiday season.
>
> Sincerely yours,
> Mrs. Betty J. Knorr

These letters affirmed that Schulz had known his audience better than the studio executives had. There was, in fact, a market for the innocent and wholesome, and even for religious affirmation. "Our theme," he told a local reporter, "is Charlie Brown's search for the true meaning of Christmas—a search that, in the larger sense, is one we're all engaged

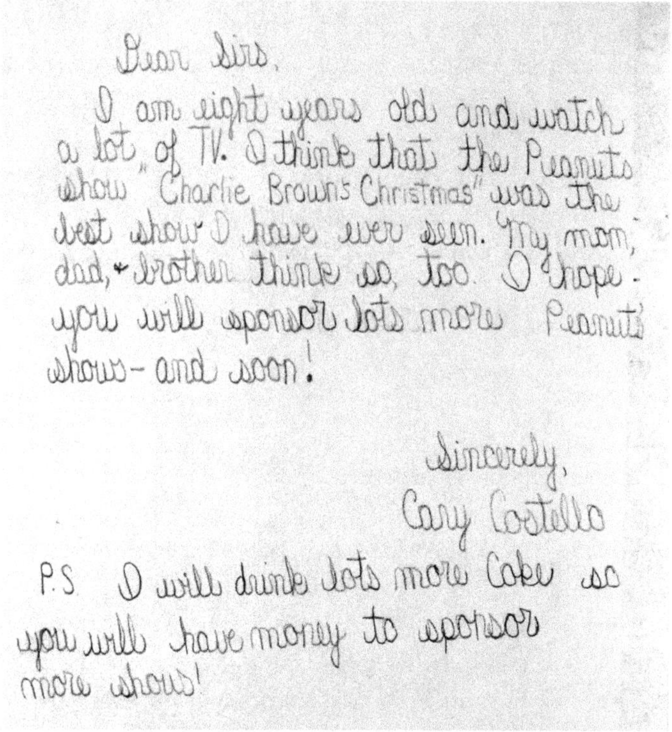

Dear Sirs,
I am eight years old and watch a lot of TV. I think that the Peanuts show "Charlie Brown's Christmas" was the best show I have ever seen. My mom, dad, + brother think so, too. I hope you will sponsor lots more Peanuts shows - and soon!

Sincerely,
Cary Costello

P.S. I will drink lots more Coke so you will have money to sponsor more shows!

Letter sent to Coca-Cola by eight-year-old Cary Costello. Costello was one of many school children who wrote in to Schulz, CBS, and Coca-Cola in praise of the Christmas program. December 1965. Courtesy of the Charles M. Schulz Museum and Research Center, Santa Rosa, California, and Cary Costello.

in."[31] He had always had a creative sensibility for the real interests of so-called middle America, and he had proven his instincts correct.

CBS immediately joined in with the celebration, ordering additional specials the very next day. Frank Stanton, president of CBS, called Schulz personally to congratulate him. "We had the most amazing reaction to this show," CBS's program chief Mike Dann said a few days later, admitting that "it was far more than we expected. We not only got letters, but schools sent in long petitions asking us to repeat the show."[32] NBC's vice president of special programming wired in his own congratulations, saying, "Sorry it was not on our network," and the president of Coca-Cola called McCann-Erickson from his office in Atlanta to ensure that the program would be repeated again the next year.

Coca Cola Company
P. O. Box 1734
Atlanta, Georgia

Dear Sir:

The Larson family would like to thank the Coca Cola Company for sponsoring "Charlie Brown's Christmas" on CBS TV. It was funny fast moving and pointedly meaningful. Your support of Mr. Schultz and his "Charlie Brown" is strengthening to we who believe in the Lord Jesus as Savior. I am encouraged to see a national company willing to sponsor not only an excellent production but also a Christian one.

Thank you again. We are looking forward to the next two, and hope there will be more.

Sincerely yours,

Clifford G. Larson,
Director of Public Relations
Kansas District
Lutheran Church-Missouri Synod

CGL:DMS

Letter sent to Coca-Cola by Clifford G. Larson. Like Schulz, Larson fought in Europe during the war. He was wounded while serving in Germany. When he returned home from the army, he attended seminary and began serving the church. December 10, 1965. Courtesy of the Charles M. Schulz Museum and Research Center, Santa Rosa, California, and Dorothy E. Larson.

Sparky had always written *Peanuts* with adult audiences in mind, but animation would redirect the base of his franchise's target audience over the years. Sophisticated as it was, *A Charlie Brown Christmas* began the trend toward being more of a children's franchise by the mere fact that it was an animated program on television. It thrived in that capacity, though, with its subsequent Peabody Award including the citation that "'A Charlie Brown Christmas' was a delight for the whole family." Schulz and his team even found themselves nominated for an Emmy Award in the category of Outstanding Children's Programming, with Sparky further nominated for his role as writer.

In May 1966, Sparky, Bill, and Lee attended the Emmy Awards without an expectation of actually winning. That night at the Hollywood

December 14, 1965

Mr. Fred W. Dickson
Advertising and Promotion
The Coca-Cola Company
P. O. Drawer 1734
Atlanta, Georgia

Dear Mr. Dickson:

May I commend you and the Coca-Cola Company for sponsoring the "Peanuts' Christmas" television special last Thursday evening, December 9. In addition, your own commercial was appropriate in sense and feeling.

It could be that many persons who wouldn't sit still for a sermon would gain some realization of the true meaning of Christmas by watching Peanuts. And having long been a Peanuts fan myself, it was good to see him featured by means of motion picture and television.

Thanks to you - and to Charles Schulz - for bringing a deeper sense of Christmas to so many through the penetrating humor of Peanuts.

Sincerely and gratefully,

Art Vermillion
Minister of Education

Letter sent to Coca-Cola by Art Vermillion, minister of education at the Christian Church of Speedway, Indiana. Near the time he wrote this letter, Art also attended a lecture by Robert Short and had him autograph his copy of *The Gospel According to Peanuts*. December 14, 1965. Courtesy of the Charles M. Schulz Museum and Research Center, Santa Rosa, California, and Art Vermillion.

Palladium, Danny Kaye and Bill Cosby hosted, with celebrity guest presenters handing out Emmys to Dick Van Dyke and Mary Tyler Moore for Leading Actor and Actress in *The Dick Van Dyke Show*, also awarded for Outstanding Comedy Series. *Bewitched*, *Bob Hope Presents the Chrysler Theater*, and *The Julie Andrews Show* were each honored for their directorial achievements, and Frank Sinatra's special won for

Lee Mendelson, Sparky, and Bill Melendez relax after winning their Emmy. 1966. Courtesy Amy Johnson.

Outstanding Musical Program. It was a star-studded affair in which the industry's top echelon was honored. When the Children's Programming category arrived, kiddies puppet show characters Kukla, Fran, and Ollie took the stage to announce the winner. To the *Peanuts* team's utter delight, the puppet group announced *A Charlie Brown Christmas* as the winner of the Emmy over its competitors *Captain Kangaroo*, *Discovery*, *NBC Children's Theatre*, and *Walt Disney's Wonderful World of Color*. Sparky, Bill, and Lee took to the stage, and Sparky grinned broadly as he accepted the golden recognition of their outstanding achievement.

When Christmastime arrived once more in 1966, Schulz drew on his 1965 success and had Linus repeat the gospel recitation to Charlie Brown in a comic strip, adding, "So who needs Santa Claus?" Letters would once again pour in to Sparky's studio, telling him that "we certainly think your Christmas message today was exactly what the whole world needs." "There is no word in my vocabulary to express my appreciation," wrote one Long Island reader. "You have enriched my life with your Christmas edition," wrote a Franciscan priest, promising Schulz to pray "the strongest prayer I know, the Holy Mass, for you and yours and your work." Readers wrote in that they shared the strip, hung it on display with their Christmas decorations, and even "scrap-booked it for future reference." One writer's commendation was driven by the astute suspicion that "more people read the Christmas story by Peanuts than from the Bible." *Peanuts* had become, for many, a rare voice of religious meaning in a perceptually secularized world of entertainment.

That year, as with every subsequent year, *A Charlie Brown Christmas* was re-aired, repeated more than any other animated Christmas special other than *Rudolph the Red-Nosed Reindeer*, which had premiered one year earlier. In 1967, *A Charlie Brown Christmas* would be watched by over 34 million viewers and in 1969 by almost 35 million. The Christmas special would ground the franchise for decades to come, and would provide a benchmark of success for all others to seek.

Despite its success, however, the special's biblical message would maintain its rarity over the years. Its enduring uniqueness may best be highlighted by one of the specials' countless homages and parodies. In the mid-1990s, Robert Smigel of NBC's hit comedy skit show *Saturday Night Live* unexpectedly honored Schulz in one of Smigel's *TV Fun House* animated sketches for the late-night *SNL*. The short opens with various televangelist and celebrity Christmas hosts physically pushing Jesus aside while they continue their routines. Walking the streets saddened by what he has seen, Jesus finds himself in front of a store window lined with televisions. Flipping through the channels with just the flick of his thumb, he becomes more and more upset until he finds himself watching Linus on the screen, reciting from the gospel. Watching this scene, the one that Schulz had insisted on, Smigel's animated Jesus sheds a tear. The live audience for the *SNL* taping sat silent. Enraptured. The animated Jesus then begins dancing a giddy Charlie Brown shrug to Guaraldi's "Linus & Lucy." The *SNL* audience cheered and hollered, connecting with not only the humor, but also the truth in the sketch.

On Schulz's birthday in 1999, Smigel wrote to the ailing *Peanuts* artist, thanking him for the moving and meaningful work he had created for so many years. Smigel wrote with a sincerity that moves the reader with a glimmer of what clearly moved the writer. After recounting his deeply felt childhood connection with the neuroses of the characters, the network comedian returned to reference his own homage, writing to Schulz,

> On the matter of breaking ground, I'm led back to "A Charlie Brown Christmas." No children's special had ever presented such a relevant, adult message, without preaching or condescending, and none has since. . . . In today's world, watching that scene from "A Charlie Brown Christmas" is probably the most religious experience many people have during the holidays. The simple honesty of that boy reading from his bible is one of the most affecting, powerful images that's been on television. And it came from one of the truly great humorists of this century.

Nearly half a century after it first aired, the profundity and rarity of Schulz's words continued to resonate in the entertainment industry.

"If we don't do it, who will?" Schulz had asked. The answer would remain "very few," as television would typically remain silent on spiritual faith. The birth of Christ was important to Schulz, and it was his insistence alone that had brought it to the special. Though some would highlight the promise of the nativity story or faith in the miracle of Hanukkah, holiday episodes and specials would as a rule stick to the conventional wisdom of a goodwill-based universalized "spirit of Christmas" instead of broaching the presumably risky subject of religion. While the dominance of Christmas on television during December inherently speaks to the implicit Christian underpinnings of American culture, studios have continued to do more to reinforce a secularized notion of the holiday through their avoidance of substantive references to the faith that many viewers demonstrably hold dear.

Schulz, however, was willing to break convention, and the outpouring of thanks is a demonstration of the power that an open approach, even if a direct approach, to religion in entertainment media can have with an audience hungry for reflections on their screens of the beliefs in their lives. Because *A Charlie Brown Christmas* fit convention in so many other thematic ways, it was able to softly but profoundly speak to the American audience, and later the world. Scene 8B had been removed, and Schulz's notion of a Give List versus a Git List would never reach cultural salience, but the message he gave in the rest of the program would resonate for decades to come. "Lights, please," Linus said . . . this was what Christmas was all about for Charles Schulz.

4

THE GOSPEL ACCORDING TO PUMPKINS

"Has it ever occurred to you that you might be wrong?"

—CHARLES M. SCHULZ

"THE CHURCH IS HAVING TROUBLE RECRUITING PEOPLE TODAY, INCIDENTALLY, simply because people now doubt everything in the world," Charles Schulz said to an interviewer in 1967, one year after his third animated special, *It's the Great Pumpkin, Charlie Brown*, catapulted Sparky's own parable of faith and doubt into the cultural iconosphere.[1] It was a transitional time for religious communities, and while membership numbers remained steady, many were still struggling with how to reach new followers. It was a transitional time for Sparky, too, though he could not fully know it at the time. His tenure as Sunday school class leader at the Methodist church was in its final years, as was his marriage to Joyce, and the success of his animated specials, though uncertain at the time, would usher in a new franchise future for the already successful strip. The themes of uncertainty and faith were perhaps fitting for this period, even if not planned that way—a nuanced coalescing that both the Great Pumpkin and the Head Beagle could appreciate.

When Sparky, Lee, and Bill began work on their third animated special, CBS once again let the team know of their own concerns for the show's success. The second program, *Charlie Brown's All-Stars*, had aired in the summer of 1966, several months after the wildly popular Christmas special. It too commanded a strong showing in the ratings, pulling in a 45 percent share.[2] It was a rather casual summer program in which manager Charlie Brown tries to lift the spirits of his struggling baseball team with the promise of uniforms from Hennessy's Hardware (which Sparky named for his United Media representative and friend James Hennessy). Though it received mostly positive feedback from critics and was nominated months later for two Emmy awards (Outstanding Children's Program and Individual Achievements of the Writer), it lacked the personal resonance of the Christmas special, and the mailboxes of CBS and Coca-Cola failed to fill up with the fan support of the show's predecessor.

The network executives were now open-minded with Schulz's writing, having far fewer concerns about what he should or should not write than before his television special debut, but regardless of what he wrote for the third show, they made it clear that it needed to be "another blockbuster"[3]—something to rival the impact of *A Charlie Brown Christmas*. CBS had purchased only two specials after the December success, and was interested in giving their valuable timeslots to programs that could make them pull ahead in the network competition, generating more profit from advertisers. According to CBS, this special would likely dictate whether or not there would be any more for Sparky and his team.

The brainstorming session Sparky had with Mendelson and Melendez proved quite fruitful. The annual scene Schulz had been drawing for seven years in which Linus believes in a legendary figure called the Great Pumpkin might be an interesting premise for the show, Sparky suggested. The idea had played well in the strips, and Sparky's two teammates were drawn to its possibilities. The richness of Schulz's suggestion was palpable, and the three had their next special. "It was one of those moments when you know something important, creatively, has transpired," Lee said.[4] Halloween specials were not yet a genre on television, but CBS was open to new ideas, leaving Sparky and his team with little direct competition. Even better, the nature of the season gave creative flexibility to the team, allowing them to load the program with some of Schulz's richest comic strip tropes without them feeling forced or inauthentic.

By the mid-1960s, Halloween had fully evolved into a secular social endeavor, connected to its ancient spiritual content only in theme, not in actual belief. Through a series of historical convergences, the Catholic celebration of All Saints' Day (or All Hallows') on May 13 had moved to November 1, redirecting the energies of the pagan rituals connected with the Celtic celebration of Samhain (pronounced *SAH-win*).[5] Samhain was believed to be a time of year in which fairies, ghosts, and demons mingle with the living,[6] and the combination of the celebrations left the evening before the Catholic observance of its pantheon of saints as a day still used to festively ward off evil spirits believed to be real. Centuries of cultural transmogrifications, though, left the mid-twentieth-century celebration as a social affair, not a spiritual one (with the name's simplification reflecting the cultural one: the eve of All Saints'/All Hallows' Day—All Hallows' Eve—Hallow Evening—Hallowe'en—Halloween). As one *Life* magazine writer described in 1941: "For young Americans, however, Halloween has no religious significance but is their glorious, traditional opportunity to scare each other to death and have the kind of fun that makes Huck Finn, Tom Sawyer and Penrod children immortals."[7]

Schulz and his team were able to trade heavily on the traditions of the season. Between the 1940s and the 1960s, trick-or-treating had evolved from a street urchin activity to a joyful, if spooky, one with children and parents going door to door in costumes with fun expectations of receiving candy. Costumes were now readily available at the drugstore, making prefab plastic masks as common as homemade costumes. The ghoulish supernatural history of the day guided many costume choices, but all were welcome. Even a World War I Flying Ace.

It's the Great Pumpkin, Charlie Brown opens with the classic harvest tradition of picking a pumpkin out of the pumpkin patch for carving. After a spooky title sequence with skeletons and jack-o'-lanterns revealing the program's title, two other gags set the context for the special—the autumnal tradition of raking leaves into a pile (Linus learns the hard way not to jump into a pile of leaves with a wet sucker) and Charlie Brown's annual attempt to kick a football that Lucy is place-holding.

Charlie Brown finds Linus writing a letter to the Great Pumpkin, the supernatural creature Linus believes appears on Halloween night with a bag of toys for all the children. "You must be crazy. When are you going to stop believing in something that isn't true?" Charlie Brown asks him. Linus responds, "When you stop believing in the fellow in the red suit and the white beard who goes, ho ho ho!" Giving up, Charlie Brown comments, "We are obviously separated by denominational differences."

After Snoopy mocks him and Lucy berates him, Linus says in a knowing aside, "There are three things that I've learned never to discuss with people: religion, politics, and the Great Pumpkin." "Everyone tells me you are a fake," he continues to write to the Great Pumpkin, "but I believe in you. P.S. If you really are a fake, don't tell me. I don't want to know."

Taking his place in the pumpkin patch, Linus awaits the Great Pumpkin's wondrous arrival while the rest of the gang ready themselves for "tricks-or-treats" before heading over to Violet's Halloween party. Charlie Brown dons a ghost costume with far too many eye holes (he had a little trouble with the scissors) and finds himself failing at each household stop. "I got five pieces of candy!" Lucy cheers. "I got a chocolate bar," says Violet. "I got a quarter," Patty reports. ". . . I got a rock," says poor Charlie Brown.

Meanwhile, Snoopy, dressed as the World War I Flying Ace, takes off in a fanciful flight atop his doghouse-turned-Sopwith Camel. Shot down by the Red Baron, he must then sneak behind enemy lines, making his way across the French countryside. Interpreting footage from World War I films into his animation, Melendez brought Snoopy's wild imagination to the screen with richly colored backdrops, realistic sound effects, and even Melendez's own altered voice for Charlie Brown's faithful beagle. "This was one of the best scenes we ever animated," Bill said. "It's probably one of the best shows we ever created. It allowed us to really break out, for the first time, with great animation."[8] Deftly executed, this Flying Ace scene would set up the dramatic moment that would bring the show to its emotional height only a few scenes later.

Having canvassed the neighborhood for treats, the gang makes its way to Violet's for the party, full of bobbing for apples, pumpkin decorations, and festive music from Schroeder, but Linus and Sally miss the events, waiting instead in the pumpkin patch all night long. "Each year the Great Pumpkin rises out of the pumpkin patch that he thinks is the most sincere," Linus tells Sally. "He's got to pick this one, he's got to! I don't see how a pumpkin patch could be more sincere than this one. You can look all around and there is not a sign of hypocrisy. Nothing but sincerity as far as the eye can see."

Just as Sally begins to lose interest, a shadow stirs in the pumpkin patch. As the figure rises up in silhouette over a large harvest moon,

Linus passes out from sheer excitement. Much to their dismay, though, it is no Great Pumpkin. It is merely Snoopy, the World War I Flying Ace, still making his way back across the countryside of his imagination. With this revelation, Sally unleashes her fury on Linus, leaving the pumpkin patch with no toys, and no tricks-or-treats.

"Hey, aren't you going to wait and greet the Great Pumpkin, huh?" shouts Linus to the departing group. "It won't be long now! If the Great Pumpkin comes, I'll still put in a good word for you." Recoiling at his own words, Linus shudders, saying, "Good grief! I said 'if.' I meant 'when' he comes. I'm doomed. One little slip like that could cause the Great Pumpkin to pass you by. Oh Great Pumpkin, where are you?!"

Waking up at 4 a.m., Lucy retrieves her shivering brother from the pumpkin patch.

Leaning on their iconic brick wall the next day, Charlie Brown tells Linus, "Well, don't take it too hard, Linus. I've done a lot of stupid things in my life too." "Stupid?!" Linus exclaims. "What do you mean 'stupid'?!" Just wait 'til next year, Charlie Brown. You'll see. Next year at this same time, I'll find a pumpkin patch that is real sincere . . . and I'll sit in that pumpkin patch 'til the Great Pumpkin arrives. . . . He'll rise out of that pumpkin patch and fly through the air . . ." Linus raves as the credits begin to roll.

The show was the hit the studio had hoped for, garnering a 49 percent share against NBC's *Star Trek* and ABC's *The Dating Game* with over 17.3 million people watching. Even more to the studio's liking, the viewer response created the demand for more. Schulz's well-paced story once again struck the hearts of viewers, wishing the best for perennial failure Charlie Brown. Packages poured in to Sparky and the studio, filled with candy for poor Charlie Brown who had only gotten rocks in his bag. Such fan response proved that the executives could repeat the show the following year with the expectations of a high viewer turnout.

The critics were once again pleased with Schulz's work as well, with *Washington Post* television reviewer Lawrence Laurent predicting before the broadcast that it would be "the week's best bet for high quality entertainment"[9] and confirming the next day that it "contained all the simple joy that had been found in 'A Charlie Brown Christmas.'" "Special praise must be given to an extraordinary and splendid musical score," Laurent wrote, adding, "And I suppose the world just might survive if a little credit were given to Charles M. Schulz, the fellow who took our grandest dreams, our fondest reminiscences and made them a delight for children and adults."[10] The *Peanuts* specials "have become the high point of the video season," wrote Clay Gowran of the *Chicago Tribune*.[11] Linus would, of course, try again the next year for the Great Pumpkin, Gowran explained to his readers, adding that "we hope he does, and that he brings the whole gang back with him." CBS agreed, putting the program on annual repeat and ordering four more specials.

Schulz and his team had packed the program with strategic assets, some intentional and others natural byproducts of the theme. The program was set largely at night, allowing for a rich color palette, even more so than that of *A Charlie Brown Christmas*, striking a provocative mood thanks to the animation team's first use of vivid watercolor artistry. As an animated Halloween special, the program was able to ride the celebratory wave of the season with little competition, given that it was in effect creating the television genre. Seasonal tropes were prominent throughout the program, including bobbing for apples, carving pumpkins, making costumes, trick-or-treating, and hosting a party. The spookiness of the season was also sufficiently captured without the program ever reaching a frightful level incongruent with *Peanuts*. Schulz went even further by purposefully integrating two of the comic strip's most iconic features to date—Snoopy against the Red Baron and Charlie Brown against Lucy's football. All of this supported the central story of Linus in the pumpkin patch, garnering the team two Emmy nominations and well-deserved praise from the viewers, critics, and studio executives.

Perhaps the most important scripting element, though, was the Halloween show's connection to Christmas. This was achieved in part by the centrality of the Great Pumpkin story, which had originated as a clever confusion between the holidays in 1959. Two days after Charlie Brown lamented that a store was putting up Christmas decorations in October, the daily strip features Linus getting ahead of himself by writing a letter to someone called the Great Pumpkin instead of Santa Claus. This connection was replayed in the television special, the words of Linus's note scrawled out above his head as they would be in a strip. The scene made clear the contest between beliefs, and could remind viewers of the Christmas special they had watched less than a year before, in which Sally had asked her brother to write out letters to Santa Claus. "You must get discouraged because more people believe in Santa Claus than you," Linus writes. "Well, let's face it . . . Santa Claus has had more publicity. But being number two, perhaps you try harder." The mood, the colors, the music, the genre, the voices, and now the explicit reference to Christmas told viewers that this was Act II to the Christmas classic that so many had loved so very much.

Like the Christmas program, the Halloween special combined Schulz's wit and natural inclination to write from what he knew. Just as the Christmas program revealed Schulz's belief that Christ's birth was important, the Halloween program reflected a number of his beliefs as well. The special was certainly not a Schulzian manifesto—none of Schulz's work ever was—but Sparky's creations could not help but reflect his beliefs, joys, neuroses, and hopes. The Great Pumpkin was no exception.

The original Great Pumpkin strip series lasted a total of eight days, making it an unmissable event for the masses of *Peanuts* readers across the country. In 1960, he doubled the endeavor with a sixteen-strip series on Linus's harvest-time faith, including two Sunday strips. Such a long run using valuable Sunday space was a clear indication that Sparky had found something he enjoyed, and he returned to these original strips for many of the key lines in the television specials.

When ideas did not work in the strips, Sparky would eventually remove them from the strip (like Frieda's cat and the boisterous Charlotte Braun), and when ideas did work, he would let the creative scene take him where it wanted to go. He rarely set out in reverse, almost never planning a declarative end that he wanted to build up to. Instead, sitting in his studio alone, he would work to produce a kernel of an idea from a humorous thought, a witty line, or an expressive doodle that he was working on. When an idea would form, his own wry sensibilities as a humorist led him to its fruitful possibilities, exploring the idea further in subsequent strips until the scene played itself out one way or another. When the Great Pumpkin idea came to him, its narrative richness could not help but pour out onto the panels. Linus would look for a sincere pumpkin patch, avoiding hypocrisy, writing letters to the Great Pumpkin, getting scolded by Lucy, trying to find understanding in Charlie Brown, missing trick-or-treating, finding hostility in a candy-less Sally, and even singing pumpkin carols. Schulz had created an addictive premise, producing more than enough ideas to fill weeks' worth of strips year after year, and allowing readers to wait in eager anticipation for October's funny papers.

Schulz's development of the Great Pumpkin storyline resonated with readers and quickly became a recognizable symbol for well-intended but misguided beliefs. The students at the University of Georgia, for instance, used a Great Pumpkin strip to illustrate their analysis of shortsighted societal flaws in their 1960 "Search for Self" literature.[12] Philosopher Alvin Plantinga would even take the idea years later as the vehicle for an analytical rebuttal to reformist epistemology that he entitled "The Great Pumpkin Objection."[13] Robert Short, a graduate student in the Department of Theology and Literature in the Divinity School of the University of Chicago, also took special interest to the pumpkin metaphor in his best-selling 1964 book *The Gospel According to Peanuts*, a work that would propel religious considerations of Schulz's work, including what the Great Pumpkin might mean, into an even broader national spotlight.

Short was at the forefront of a wave of clergy and religious thinkers taking a theological interest in popular culture. Some, for example, were finding spiritual meaning in the works of popular music, such as folk-rock duo Simon and Garfunkel. "The problem is," said the duo's Paul Simon at the time, "that some religious people are like English majors and can find religious significance in 'Ba Ba Black Sheep.'"[14] When one of his graduate school theology professors brought in a *Peanuts* strip to explain the day's lesson, however, Short was given the chance to explore more than mere nursery rhymes. Trained in various ways to interpret a text beyond simply exploring what the author had intended, Short was captivated by what could be done with Schulz's work and how it might be deployed for other ends. "There was a whole group of us that began reading *Peanuts* religiously, if you'll pardon the very bad pun," Short said,[15] adding that many of his classmates switched their allegiances from Walt Kelly's *Pogo* strips to Sparky's *Peanuts*. Short began compiling his own thoughts on *Peanuts*, keeping a complete file of every strip and noting which strips could be used to illustrate a spiritual idea. He soon developed a sufficient set to share with audiences, and the audiences that came out to hear him could not get enough.

With his insights gleaned from the comic strips turned into a public presentation, Short traveled across churches, entertainingly clicking through slides of *Peanuts* comics as he explained theology to captivated audiences. Short was not divulging Sparky's religious beliefs to audiences, nor was he overtly making claims about Schulz's artistic intentions. He knew little of either. He was not even discussing explicitly religious strips penned by Charles Schulz, as the cartoonist had only recently begun including such overt references in his syndicated work. Instead, much like Paul Simon's English major, Short had found significant theological themes represented in an array of typical *Peanuts* strips. Lucy's torment of poor Charlie Brown, for instance, could be seen as a representation of original sin. Drawing on literary and philosophical giants like Kierkegaard and Hegel, Short would then make bold interpretive claims, even going so far as to argue that Snoopy was the "hound of Heaven," representative of the fallen but faithful Christian whose best attributes mirror those of the Lord—the beagle could cause trouble, but ultimately he was loyal, watching guard, and bringing happiness to the gang. Presenting these ideas with dynamic expression, giving wild voices to the characters as he read strips out loud, Short quickly found that he had struck a rich vein that could carry him even further.

Short would extend the reach of his success by publishing his thoughts in book form. He completed his manuscript, wrote to Schulz asking for permission to include actual strips, and was pleased when Sparky gave his blessing. "I told him that I would certainly be pleased if his book were published," Sparky said, "but I wanted no one to think that we had collaborated on his work. This is my philosophy: Always accept the compliments and praise, but avoid the blame."[16] Tadashi "Tad" Akaishi, a Japanese native and former Los Angeles minister with a doctorate from the San Francisco Theological Seminary, was working at John Knox Press at the recommendation of a friend when Short's book proposal came across his desk. Given the social cachet *Peanuts* commanded at the time, the book was too attractive for Tad to turn down. After formally obtaining the licensing rights from the syndicate to include strips in the book, Tad took Short's book of "theological literary criticism" to print with wild success.

The Gospel According to Peanuts sold a steady average of almost 4,000 copies a week, with over half a million copies sold by the end of 1966 thanks to fifteen rounds of reprints. The book's popularity allowed Short to achieve his goal of spurring theological thought in his audiences across the world. "Art, like Christ," Short wrote, "casts us back upon ourselves for a searching decision: 'Who do you say that I am?' they ask. For in both cases, the answer is never self-evident. . . . Art can also bring about some radical shifts in one's intellectual presuppositions. It does this by providing 'conversation pieces' that attract one's attention while moving the basis of conversation onto entirely new grounds."[17] By harnessing art as a vehicle for thought, Short was able to offer readers an accessible way to consider important spiritual concepts, to consider what it might mean to be a sinner in relationship to a loving God.

The fact that *Peanuts* was the art Short chose to use, of course, is what moved the books off from the shelves. "It is not unusual for Peanuts followers to buy everything in sight, stacking the books in piles that presently may reach the ceiling," a *New York Times* literature columnist wrote of the diverse *Peanuts* books in 1967.[18] The success of Short's work could have been seen as riding the coattails of Schulz's success, but Short had played his own important role in propelling Schulz to even greater visibility. He had been showcasing *Peanuts* in churches and on college campuses for years, and the success of his book[19] now extended Schulz's own reach further; it was a dramatically magnified version of what the church bulletins had done in local congregations.

Schulz would make it clear over the years that Short's ideas were Short's, not his own, but he wrote to Short soon after the book was published, saying, "I am flattered that you have made such a very thorough study of the comic strip and have come up with such remarkable conclusions. I couldn't be more pleased."[20] Likewise, Short would endeavor to make clear that his was a work of interpretation and adaptation, not biography, even though some in his audience would often insist that various strips simply must have had a theological motive behind it. "If I allowed myself to see in my cartoons what you see in them," Sparky joked with a rabbi friend working on similar books[21] many years later, "it would paralyze me and I would never be able to draw."[22]

"I usually tell most of these kids who are very serious about all of these things that happen in *Peanuts* that I'm not sure that every one of them has this kind of significance to it, that sometimes you're attempting to amuse us," Short once explained to Schulz. For audiences

Robert Short and Sparky discuss each other's work on a television broadcast produced by KPIX/San Francisco. Sparky holds in his hand a copy of Short's *The Gospel According to Peanuts*, the popular work of the man he met in person only shortly before the cameras began rolling. Courtesy of KPIX/San Francisco.

not familiar with approaches to literary criticism, and perhaps because of the heavy hand that Short used to write his book, Sparky's personal agency in the matter would routinely get obscured. From its very publication, the book has been routinely misinterpreted as a description of Schulz's hidden intentions secretly embedded in each strip, a misreading that frustrated Schulz. In 1972, he went so far as to say to one reporter that "it's almost a pity that book was published. I have had to explain things in it so many times and basically it isn't my book." Resisting the reporter in a rather uncharacteristic way, Sparky stopped the line of conversation with the reporter, saying haltingly, "No, I'm not going in to that," and turned away.[23] The constant barrage of misquotations and misinterpretations had worn on Schulz, and for once, he let it show.

Despite the routine misreading, Sparky had nonetheless been quite flattered by Short's treatment of the strip. "This is what makes me so happy, that you are able to use the strip in this way. This delights me to no end," Schulz said to Short during a television appearance they made together, meeting just hours before hosting a half-hour program about their works.[24] It was flattering to have someone spend such serious energy on his work, and the impact was, of course, quite positive for the syndicate. The book was, as Schulz would describe many years later, part of a "whole series of fortunate circumstances" that allowed *Peanuts* to become so successful.[25] Short certainly reaped rewards from the endeavor as well, traveling domestically and internationally to give talks on his book almost every day of the week after the book was published. Sparky had questioned Short's decision to do speaking tours instead of using his knowledge, resources, and skills as a full-time shepherd of his own church congregation, but Short eventually did take a pastorate position in 1991 at the First Presbyterian Church in Brighton, Michigan. He would later be the pastor of the First Presbyterian Church in Monticello, Arkansas, sending Sparky copies of his sermons over the years. Though his theology would shape into perhaps a slightly more radical Christian universalism than Sparky would espouse (in 2001, Short began his own church in Little Rock called Christianity Without Doom and Gloom), Sparky would continue to refer to him as a "wonderful guy" and "a very nice man"[26] through his last years. Short visited Sparky in California, even attending Sunday school with him once at the Methodist church. The two were collegial friends early on, and in their careers, they certainly had served each other well.

Robert Short died in 2009, nearly half a century after his first book hit the market. The influential text had been possible only because Schulz's own work was itself so influential. Already a sufficient part of the cultural vernacular, Short could use the art as a vehicle for thoughts not inherently in the strips. The Great Pumpkin saga was one such artistic expression that he could use, given how successful Schulz had been with the series. Short discussed Linus's faith in the Great Pumpkin as a negative exercise in misguided faith, going so far as to call it representative of "religious heresy" in its theistic confusion and overreliance on mere sincerity. "Schulz seems to be in agreement with Kierkegaard, who said, 'Evil, mediocrity, is never so dangerous as when it is dressed up as 'sincerity,''" Short wrote.[27] Though Sparky made great efforts to clarify that Short's words were only interpretations of what one could illustrate through any art, in this instance no leap was necessary. The

Great Pumpkin had clearly already taken cultural root as a critique of misguided faith.

Sparky's successful supernatural squash had been in the strips for years before Short's book then made it even more salient. Two years after Short's book hit shelves, Sparky's television special *It's the Great Pumpkin Charlie Brown* then embedded the trope as a holiday icon, re-inscribed yearly by the much-anticipated re-airing of the Halloween special. The myth at the heart of the show would provoke decades of speculation over its meaning—from Plantinga's philosophical use to turn-of-the-millennium online message board posts asserting that the cartoon was "a great anti-religion teaching tool!"[28] and that it should be claimed for "atheists, agnostics, and freethinkers."[29] Such claims of atheism and agnosticism bent the issue much too far, made possible by Schulz's open style that lent itself easily to diverse interpretations. Nonetheless, a call to "freethinkers" was in fact something closer to a Schulzian perspective.

Schulz did not initially intend to make a theological statement with the Great Pumpkin, and many of the Halloween strips remain non-religious. Yet, almost without the need for such explicit purpose at the start, some of Schulz's views on faith trickled in as he found it a rich creative space for making amusing commentary on religion. He would humorously expose the trials of door-to-door evangelism as Linus tries to hand out tracts to neighborhood families, and he would critique the influence of false prophets as Marcie undergoes "deprogramming" after falling under Linus's sway. After Marcie is rescued, Sally opens her Bible to look up all of the Scripture warnings of false prophets. "Jeremiah, Matthew, Luke, John . . ." she says, thumbing through the pages for her Sweet Babboo. "I think you're off the hook. I'm almost to the end, and I haven't come across your name."[30]

In its tension with Christmas, the Halloween plot also gave Sparky an opportunity to comment on one of his most deeply held misgivings about the practices of religious communities by explicitly vocalizing his resistance to denominationalism. "Santa Claus is twice the man the Great Pumpkin is!" Lucy shouts at Linus in a daily strip on October 29, 1960. "You're crazy!" Linus says. "The Great Pumpkin doesn't even exist!" Lucy counters. As they continue back and forth, a helpless Charlie Brown comments, "I'm always disturbed by denominational squabbling."

Peanuts © Peanuts Worldwide LLC. Used with permission. October 29, 1960.

Though he believed in its core message, Sparky had even begun to resist some of the hierarchical organizing happening within the Church of God, something he had gotten a taste of as early as his time in Minnesota when serving on the pastoral search committee after Cliff Thor moved in 1957. Sparky had hoped without success that Brother Forbes would return, but "being on this committee has convinced me that the whole business of pastoral selection is a slipshod one at best," he told Forbes, apologizing for the "mockery" that he felt was taking place by asking Forbes, one of the church's own former pastors, for references during the process.[31] It was something of a sour note for Sparky to experience shortly before moving to California at Joyce's urging, though he still kept in touch with his closest church friends, many visiting him out west.

Schulz felt strongly about such divisions in churches, lamenting that competition and exclusion were taking away from the call to love one's neighbor. Just one year before he introduced his readers to the Great Pumpkin, Schulz expressed his views on denominationalism for the small readership of *Lookout*, the student newsletter of Cascade College, a Christian university located in Oregon:

> Only a very religiously blind or biased person can read the New Testament, and listen to the words spoken by our Lord and not come away knowing that the one central message is to love your neighbor. We in the church of God seem to find it much easier to try to win people over to our thousand and one different doctrines than we do to love people into the Kingdom of Heaven. Our actions are absolutely no different from the actions of people who belong to political parties, and try frantically to win others to their way of thinking. The truly evangelistic Christian has to learn to be very long-suffering as he sees his loved ones turn aside from

> God time and time again, and he must indeed be filled with Christ's love to see these same people be won over to a Christian experience by the actions of some other Christian church. If one cannot rejoice over such a conversion, one is then alike with the members of the political parties who insist that you think exactly as they do, or you are all wrong.
>
> In my daily mail from readers who write from all parts of the country, I receive letters from members of various religious groups, Jewish, Catholic, Lutheran, Methodist and others, and I always rejoice that we can be brought together by something like the characters in a comic strip, and I try to feel the brotherly spirit that can exist there rather than to try to think of how we must differ so greatly in doctrine. With all the world in strife, and with millions not knowing or caring for Christ, why must we be so ready to differ with those who do love Him? I am as fanatical as the next one in regard to the fundamental teachings of the religious movement to which I belong, but I hope that I can increase daily in my respect for others who are in parallel beliefs. Jesus said, "I desire mercy, and not sacrifice."
> CHARLES M. SCHULZ, Creator of "Peanuts"[32]

Those with parallel beliefs should not be discarded out of mere difference, Sparky knew, having entered his theological studies with a sense of open-mindedness. He would at times be burdened by feelings of aloneness, occasionally panged by a sense that perhaps he was not even loved. This was not a debilitating depression, but it was a melancholy anxiety that he would from time to time have to get through. Conversely, he found Christ's call to love and minister to be the features that should override any human impulse to reject or judge. Churches, according to Sparky, thus had no business creating artificial borders that would make others feel unwanted, unworthy, or unneeded. They certainly should not be basing their message on fear or condemnation, he believed, though he understood the persuasive power that these messages often had as means of reinforcing a congregation's numbers, identity, and offering plate. "Some of the hate preaching which goes on in the guise of religion is really frightening," he said.[33]

Not unlike the storylines Sparky would revisit throughout his career in which Sally and Peppermint Patty bring religion to their classrooms, the Great Pumpkin saga gave him a context in which to comment on the difficulty in expressing one's faith in public, knowing that individuals

"ALL RIGHT.... A MOTION HAS BEEN MADE AND SECONDED THAT EVEN THOUGH FRED, HERE, INTERPRETS THE STORY OF JONAH AND THE FISH ALLEGORICALLY, HE CAN STILL BE PERMITTED TO ATTEND OUR YOUTH FELLOWSHIP PICNIC."

Young Pillars. March 17, 1963. © 1989 Warner Press, Inc., Anderson, Indiana. Used with permission.

with different beliefs, even parallel beliefs, were not always treated with respect. While he was vocal about his faith in certain contexts, he also knew that some would disagree with his own views on the Kingdom of God, and at times he had to be pressed to share his perspectives in more than broad strokes. To do otherwise may result in social chastisement. Linus went through such social pain when he attempted to share his religious beliefs in Schulz's 1972 animated special *You're Not Elected, Charlie Brown*; his political fallout matched the social shame he had felt in the Halloween special. In the election show, Linus tells his classmates in his first public speech that if elected as class president he will "purge the kingdom" and "bring down the false idols in high places" in their "spiritual Babylon," statements that make the school principal turn rather pale. After all, as he tells Violet, they are "in the midst of a moral decline." Though Linus ends up winning the election by a slim margin of one vote, it's not without a political fiasco caused by Linus sharing his faith in his final speech.

"Linus, this is your last speech of the campaign, so go out there and give it all you've got," Lucy says. Linus takes the stage amidst cheers from a packed elementary school crowd and announces, "Mr. Chairman, teachers, and fellow students—this will be my last speech before our election." From her seat in the crowd, Lucy tells Charlie Brown, "We've got it cold."

"I want you to know that I have enjoyed this campaign," Linus says amidst cheering. "And it has been a pleasure to meet so many of you. And I have appreciated your support. Therefore, I have a little surprise for you." As more cheers pour in, one kid in the audience yells, "Tell it like it is!" Doing just that, Linus declares, "And, as a change of pace, rather than campaign talk, I decided to say a few words about the Great Pumpkin." Sunk by Linus's decision to share his peculiar beliefs, Lucy and Charlie Brown can only yell out "Aaugh!"

Unlike in previous speeches, where he was met with routine praise and robust cheering, this speech ends with Linus walking offstage, head hung low, in a sea of laughter from the crowd, confessing to himself, "I've blown the election."

Linus was not alone in the risks brought on by sharing one's sincere faith, Sparky knew. Over the years, Sparky had endured journalists and faithful readers at times misquoting or misinterpreting the cartoonist's religious perspectives. At times, Sparky doubted if he would ever find real understanding. And, of course, even when he did find understanding, there would be some who would disagree with his theological perspective. At times, such a conundrum was more than enough to keep Schulz from being overly expressive about his spiritual beliefs. Yet he had still developed enough of a personal voice in his strips that glimmers of his beliefs could not help but shine through, even when he had no interest in being actively evangelical or argumentative. "When a person has to turn out something funny every day of every week of every month of every year, and this goes on year after year after year, you obviously have to draw upon every thought which comes to your mind! Everything that you know becomes part of this comic strip," Schulz realized.[34] In the Great Pumpkin, his awareness of social fallout and his recursive relationship with faith and narrow certainty offered what for some readers might seem like a paradox of openness and belief. He believed, according to his own statements, but he could not help but have doubts in overconfident dogma. He was sincere in his own beliefs, but sincerity did not justify being judgmental, nor did it justify hubris.

Doubt was a natural byproduct of such a personal and studied relationship with Scriptures. Reading diverse interpretations from various commentaries talking about troubling passages from the Bible, Schulz could not help but doubt theologians' definitive stances on complex ideas. "I'm always a little bit leery of people who are sure that they're right about things that nobody's ever been able to prove, and never will be able to prove," he said.[35] No one person or denomination could have all the answers, Schulz firmly believed, finding little pleasure in those that would immaturely think otherwise. Linus's blind faith in the Great Pumpkin satirizes such misguided devotion. "I've written a book on my experiences with 'The Great Pumpkin,'" Linus says to Charlie Brown in a strip from November 4, 1960. "I call it 'My Belief was Rudely Clobbered.'"

Schulz would always have doubts about the various beliefs that he and other spiritual thinkers held to be true. "I think that we have distorted many of the things which [Jesus] said, so much so in the church that we have lost these things," he said in 1967.[36] Unlike many in church circles, Schulz was willing to doubt such distorted certainties that others insisted upon. Maturity demanded that he do so. Such an allowance for doubt was not a dismissal of truth or belief, however—quite the opposite. Schulz experienced doubt because he also experienced belief, and he worried that others were avoiding the church because they doubted too much.

In a strip series from 1980 that would last for seventeen dailies, Schulz set Linus squarely at the center of this tricky equation, offering his readers a potent line that would exemplify Sparky's own relationship with doubt and faith. The June 3–21 series, which developed organically for Schulz, without tight narrative direction or staging, finds Charlie Brown heading off to summer camp with the gang—Linus, Lucy, Peppermint Patty, Marcie, Sally, Eudora, and even Snoopy the World War I Flying Ace. The camp turns out to be a church camp of sorts. "This new camp we're all going to looks kind of interesting," Linus says to his sister. "They have guest speakers and discussion groups." More than that, though, they had prayer before breakfast, inspirational choruses sung around the campfire, and no comic books.

The camp was also fraught with the burden of end-times preaching. Schulz painted the counselors in a negative light for scaring Peppermint Patty with the talk of the end of the world. "Aren't you scared, Marcie?" a distraught Peppermint Patty asks from bed one night as she recounts being told that they were in the last days. "Doesn't that bother you? Aren't you terrified?!" Such speculative theology had always frustrated Schulz, knowing that intelligent theologians had disagreed on their interpretations of the unknowable future for millennia. "I think this is irresponsible preaching and very dangerous," Schulz said, "and especially when it is slanted toward children. I think it's totally irresponsible, because I see nothing biblical that points up to our being in the last days, and I just think it's an outrageous thing to do, and a lot of people are making a living—they've been making a living for 2,000 years—preaching that we're in the last days."[37] How could a camp counselor know they were in the end days, when the people in the Apostle Paul's day thought the very same thing? For Schulz, he couldn't, despite what many in the church would rather proclaim.

Later in the series, Sally becomes the victim of naïve criticism when she attempts to pray in public, she too feeling the pressure to get her public spirituality right or not display it at all. During one of their meetings, Sally is asked by the off-panel leader to pray. "Yes, sir?" Sally says. "You want me to what? Lead in prayer? Out loud?! Me? But. . . ." Linus, a confident theologian himself, encourages her out of the corner of his mouth, saying, "Go ahead, Sally . . . You can do it . ." The ever-earnest Sally, who has a history of getting her homework assignments jumbled up to the detriment of her report card, again gets a cue a little wrong, closing her eyes and praying, "Now I lay us down to sleep . . ." Support is not what she received in return, but rather laughter—shame-inducing laughter.

In the next, penultimate strip in this series, a calm Linus cannot seem to keep a burning question to himself, a question that is prompted by the misguided actions of the church camp counselors. "May I ask a question, sir?" he says. "I don't really wish to interrupt . . ." Charlie Brown then says, "I think I'll leave . ." (He realizes that Linus's question could end with nothing short of a scene.) "I also don't wish to be rude . . ." the

Peanuts © Peanuts Worldwide LLC. Used with permission. August 9, 1976.

young Van Pelt continues. "Just as a matter of curiosity, sir . . ." he asks as Eudora likewise leaves the room. "Has it ever occurred to you that you might be wrong?"

"Has it ever occurred to you that you might be wrong?" This line had become important for Schulz, emblematic of the twin pillars of security and insecurity in his belief. He was confident enough in his own scholarship to know that many others interpreted the Bible and church operations foolishly, often to the detriment of others. "All too often it happens that the weak ones have to bolster up and tolerate this persecution of the strong ones in the church," Schulz told Robert Short. "And this is what happens to our young people—they come into the church and they are immediately beaten down by the older element who want them to shape up and to be what they think they should be."[38] Schulz knew enough about the Scriptures to know that there was an immense amount that he did not know, and he desired that he and others might be reflexive and open about their theologies without ostracizing or shaming those with different studied ideas.

Schulz had first used the "have you ever considered" line in a 1976 strip in which Snoopy sits atop his doghouse with his typewriter. "I hear you're writing a book on theology," Charlie Brown says to him. "I hope you have a good title." "I have the perfect title . . ." Snoopy thinks. "Has It Ever Occurred to You That You Might Be Wrong?" Sparky became fond of ribbing friends and family with this question when they would espouse an idea he disagreed with, but it was more than a humorous line for the humorist. It should be a personal commitment. The first inclination may be to assume that Schulz was emphasizing the wrongness of theology in these strips or in his conversations, that he was skeptical of any faith. For Schulz, though, the important comportment was not

Sparky's father, Carl, stands beside the car with their family dog, Spike. 1930s. Courtesy Pat Swanson.

toward wrongness, disagreement, or difference. Such was the tendency of immature denominational thinking or of hopeless doubtfulness. What was more deeply important in the lines of Linus and Snoopy was that one should allow additional studied perspectives, even the possibility of being wrong, to "occur to" oneself when considering complex ideas like theology. This was the mature thing to do.

Linus's relationship to faith, holding deep beliefs with the need for critical reflection, modeled not just Schulz's approach to faith, but the broader complexities of his personality as well. He was simultaneously plagued by abject feelings of outcast awkwardness and a competitive drive motivated by a sense of strong-willed superiority. At times he would describe his art as just being in the business "to draw funny pictures,"[39] while at other times he would boast that his unique style and voice had elevated the art. He was, as he would point out, the first to introduce the "slight incident" as the basis for a strip, offering very little action in the panels compared to his contemporaries. He claimed with pleasure that he was the first to use authentic musical scores in a strip, the first to use extensive theological references in a strip,[40] even the first to introduce a Catholic nun in a Protestant magazine cartoon.[41] At times he was withdrawn and socially anxious, while at other times he was witty and romantically charming. He was complex and at times somewhat paradoxical, and his relationship to faith could be nothing different. One should allow for belief, but not with naïve certainties; one should allow for doubt, but not doubt everything.

Charles Schulz had very real and very personal spiritual beliefs as well as serious misgivings about the church and dogmatic theology; both ends of his spiritual spectrum would occasionally come out in his strips, from Linus's Christmas proclamations to his misguided evenings waiting in the pumpkin patch. Of course, not every strip or every gag held deep meaning for Schulz, even if books like *The Gospel According to Peanuts* inadvertently gave readers the impression otherwise. During their television broadcast together, Sparky told Robert Short,

> Sometimes the only significance is that you know the post office closes at five o'clock and its ten o'clock in the morning and you have to get something done and wrapped up and to the post office within the next few hours, so the only significance is that you draw something that is as simple as possible because you just have to get it in there. Drawing a comic strip is like running up a glass hill—you do real well, you go running up, and you almost reach the top, which to me is getting a three or four week lead on your schedule, and then you go sliding back down and suddenly you're right on top of it again.

As he battled that glass hill, Sparky often found his footing in the shadows of his own beliefs. The Great Pumpkin was one such occasion. It was not a declaration, as some would misinterpret it to be, nor was it the seeds of some unrecognized atheistic doubt. Instead, it was a reflection of the complexities of Charles Schulz's very personal and purposefully studied faith.

Awarded with an honorary doctorate, Sparky enjoys a laugh with the crowd as he delivers his commencement address at St. Mary's College in Moraga, California. 1966. Photo courtesy of St. Mary's College.

In May 1966, only a few days after the Emmy awards and while the team continued on the Halloween special that would highlight in broad watercolored strokes some of the misgivings Sparky held, Sparky's father, Carl, died of a heart attack. Back in the Twin Cities, the respected barber had been serving as an usher in his new wife Annabelle's Lutheran church, but he was visiting his son Sparky at Coffee Grounds when he died. "He probably died within three or four minutes," Sparky recalled to Marvin Forbes of the night during his stay that Carl died, "although we worked amateurishly on him for half an hour waiting for the ambulance to come."[42] Sparky could not bring himself to make the long, emotional trip back to Minnesota, where the funeral for his father would be held. He called and asked Bernetta Nelson to help with the service as she had done for his mother.

That same summer, Sparky was awarded his second honorary doctorate, this time from St. Mary's College in Moraga, California. His "astute analysis of human objectivity, is essentially theological; his basic inspiration is deeply Christian," the university's president said in his citation to confer the degree. "Today it is our honor to cite this 'master of wisdom' as philosopher and psychologist, as an artist and an author, as teacher and cartoonist preeminently gifted with a profound sense of humor and a profound understanding of the vicissitudes of human existence."[43]

Delivering his own address as the guest of honor at the commencement, Sparky offered some of his inspiration and insights to the graduation's audience, bookending his talk with a verse from Romans that speaks of the Holy Spirit's role in taking the deep, hard to utter prayers to the Heavenly Father. Sparky spoke of his appreciation for being honored by the school and of his continual surprise by readers' emotional responses to his work. He told stories of strips that brought laughs and grumbles, and he shared with the audience the story of how his Christmas special had met resistance for its religious content. He then led them through passages in the New Testament in which the devil offers Jesus the kingdoms of the world. "The devil was lying!" Sparky explained, for the devil did not have such authority.

He then took the audience to the Sea of Tiberius where Peter and others are gathered by a fire with Jesus, recounting the story of Jesus repeatedly asking Peter if he loved Him. Telling how Jesus asked a third time, Sparky pondered deeply with the commencement audience over what emotions of anguish Peter may have been feeling being asked yet again. Yet Peter answered with what Sparky described as "the answer of supreme faith," telling Jesus, "Lord, you know everything; You know that I love you." "When the excitement of these days passes away," Sparky said to the audience in closing, "and when some of the visions begin to grow a little dim; when it becomes impossible to put into words the prayer you want to speak, then we must be able to lift our heads up, and say with all faith as Peter did, 'Lord, you know that I love you.'"[44] Such was the gospel for Sparky. It was a gospel of faith that circumvented any dangers of essential doubt. He had misgivings about certain elements of the church, and he could not rest assured in strict dogma, but according to his own words, one could hope through all of that, believing that the Lord might still know of one's love and faith. Perhaps in some ways, sitting alone in the pumpkin patch, somewhat misguided as he was, Linus might have had the right idea after all.

5

MAKING THE STRIPS COUNT

"If we are all members of the priesthood, why cannot a cartoonist preach in the same manner as a minister, or anyone else?"

—CHARLES M. SCHULZ

"DO YOU THINK I'M A DEMON? DO YOU THINK MAYBE THEY'LL STONE ME?" Linus asked, understandably concerned. He had, after all, caused the winds and the rains to cease after chanting an ancient and powerful incantation—"Rain, rain go away, come again some other day."[1] Sitting in his studio, Charles Schulz thoroughly enjoyed that his life revolved around coming up with these amusing episodes. With a personal library of books by his side and a small staff down the hall, he sat at his well-worn drafting table daily, trying out sketches on a legal pad before tossing the trial ideas into the wastebasket. "It's hard to convince people when you're just staring out of the window that you're doing your hardest work of the day," he joked.[2] As the ideas would come, he paired his knack for witty insights with his craft for drawing endearing images and set his cast of *Peanuts* characters to paper in India ink with enviable speed.

When they were younger, Sparky's children might surprise him with a welcome interruption in his studio, and later in life, he might take a phone call from a famous friend. Sometimes he would simply fall asleep in his chair trying to think of an idea. He refused to acknowledge "writer's block," something that he considered an "amateur's problem,"[3] but he admittedly had days where he could not think of ideas, and he would "go home kind of disgusted" at the day's stall. Schulz held himself to a high standard, fearing that one day he might not recognize when

In his studio, Sparky smiles as he looks at the original drawing of his July 9, 1969, strip in which Charlie Brown asks Lucy, "Do you ever wonder if God is pleased with you?" Courtesy of the Charles M. Schulz Museum and Research Center, Santa Rosa, California.

his own work was no longer funny. "The dangerous thing—and I have seen it on the comic pages—is when you lose the ability to judge what you have done," he said in a speech at the National Cartoonists Society Convention. He would admit only rarely that he would take advice from others, once doing several stories without Snoopy after receiving a number of letters worrying that the dog was taking over the strip. "I listen to such criticism, if it's valid, I do something about it," he said.[4] But while the possibility of a slump would weigh on any artist, Schulz had grown confident, even defensive and competitive, in his art. "I'm a combination of an egotist and a humble person," he once confessed.[5] It was his work, succeed or fail, and with his strip syndicated in 2,600 newspapers at the height of its popularity, published in seventy-five countries and thirty-one languages,[6] calling his work a success would be something of an understatement.

Unlike other comic strip artists who hired out others to do lettering or even major syndicates which found new artists to grind out a comic strip long after its creator had quit, Schulz insisted on doing all of his own work for the newspaper strips. "That would be like Arnold Palmer having someone hit his chip shots," he said of the idea that someone else even do the lettering.[7] Not only did he find himself most suited to execute his artistic vision correctly, he simply loved what he was doing. He had wanted to do it since he was a young boy, watching through the window as the comic pages rolled off the presses of the *St. Paul Pioneer Press*. As the *Peanuts* franchise had grown, though, he had allowed others to create products for other media. Though Schulz guided their projects, keeping an eye on the progress, Bill Melendez was given freedom in animation, Connie Boucher of Determined Productions had ushered in a merchandizing empire, and friends of Schulz's created *Peanuts* series for comic books.

Among these comic book artists were his Art Instruction billiard buddies Jim Sasseville, who also did artwork for Schulz's short-lived second mainstream comic, *It's Only a Game*, Tony Pocrnich and Dale Hale, each having moved out to California to be Sparky's assistant, and an East Coast minister friend, Roger Palmquist. Like many ministers who enjoyed Sparky's mainstream and church panels, Roger wrote to the artist, beginning a series of correspondences. The two met during a trip Roger took to Minnesota, and they became friends. When Sparky moved to California not long after, Roger and his wife, Lois, took advantage of Roger's sabbatical and followed them west to Coffee Grounds. Roger took art classes in San Francisco and absorbed as much as he could while visiting with Sparky, who was settling into the new home. When Roger returned to the ministry back east, he and Sparky kept in touch by letter. "We finished Jeremiah in Sunday School last quarter. I enjoy very much the teaching of the class," Sparky wrote. "I now feel that I am expert enough to know that it is a rare person who really understands the book. I know I don't. I miss our conversations about things of the spirit, but I have prayed for your happiness, your welfare and the success of the mission that you both are working in. Please face westward now and then, and wave."

It was not long before Sparky could offer Roger an invitation to do more than wave. Roger was an adept artist himself, and Sparky wanted him to work on *Peanuts* comics that would run inside the *Tip Top* comic books produced by *Dell*, along with *Nancy* and *The Captain and the Kids*. Schulz had already hired the others from Art Instruction to create eight-page episodes, keeping a loose watch over their work to make sure their stories matched his desired tone and that they got Charlie Brown's deceptively difficult round head right. Roger had a good line, and Sparky assured his friend that he was up to the task of contributing as well, telling him, "Your cartooning puts me to shame. You draw better than I do, and you are a minister too."[8] Roger gratefully accepted the opportunity and the warm praise from his new friend, sending in his stories and art and enjoying the $25 a page he received in return. Dell's last issue of *Tip Top* ran in 1961, ending Palmquist's short work with *Peanuts* in the winter of 1960. He continued his own art through chalk-talks and illustrating books, eventually settling back into full-time pastoral ministry.

Sparky did not give out praise indiscriminately, and he had very strong opinions about the shoddy artwork of some of his peers, which he would only rarely share when pressed. In his early years with the syndicate, Schulz strove to avoid provoking harsh criticism or pushback, for fear that he would lose the trust of a newspaper editor that a salesman had worked so hard to convince to purchase *Peanuts* for the paper. As his success grew, though, Sparky became increasingly confident in asserting his voice. When one editor, for instance, balked at Sparky's addition of Franklin, an African American character who would attend school with Peppermint Patty, Sparky did not flinch,[9] having reached a point where management across the syndicate structure had few options but to respect the wishes of their biggest success.

Over the years, Schulz had insisted that the syndicate allow him to draw his *Young Pillar* church panels, and with the show of support from clergy across the country, he had found his spiritual voice in the comic strips, even insisting that it be included on network television in *A Charlie Brown Christmas*. Though such religious references were received with overwhelming support from diverse audiences, they did at times prompt criticism, often coming from readers who were not disparaging his religious interests but instead who believed that Schulz had gotten a particular passage wrong. One reader even scribed Hebrew text in his letter to Sparky, telling the artist that a strip in which Linus must recite an unexpected passage from Jeremiah in their Christmas program was obviously based on an incorrect translation of the Hebrew.[10] Schulz's broad appeal to churchgoers had won him significant momentum throughout his career, but there would always be those deep within the ranks that would insist that he conform to their particular view, their particular hermeneutic interpretation, and theirs alone.

These responses lasted his entire career, with a reader of the October 17, 1993, strip censuring Schulz for not knowing the context of the verse he was quoting. In the strip, a boy joins Peppermint Patty and Marcie on their bench at lunchtime, telling them, "Move over, little girls . . Let a man sit down!" and "Girls are always getting in the way." Marcie counters his misogyny by explaining, "Miriam was Moses' older sister . . in chapter twelve of the book of 'Numbers' she asks 'Has the Lord spoken only through Moses?'" When the boy doesn't understand what Marcie's trying to say, Peppermint Patty explains it simply—she slugs him. While Schulz allows Marcie to use the verse to defend the equality of women, the actual verse is followed by Miriam complaining about Moses's Ethiopian wife and being cursed with leprosy for begrudging Moses's authority even though she too knew their God. "If your Bible does not contain the entire chapter, we have included a copy of the entire story. Please read it carefully. It'll be extremely unfortunate if you allow your perversion of the meaning of the Word of God to stand," one letter of criticism to Schulz read. "Now, I am not stupid enough not to know that this episode goes off in a different direction," Sparky said, having led studies of the Scriptures many times over. "How they could imagine I could even find such a quote without having a reasonable knowledge of the Old Testament is beyond me."[11] Though it was a cheeky choice on his part, Schulz used the verse simply because he thought it would provide Marcie with a witty response to the bully. Some readers clearly disagreed.

In 1970, with his work read by nearly 100 million daily readers, Sparky drew diverse responses for a strip that was not particularly new to his comic, but that nonetheless caught the tides of the times. On July 20, Linus comes to Lucy as she sits in front of the television. "I have a question," he tells her. "What would happen if there were a beautiful and highly intelligent child up in Heaven waiting to be born, and his or her parents decided that the two children they already had were

Peanuts © Peanuts Worldwide LLC. Used with permission. July 20, 1970.

enough?" Without turning from her program, Lucy replies, "Your ignorance of theology and medicine is appalling!" "I still think it's a good question . . ." Linus says. Schulz had been making similar "population control" jokes in his strips since 1959, when Linus hollers at Lucy, who thought that times were too uncertain to bring a baby into the world: "What are you gonna do with all those babies who are lined up waiting to be born? You can't just tell them to go away and wait for another thousand years, can you? Can you?"[12] A week later, when he finds out that Lucy wishes he had never been born, Linus exclaims, "Why, the theological implications alone are staggering!"[13]

Many readers viewed his July 20 strip as a statement about overpopulation, drawing both supportive and harsh responses from diverse perspectives. "The world is polluted with people," one letter lamented, chastising Schulz for his "soap opera dramatics" that "don't have much romantic appeal." Another suggested, "Perhaps Linus should ponder this question, 'What would happen if there were a beautiful and highly intelligent child here on earth already born and he was unable to get food or water or an education because the world was overpopulated?'"

Still others saw the strip in a different sociopolitical light, given their historical moment. While the U.S. Supreme Court would not begin reviewing the historic *Roe v. Wade* case for another year, the debate over abortion laws was in full swing across the American populace in 1970, and many readers expressed their distaste or appreciation for Schulz braving the subject in a strip. Among them was long-time *Peanuts* follower and governor of California, Ronald Reagan. Reagan had begun occasionally writing to his clever California resident Charles Schulz and the two struck up something of a friendship, albeit distanced by the celebrity of their different offices. Weeks after reading the 1970 unborn child strip, Governor Reagan wrote to Schulz, saying that the strip "continues to haunt me in a very nice way." In the letter, Reagan explained how he believed "our religion does justify the taking of life in self defense," thus allowing for abortion in the case of the pregnancy threatening the mother's life. The California Supreme Court had recently struck down the California statute that sought to restrict abortions,[14] and Reagan lamented to Schulz that a psychiatric loophole was nullifying any of the protections against abortion that the governor had hoped to maintain. "I didn't mean to let you in on all my problems but just to give the background of why you touched a nerve with your strip the other day," Reagan wrote to Sparky, believing that his friend might understand.

"It was not my intention to get involved in a contraception or abortion debate," Sparky said a few years later, trying to distance himself from the political issue. "My point was simply that people all too frequently discuss things that they know little about."[15] Distancing himself publicly made commercial sense, and perhaps he had honestly not expected such poignant responses related to abortion to fill his mailbox, let alone one from the governor, but it is highly unlikely that Schulz was unaware of the political reality of his strip as he sent it off to the syndicate. Not only was the topic common fodder for newspaper and television reports, but just two years earlier, Sparky's own eldest daughter, Meredith, only eighteen at the time, had an abortion. Sparky and Joyce had sent her away to high school in Switzerland with the hopes that it would get her away from a bad crowd mixed up with alcohol and drugs that Joyce believed she ran with. When she returned home pregnant, according to Meredith, she was told by her parents that she would have an abortion. If Sparky had religious objections to the choice, he did not ever say so, and as Meredith saw it they would have been secondary to the societal or career pressures their family would have been under in that era. "He's not going to stick his neck out when he's climbing the ladder of success. He couldn't. He couldn't. He was strapped. I understand that," she said. "I can only imagine being them in that time." As Meredith recalled, her father's friend Dr. Bob Albo suggested Sparky send Joyce and Meredith to Japan for the procedure, given that California's laws restricted abortions at the time. "So that's what we did."[16]

Sparky enjoyed his friendship with the Reagans. In 1967, Reagan proclaimed May 24 Charles Schulz Day, and in 1969, honored him with the state's Creative Citizenship Award. Nancy Reagan even once instructed her limousine driver to make a detour by the studio just to visit Sparky, but the governor and Sparky certainly had different experiences with the question of abortion. The power of Schulz's strips, especially when dealing with such a provocative issue, was that they allowed the reader to fill in the strip with critical information from the reader's own perspective. In fact, Schulz's strips often required they do so.

As many comic theorists explain, comic strips are a particularly engaging medium for readers because their very structure asks that the reader take part in the action. The white space between panels, known as the "gutter," is an intrinsic feature in most comic art, and "despite its unceremonious title," theorist Scott McCloud explains, "the gutter plays host to much of the magic and mystery that are at the very heart of comics."[17] When readers come to the end of a panel, there is a gap not only between the two rectangles, but also the action contained in each, and the reader must then fill in what happened, creating a sense of mental "closure" so that the episode makes sense. As the reader fills in this narrative leap, they begin to connect with the scene, for they helped create it.

Aristotle described a similar process in the fourth century B.C. in his treatise on rhetorical persuasion. One of the most powerful forms of argument, he explained, was the enthymeme (pronounced EN-thu-meem).[18] This type of statement was a "rhetorical syllogism"[19] in which an audience supplies a missing premise[20] to complete the speaker's argument for him/her.[21] Like the gutter in a comic strip, the enthymeme becomes an increasingly engaging argument since the audience is involved in co-creating it. In some of his most provocative strips, Schulz employed this enthymematic approach, requiring that readers not only fill in the spatial and temporal action of the gutter, but also critical conceptual elements in order to complete the meaning of the strip. The trouble, of course, with enthymemes is that while more power given to the audience may result in a more potent impact, it also diminishes the artist's ability to control what direction the audience will perceive the argument is going. The earnest letters of both criticism and support that flooded in after certain *Peanuts* strips proved this effect to be very real for Schulz. It allowed him to express his thoughts, court diverse audiences, and then avoid expressly dictating which interpretation was correct.

Schulz's open verbal style was highlighted by the open visual style he had brought in from the world of magazine cartooning. Compared to the densely drawn and narrated adventure and soap opera strips that were common when *Peanuts* first began running, Schulz simply put less ink on the paper than his peers. In this void, child characters then gave voice to surprisingly introspective and insightful ideas not typically explored by strips trying to lure in and entertain newspaper readers. By stripping away needless details, Schulz was able to pour his own thoughts out with an authenticity that connected with diverse audiences, inviting even some of his most resistant readers to consider his ideas.

"I'm at my happiest when I have a good idea and I'm drawing it well, and it comes out well and somebody laughs at it," he said. "This is what I enjoy doing more than anything else. If there is such a thing as being born to do something I think I was born to draw comic strips."[22] In the 17,897 *Peanuts* newspaper strips that he created throughout the strip's nearly fifty years of original content, Schulz poured himself onto the page. In contrast to many of his predecessors and contemporaries, he employed a sly humor that was more thoughtful than vaudevillian. He had an instinctive and professional sensitivity to what worked in his strip, eliminating elements that failed even after they were published, such as when Linus wore eyeglasses for a season, a choice which had made it difficult for Schulz to give Linus's eyes expressiveness. When ideas did work, whether immediately like the illusory Great Pumpkin or gradually like the upended Woodstock, he perfected them, making them part of his repertoire of scenarios in which to humorously explore the universal themes of hope and grief, joy and failure. "A cartoonist is someone who has to draw the same thing every day without repeating himself," Schulz said,[23] and his recurring motifs, like Snoopy at his typewriter and Lucy at her psychiatric booth, provided him the foundation for his introspection and wit.

"The strip is very personal and all the things in the strip are things that I think about," he explained.[24] "Of course, you can grind out daily gags but I'm not interested in simply doing gags. I'm interested in doing a strip that says something and makes some comment on the important things in life."[25] The openness of his style and the dependability of his tropes, also founded in the reliability of his distinct characters'

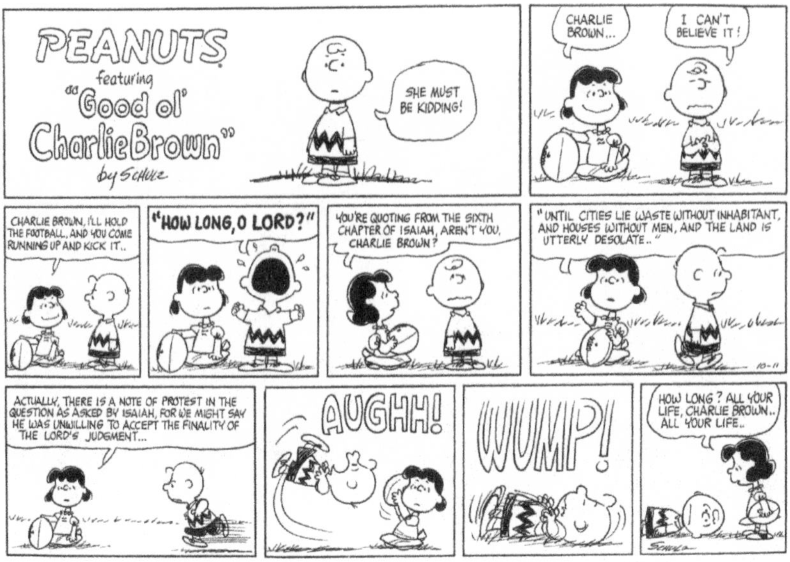

Peanuts © Peanuts Worldwide LLC. Used with permission. October 11, 1970.

idiosyncratic personalities, allowed Schulz to explore important issues, even if through humor. While many strips were lighthearted, with Charlie Brown failing to fly a kite or Lucy being shunned at Schroeder's piano, others tapped into heavier subjects like feminism, war, and, of course, theology. When Schulz published a collection of his strips with religious references entitled *And the Beagles and the Bunnies Shall Lie Down Together*, he was surprised by their ability to fill even a small paperback volume. Over the course of his career, he would develop enough that could have filled several sequels.

Of the 17,897 newspaper strips, more than 560 (3.2 percent) contain a religious, spiritual, or theological reference.[26] While this may seem like a small portion of the total *Peanuts* collection to some, the number is substantial when compared with other recurring motifs Schulz employed—Schulz only drew 415 strips (2.3 percent) in which Snoopy dons the persona of the Red Baron's nemesis, the World War I Flying Ace, and he only drew 61 strips (0.3 percent) of the iconic football scene where Lucy pulls the ball away as Charlie Brown tries to kick it.[27] If totaled after 1958, when Schulz first made his religious references explicit

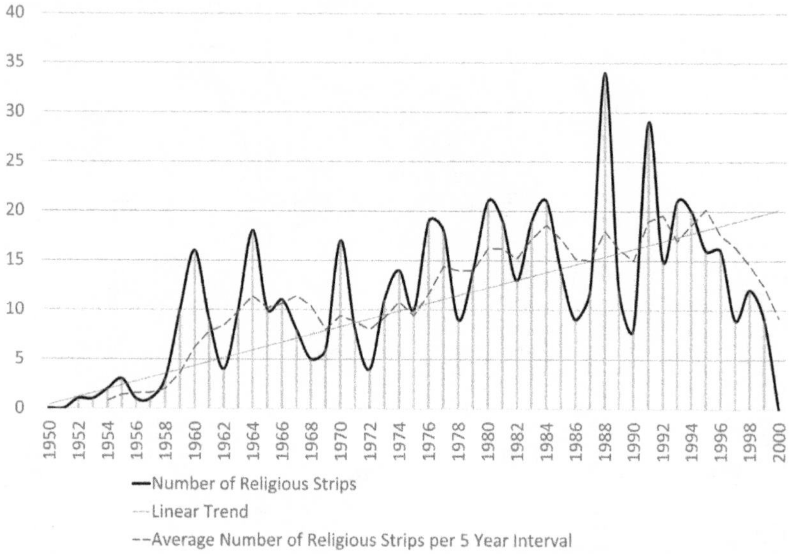

Frequency of religious references in the fifty years of *Peanuts* newspaper strips.

through his Christmas pageant scene, the religious references comprise 3.7 percent of the strips, averaging two weeks' worth of strips per year.

Though Linus and the Christmas scenes have endured as the most iconic religious references, serving as a lightning rod for those interested in Schulz's religious voice,[28] the occasions and characters involved in the religious references vary greatly across the strips. Christmas episodes make up only 11.4 percent of the religious strips, and nearly every major character makes a religious reference at one time or another, each even taking a turn in explicitly quoting Scripture. "In the sixth chapter of Proverbs, it says, 'Go to the ant, thou sluggard.. Consider her ways, and be wise,'" Franklin tells Peppermint Patty.[29] Charlie Brown explains to Snoopy, "As it says in the ninth chapter of Ecclesiastes, 'A living dog is better than a dead lion.'"[30] Sally, on the other hand, struggles at times to recall her Bible verses: "Maybe it was something Moses said, or something from the Book of *Reevaluation*."[31]

The frequency of the references in a particular year mirrors Charlie Brown's classic shirt, zigzagging across the decades as Schulz found great creative inspiration in matters of the spirit one year and little the next, but the overall trend was continued growth. In the late 1980s, the rate spiked with over thirty strips in one year as Sparky revisited questions of religion and public schools in two series, making humorous the narrow-minded interpretations of the so-called "separation of church and state"—Sally takes her new "Praying Doll" to class in February, only to be scolded by the principal, and in December, the school board cancels the Christmas play she was directing because of its religious content, including Joseph driving his family to Egypt in a '56 Thunderbird.

In 1972, by contrast, *Peanuts* had merely four religious references, the lowest number in any year following 1958. That summer, the Schulzes had moved north 20 miles from Coffee Grounds to Chalk Hill Road outside of Healdsburg. Joyce had fully transformed Coffee Grounds, had built a beautiful world-class ice arena in Santa Rosa after the community's had been closed down, and was looking for new space on Chalk Hill Road for their horses and her construction creativity. They deeded Coffee Grounds to the First Assembly of God of Santa Rosa,[32] benefiting from the tax write-off, but Chalk Hill could provide no marital benefit for a couple separated by the strain of diverging personalities. Nineteen seventy-two thus saw the culmination of a difficult time in the Schulz household. That year, Sparky's marriage to Joyce ended.

"Opposites attract, but they were so totally opposite," said Elaine Ramsperger with sadness but little surprise; she was a friend to both Sparky and Joyce during their time in Minnesota.[33] Their distinct interests and personalities had supported each other for many years—Sparky was able to realize his dream as a cartoonist; Joyce was able to find her voice building; each could take part in the joys of having a family. The move to Chalk Hill Road, by contrast, was almost a performance of the schism that their diverging interests and personalities had created. As Joyce looked for more room to exercise her architectural creativity, Sparky was acquiescing to a decision that took him away from all of the comforts and amenities he had so thoroughly enjoyed in their home of more than a decade. "Buying the ranch was mom's exit since she surely knew dad would never be comfortable there," Monte said. "Gone were his studio, his four-hole golf course, his tennis court, and our baseball field. And the three miles of gravel and dirt road access across several cattle guards would have ruined his willow green Jaguar XKE, so he sold it and drove off the ranch for good in a brown Pinto."[34]

In 1970, Sparky had begun a romantic relationship with a young journalist he met at the café inside the ice arena Joyce had designed with contractor Ed Doty. Sitting in the Warm Puppy Café, Sparky could order his regular meal, read the paper, and watch the figure skaters and hockey players practice through a large wall of windows. It was there that he met Tracey Claudius and began a nearly two-year romance.[35] They met for an occasional outing in San Francisco, and while questions would remain about the specific nature of the affair,[36] Sparky expressed his desire to be with Tracey in a series of private notes and letters, embellished with personalized drawings of Charlie Brown and Snoopy. He gushed sweet and romantic, telling her he loved her and that he looked forward to visiting a bookstore where they would "wander quietly off into a corner where I will put my arms around you, and say 'Hi, Sweetie . . .'"[37] In one note, he thanked her for introducing him to the music of the off-kilter *Jacques Brel is Alive and Well and Living in Paris*. The music was haunting and deep, burdened by disappointed hope in religious motifs.

In 1969, Sparky had written to Roger Palmquist, telling him that he was still enjoying teaching but that he wondered if he was being effective any longer. In December 1971, though, *Newsweek* revealed in their cover story about Schulz's enterprise that the cartoonist had recently stopped attending church. He had been attending faithfully since the late 1940s and had led discussion on the Bible at Sebastopol United Methodist Church for a full decade, giving his faithful class members each a copy of the Abingdon Study Bible when the group finished the Scriptures for a fourth time. But as of 1971, his formal involvement with a church was over, and Pete Coleman graciously took over the duties of leading the class. "He insists that his religious convictions remain unshaken, and a Bible in the top drawer of his desk seems to provide well-thumbed evidence of that," the journalist wrote of the lay theologian.[38] Sparky attempted to offer an explanation, one that he would continue to use for decades,[39] saying that he had left his role as leader of the Sunday school group because "I simply had nothing more to say." Repeated study was nothing new for him, though, and he had literally made a career out of saying the same thing twice without repeating himself, making it unlikely that he stopped attending church simply because he had nothing new to say. While he would never comment on such, it was perhaps more likely that within the tumult of a failing marriage and while in the midst of a private romantic affair, he no longer felt comfortable leading a study of the Bible. He still loved the Scriptures, he told Jim Phelan in a 1971 interview for *Penthouse*, but even after his affair had ended in the summer of 1972, any possibility of returning to the Sebastopol services was all but erased with the Schulzes' move to Healdsburg.

In late 1972, the marriage with Joyce was over. Joyce filed the papers for divorce, Sparky had his wedding ring cut off with his visiting former pastor Fred Shackleton on hand to offer support, and he then moved into his office at the ice arena. While at the rink, Sparky found not only solace in his drawing and his routine, but also the beginning of the next exciting chapter in his personal life. Even before the papers had been filed, he had met Jeannie. The two crossed paths in the Warm Puppy while waiting for their daughters to finish their skating practices. Sixteen years younger than Sparky, Jeannie was active and energetic, skilled at motivating and leading, and a fan of the tennis courts. She was married at the time to her husband, Peter Clyde, but was captivated by the warm and ambitious Sparky. The two offered each other a new exciting relationship, a welcomed new partner for Sparky and an unexpected one for Jeannie.

Joyce remarried in August 1973, starting a new life with contractor Ed Doty, and Jeannie left Peter. Jeannie and Sparky purchased a new home in Santa Rosa, a former bishop's residence, and they were married on September 22 in the small chapel on the grounds by a minister down the street that Jeannie had asked to perform the ceremony, neither she nor Sparky being active in a local congregation. "She is a gentle little girl, and I know you would like her very much. I was greatly tempted to ask Marvin to come out to perform the ceremony, but I didn't want to obligate him," Sparky wrote to Ruth and Marvin Forbes, inviting his former pastor to visit their new home. "I know we could spend the whole night talking and I hope that it will happen."[40] He sent a picture of himself and Jeannie to Palmquist, telling his minister friend, "She is a neat little girl, and we are doing our best to try to start over."[41]

While their new home had its own religious history, Jeannie did not share Sparky's affinity for biblical study, but they nonetheless found themselves thematically compatible. As a young child in California, part of a nominally low-Episcopalian British family that had immigrated to the United States, Jeannie had visited an array of churches, her mother insisting that they experience a wealth of perspectives, even Quaker services. Jeannie would find the discussions of spirituality interesting, and though she did not engage in deep study of her own, she and Peter Clyde had attended several different Episcopal churches while in college and had enjoyed late night dorm discussions about religion. When they moved to Hawaii in 1959, they even led prepared Sunday school lessons at a Congregational church before moving to Santa Rosa in 1962, at which time they began attending a Presbyterian church. "We belonged to the couples group," Jeannie remembered, "and as part of the educational component we had groups from different religious denominations come to speak to us—Hindus, Jews, Mormons, Islamic sects."[42]

Jeannie developed something of a loosely cosmopolitan view on spirituality, concerned more about actively doing good as a person than determining whether any particular prophet was divinely inspired. She and Sparky talked casually about attending church, but the plans never materialized, though Jeannie would insist for years that they attend the Christmas Eve carol service at the local Presbyterian church, stopping only after the service no longer included congregational singing. Occasionally, she would mention one of her more worldly views on spirituality, and Sparky would jokingly chide her for the nonsense, but neither pressed each other on their beliefs. Marriage to Sparky opened wide new and exciting doors for her, and their lives together were big enough for her to find ample opportunities to love and support him. Unlike marriages that struggle because of diverse faith perspectives, their differences did not become stumbling blocks, in part because of her youthful admiration and positivity, and in part because of Sparky's non-confrontational approach to faith.

Sparky had developed a curiosity in hearing what others thought but would typically not try to convince them of his own position. Jeannie and other friends of Sparky's would marvel at the sometimes reserved man's willingness and skill to interject provocative ideas, making their friends unexpectedly consider some weighty idea that came to the artist's mind. At a dinner party attended by Robert Short, Sparky kept everyone amused by interjecting the same non sequitur question into the conversation: "What did Jesus mean when he said, 'I saw Satan fall like lightning from Heaven'?"[43] Later, he would discuss the Luke 10:18 reference with Short, wondering if Jesus laughed in that moment.

On a trip to Europe, Sparky and Jeannie had a chance to catch a meal in Paris with prominent Italian philosopher Umberto Eco, who had flatteringly called Schulz's characters "monstrous infantile reductions of all the neuroses of a modern citizen of the industrial civilization."[44] "We hit it off real well," said Sparky, enjoying his time with such a rich thinker. But it was the cartoonist who would catch the philosopher off guard, asking him without preamble, "Do you believe in Jesus Christ?" Remembering the scene vividly many years later, Eco would admit, "I felt a little embarrassed" by being unprepared for such a poignantly direct question. "I had the highest opinion of the historical role of Jesus Christ," said Eco, but he was no longer a believer as he had been in his youth.[45] Schulz was satisfied, though, with their conversation. "When I'm with somebody like that," he said, "I don't want to waste time telling him all about myself and discussing where we live and all of that. I want to find out what they think . . . who they think Jesus really was. Did Jesus have a dog, and all that sort of thing."[46]

Sparky's clever, inquiring mind could not help but consider such matters. "Did you ever wonder whether Jesus knew that at his birth other children were killed because of him?" he questioned. "If he did know, how did he carry that burden? I read something about that once."[47] In the strips, Sally would more tamely muse, when she heard that David defeated Goliath with a stone to the head, "What did Goliath's mom say about that?"[48] "How do you come up with those things?" Jeannie and Sparky's friends would wonder. Even though she and many in their social circle were not as personally invested in such inquiries, Sparky was never in short supply of an audience, allowing his ponderings to flow out of his own quick mind and into the day's comic strip. And he did so with much higher frequency than his peers.

Even after Sparky had proven to editors that religious content was acceptable for the mainstream market, *Peanuts* remained the leader, producing upwards of seven times as many religious references as others on the page.[49] From 1979 to 1987, barely half a percent (0.6 percent) of strips in the *Los Angeles Times* contained a religious reference,[50] while during that same period, Schulz averaged 4.4 percent. Of course, readers would be able to occasionally find religious references throughout other properties on the comics pages over the years after Schulz had broken the taboo, such as in panels of *Family Circus*, *Ziggy*, *Fred Basset*,

Frank and Ernest, *Andy Capp*, *Marvin*, and *B.C.*[51] Archie comics even had a non-canonical run in which the gang evangelizes, complete with the steps to salvation at the back of the issue.[52] Underground and online distribution methods later paved the way for further genres of religious comics that would expand as Sparky's career came to an end.[53] The comic book and graphic novel industry would likewise find a trend in making fantastic the supernatural, with titles such as Superman's *Kingdom Come* and characters like Mephisto and the Son of Satan. Some evangelical artists would even robustly embrace the power of the medium, translating the Bible into comic panels in such works as *The Comic Book Bible* and the stylized *The Manga Bible*.

Throughout his career, there would be those who would criticize Schulz for incorporating the high thoughts of religion in the low art of a humor-driven comic strip. To have the things of the divine anywhere near a strip about kite-eating trees was pure sacrilege in the eyes of some readers. Schulz himself thought that one could misuse spiritual references, saying, "I hate shallow humor. I hate shallow religious humor. I hate shallow sports humor, I hate shallowness of any kind."[54] But he believed that he was treating his faith and its sacred texts with a certain amount of dignity, a quality he sought throughout his work, and he was proud of his approach. He believed that his medium—humor—was a good fit for matters of religious faith. "Religion without humor is a worthless religion. Humor is part of man and man never would have survived without humor. It's the only thing that makes life palatable—if that's the word. And to say that there's no room for humor in religion is like saying there's no room for humor in life. The scriptures themselves have quite a few incidents of humor—probably more than we realize," he once told a group of young Christians. "Of course, I do believe that the scriptures are holy, but I do not believe that the Bible itself is a holy instrument to be worshipped. After all, the words are only the words which men put down under inspiration." The artist then added, "If we are all members of the priesthood, why cannot a cartoonist preach in the same manner as a minister, or anyone else? And from some of the preaching I hear on the radio, I think cartoonists should do more of it and the radio preachers should do less of it."[55]

Though his religious references had opened up the opportunity for others to do the same in comic strips, his insights remained comparatively sharp and his references unique. While others relied on routine Old Testament tropes (Leonard Greenspoon contending that these four account for as much as 75 percent of other strips' references: Noah and the ark, Moses and the Ten Commandments, Adam and Eve, and the creation of the world, with an infrequent number then referencing the New Testament's nativity and Sermon on the Mount),[56] Sparky drew on his own well-studied knowledge of the Bible's Old and New Testaments, referencing biblical characters like Elijah, Job, Jezebel, Jeremiah, Gabriel, King Solomon, Matthew, the Apostle Paul, and more. Even Jesus. Bringing in a wooden yoke to school for his report, Linus tells Charlie Brown, "I'm going to tell how the yoke is a symbol of subjugation of one individual to another, as Esau to Jacob (Genesis 27:40). Then I'll tell how the yoke was sometimes placed literally on the neck of a person reduced to submission . . . My reference will be Jeremiah 28:10. Then I'll tell of the yoke placed on Israel by Solomon and Rehoboam (I Kings 12:9) and wind up talking about the yoke of sin suggested in Lamentations 1:14 and the 'easy' yoke of Matthew 11:29. I think that will cover the subject pretty well." As Linus walks away, Charlie Brown turns to his friend and hollers his own lament, "What about the 'Yoke of Inferiority' you've given me?!"[57]

In seventy-six different *Peanuts* strips, Schulz made clear to readers that he was drawing inspiration from the Bible, having characters directly reference thirty-two different books of the Bible, such as when Linus asked Miss Othmar, "I was wondering if you'd care to reconcile our failure to say 'Grace' before drinking milk with the story of Daniel in the sixth chapter of that book,"[58] or when Sparky took to scriptural interpretation, having the characters debate the meaning of Job.[59] In twenty-three of those strips the characters paraphrased ideas and biblical stories, but in fifty-three strips, the characters directly quoted passages of scripture, verbally noting that they were doing so. In another thirty-four strips, the scriptural reference was inferred by putting quotation marks around the character's biblical recitation; in six of these strips the characters were shown reading from an unlabeled Bible. In yet another thirty-two strips, Schulz drew upon his biblical vocabulary and embedded scriptural passages into the dialogue without quotation marks at all. Walking in the rain on October 23, 1973, Charlie Brown says to Linus, "The rain falls on the just and the unjust," which some may have recognized as a quotation from Jesus, recorded in Matthew 5:45. As they continued through the downpour, Linus responded to his friend, "That's a good system!"[60]

The vast majority of Sparky's religious references draw on Christian idioms, texts, and practices. It was the tradition he knew, so it was natural that this was where he would find ideas. "I never draw about anything unless I feel that I have a better than average knowledge of my subject," he described, consulting his library for proper terms or occasionally asking a practitioner friend from another field before using other terms.[61] Some of his religious references crossed traditions, such as the more than two dozen strips in the 1990s in which a voice speaks back to Charlie Brown out of the dark as he lies awake at night. "Sometimes I lie awake at night, and I ask, 'Where have I gone wrong?' Then a voice says to me, 'This is going to take more than one night.'"[62] Others drew more explicitly from non-Christian origins, including those referencing omens and paranormal forces (such as when Snoopy gets a divining Beagle Board),[63] supernatural beings (such as when Snoopy laments about the tennis gods being against him),[64] mystical practices (such as when Woodstock takes up the art of reading not tea leaves but supper dishes),[65] reincarnation (such as when Charlie Brown tells Linus that you can only come back after you die if you have had your hand stamped),[66] and the strip in which he referenced a proverb from Persian literature[67]—"An unjust king asked a holy man, 'What is more excellent than prayer?' The holy man said: 'For you to remain asleep till midday, that for this one interval you may not afflict mankind.'"[68]

Sparky poked fun at many of these traditions, some of which he personally found groundless, but he was never hostile in his strips. Over the years some would presume that he was anti-Catholic or anti-Semitic. He was neither, though he did disagree with the bureaucratic or hierarchical practices of any faith tradition. He was proud to have introduced nuns into his *Young Pillars* panels, and on a few occasions he referenced Judaism in *Peanuts*, having Linus wish a local Santa Claus a very Happy Hanukkah, leading to a discussion of Judas Maccabaeus and the cleansing of the temple.[69] He had simply not grown up in a Jewish culture, so as with all of the strip's non-Christian themes, these references were minimal.

cms
"PARDON ME, BUT I'VE NEVER TALKED WITH A NUN BEFORE. DO YOU SPEAK ENGLISH OR LATIN?"

Young Pillars. February 7, 1965. © 1989 Warner Press, Inc., Anderson, Indiana. Used with permission.

Stretching himself into other arenas came with occasional risks. While he had built up support from great swaths of Christian communities, he did not always carry the same in-community ethos with others. Referencing the death premonitions in *I Heard the Owl Call My Name*, a best-selling story of an Anglican vicar learning from the native Kwakiutl First Nations community he witnesses to, Schulz once had Snoopy predict his own stomachache by explaining, "I heard the beagle call my name!"[70] A professor of American Indian Studies wrote Schulz a scathing letter, telling the artist that such disrespect should have subsided in the "somewhat more enlightened age" of the mid-1970s. "Since you profess to be a Christian," he wrote, "it might be more appropriate to make light of your own faith rather than that of the American Indian."

Schulz did make a habit of using his own faith as a source of light humor in the strips. His primary use of religious references was as a source of humor, using a scriptural or topical element in the dialogue similar to the way he might comically reference Tolstoy or ice hockey. Such strips were simply intended to elicit a chuckle, and religious notions were often simply another piece of inspiration from which Schulz might create a humorous moment to fill the panels of a strip. These strips drew upon a variety of themes, including prayer, sacred music, evangelism, prophecy, biblical stories and characters, church camp, Heaven, and, of course, the sacred meaning of Christmas. The characters even attend church, featured in over forty strips, almost all occurring after Schulz no longer attended, including Sally as an unexpected teacher of a Bible school class in the early 1990s. She, of course, has trouble getting through to the minister's son, Larry, who is quite sure that it was the Great Gatsby who defeated Goliath.[71]

"I don't have any axes to grind or beliefs that I want to convince people of," Sparky would say.[72] He simply wanted to draw funny pictures. And he did just that, at times drawing upon his decades in the church as a rich source of material. Yet his strip routinely stirred readers to new depths, revealing truths about the internal self and external society that the adventure and soap strips never did. In this same way, his religious strips at times exposed truths about faith or questions about the divine that one might not otherwise consider during their morning routine of reading a disposable newspaper. "Cartooning is preaching," Sparky admitted when pressed. "And I think we have the right to do some preaching."[73] In *Peanuts*, he provoked readers to reconsider narrow religious dogma through strips critical of denominationalism and through his criticism of apocalyptic end-times preaching. Such narrow-mindedness was anathema to him. "We are more confused now than the Scribes and the Pharisees ever were," he once lamented, listing points of contention such as speaking in tongues, prayer languages, ordinances, and the return of Christ. "We can list them by the dozens," he said. "It's frightening, isn't it? What have we done to this marvelous faith?"[74]

At other times, though, Sparky used his strips as a way to express his own inner spiritual inquiries. "Is God pleased with me?" he wondered through a strip, and Sparky allowed readers a glimpse of his own ways of thinking through the personal, social, and theological components of prayer in forty different strips on the subject. "You'll pray for me? Why? I'll pray for myself!" Sally hollers at a TV host on the screen.[75] When

Linus asks his sister, simply, "Do you ever pray, Lucy?" the older Van Pelt belts back, "That's kind of a personal question, isn't it? Are you trying to start an argument? I suppose you think you're somebody pretty smart, don't you?"[76] In 1974, not long after Sparky had left the church and was remarried, he invoked a scriptural passage dear to him when Linus quotes to his sister, "Likewise the spirit helps us in our weakness; for we do not know how to pray as we ought, but the spirit himself intercedes for us with sighs too deep for words. Romans. . . . Eighth chapter!"[77]

Sparky had found a home in the Church of God as a young man aspiring to be a professional cartoonist. His friends and mentors in the church inspired and supported his desire to personally study the Bible, finding verses like Romans 8:26 to be something not just to be taught by a preacher but to be engaged by the individual. The Church of God gave him the structure and language to guide his theological thought, and the more he studied, his beliefs simultaneously became more substantial, complex, and personal. When he and his family moved to California, he found himself without the comforting support of the Church of God movement, but found instead a new community of studiers in the Methodist church. After leading and studying in that new environment for over a decade, his role in his Sunday morning Bible class came to an end. By the time he left the structure of the church, his religious voice was nothing if not genuinely personal, and he was never without an audience for such spiritual inquiry. He had friends and family to whom he could lob an unexpected theological firecracker, and perhaps more personally, he had his strips.

"I think of myself as Charles Schulz. But if someone wants to believe I'm really Charlie Brown, well, it makes a good story," Sparky once said.[78] His own personality was not relegated to one character but was spread across the cast, each taking a turn sharing his spiritual voice. Sparky could at times be melancholy, contemplative, distant, charming, and often full of joy. His joys, as his son Monte remembered them, were many. "Dad's joys were in movies and golf and trips with his friends, teaching me to throw the knuckleball, or Jill to ride a bike, or Craig to drive a car. They were in a bowl of tapioca pudding or a tuna fish sandwich at his table at his ice rink with his friends joining him for lunch."[79] And, of course, he also found joy in drawing his strips. The reader was then often able to join in the delight, even through the humorous religious moments. "Faith is positive. Humor is proof of faith, proof that everything is going to be all right with God, nevertheless," he once said.[80] He pushed his own humor industry to new heights through not only his innovative artistic and narrative style, but also his willingness to allow his spiritual self to fill panels on the page, doing so as much as he did with the other recurring *Peanuts* motifs. His well-studied voice imbued the strips with authority; his joy kept the strips from being bitter; his thoughtful insights provided readers with their daily laugh. Some mornings, as the paper was read over a cup of coffee, a religious reference would even offer readers a new way of pondering their own personal faith.

6

FILLING THE SCREEN

"In television it is difficult even to carry on a conversation, let alone philosophize."

—CHARLES M. SCHULZ

RESTING THEIR HEADS ON A GRASSY HILL, CHARLIE BROWN, LINUS, AND LUCY stare up into the afternoon sky. As they lay in enviable stillness, the clouds overhead slowly tumble, wander, and slip past. "I could just lie here all day, and watch them drift by . . ." Lucy says. "If you use your imagination, you can see lots of things in the cloud formations . . . What do you think you see, Linus?"

"Well, those clouds up there look to me like the map of the British Honduras on the Caribbean . ." says Linus, as Charlie Brown sits up in surprise at the detailed interpretation. He leans back to try another look while Linus continues: "That cloud up there looks a little like the profile of Thomas Eakins, the famous painter and sculptor . . . And that group of clouds over there gives me the impression of the stoning of Stephen . . . I can see the Apostle Paul standing there to one side . . ."

The expressive shock lines around Charlie Brown's eyes that had appeared at the sound of such deep insight retreat when Lucy invites him to join. "Uh huh . . . That's very good," she says of her younger brother's biblical interpretation. "What do you see in the clouds, Charlie Brown?" Lying back once more, a somewhat baffled, somewhat innocent, somewhat perpetually outclassed Charlie Brown answers, "Well, I was going to say I saw a ducky and a horsie, but I changed my mind!"[1]

When newspapers ran this Sunday strip, August 14, 1960, letters flooded into Sparky's studio, as they were prone to do over his career, overwhelmingly praising the scene and its biblical import. With the strip's popularity, it was a natural decision for Sparky, Bill, and Lee to use the episode as the opener for their first theatrical feature, 1969's musical *A Boy Named Charlie Brown*. Soft daisies were added to the hill and engagingly off-kilter child voices brought the scene to life to the joy of audiences—so much so that audiences once literally applauded when Charlie Brown delivered the endearing punch line.

Sparky's team had established the rhythm and techniques for bringing the strip to the screen thanks to the successes and challenges of their first three specials. In 1967, they began the exciting work of exploring the possibilities of the longer cinematic release format. As a feature film it could be shown worldwide, not limited by domestic mid-century television distribution, bringing wholesome family entertainment to neighborhood cinemas across the globe. Their animation had been a smash hit in living rooms, and it was time to expand their momentum beyond the home. "We were astounded to discover, however, that all of the major film companies turned us down," Lee remembered with some bewilderment. "It was like reliving a bad dream all over again, and we still heard the same reasons why an animated feature was a bad investment."[2] Studios simply did not see the comic strip as lending itself naturally to a profit-yielding feature film. Walt Disney could make it happen with classic fairy tales, but few believed Schulz could do it with good ol' Charlie Brown.

Lee and Sparky had developed a good relationship with CBS president Frank Stanton (soon after the Christmas special, Sparky had sent him a large drawing of Snoopy under a note reading, "To Mr. and Mrs. Frank Stanton with every best wish for 1966—Joyce and Charles Schulz"), and the team had quickly gone to work on *You're in Love, Charlie Brown* after the Halloween program netted them four more specials from CBS. Dropping by Stanton's office to talk television, Lee mentioned the feature idea as an afterthought. Much to his delight, Stanton saw promise in the idea and suggested the possibility of CBS's own theatrical film division (eventually named Cinema Center Films or CCF) producing the film. CBS had purchased Republic Pictures' North Hollywood studio earlier that year, and was hoping to turn a strong profit by having its own studio from which to release films into theater and then later replay on television. It had gotten expensive for broadcasters to lease film licenses for teleplay.[3] CCF would reportedly cost CBS tens of millions in losses before it was shut down in 1972,[4] its final film being *Snoopy Come Home*, but it nonetheless opened the door for this first theatrical feature from the *Peanuts* team.

The deal for the feature had been quickly made with CCF, and *A Boy Named Charlie Brown* premiered on December 4, 1969, at Radio City Music Hall in New York City, a week earlier than originally planned, accommodating extra viewers. "The film broke every major record of the thirty-seven year history of the Music Hall," Lee said, "including the greatest advance sale, the greatest single day, and the greatest single week."[5] The musical film focused on Charlie Brown's unexpected triumph at a local spelling bee, causing him to attend the national competition with the typical worrisome anxiety one would expect from the depressed optimist. It was nominated for an Academy Award (and later for an Emmy when it was broadcast on CBS in 1976), and the critics' reactions ran the spectrum from praise to tepid approval to distaste. "It's difficult—perhaps impossible—to be anything except benign towards a G-rated, animated movie that manages to include references to St. Stephen, Thomas Eakins, Harpers Ferry, baseball, contemporary morality (as it related to Charlie Brown's use of his 'bean ball'), conservation and kite flying," wrote *New York Times* critic Vincent Canby. "The pleasures of the film are the delicate, unspectacular ones of the original comic strip," he continued, feeling compelled to add that the three Rod McKuen songs ("A Boy Named Charlie Brown," "Champion Charlie Brown," and "Failure Face") in the musical were a "really dreadful contribution to the film,"[6] a general consensus among many reviews. Other reviewers praised the overall tone; Gene Shalit wrote in *Look* magazine that the clouds scene was "completely perfect" and "Charlie Brown's first film is so cheerful I can hardly wait for his next one!"[7] The team took the diverse notes in stride. Sparky noted two years later that "we have learned a good deal since we made that one, and we have high hopes that people will really like this new feature, [*Snoopy Come Home*]." The ever-competitive Schulz wanted it to be "ten times better than the last movie."[8]

As the studio executives had originally told Lee when they rejected his film pitch, one of the unique challenges in making a feature-length *Peanuts* film was that the source material was so minimalistic. Sparky had prided himself on the development of the slight incident in his strips, which did not seem to lend itself naturally to extended storytelling. In order to maintain Schulz's segmented narrative pacing, and to simply fill the time, musical "specialties" were added to the script. These included numbers from the characters (like Charlie Brown's mnemonic-device spelling practice tune, "I Before E"), scenic action set to the Rod McKuen songs (like Charlie Brown failing at flying his homemade kite while McKuen croons a wistfully subdued opening number), a patriotic homage to the red, white, and blue to open the ball game, and, of course, a display of talent from toy piano aficionado Schroeder.

The need to extend the strip content with specialty fillers had certainly been a creative challenge for the team, but it also provided them with unique opportunities to try new techniques. "Fortunately, working with Lee and Bill is very easy," Sparky said, "for each of us never encroaches upon the others' area of responsibility. I know what I want in the movie, but I also know my limitations and am perfectly willing to allow the animators to use their imagination where it is demanded for scenes."[9] One such scene that called for a confluence of animator imagination and writerly interest involved Schroeder at the piano, playing the Adagio cantabile movement from Beethoven's Sonata No. 8, *Sonata Pathétique*. In this three-and-a-half-minute scene, which one reviewer called "beautifully done" as "an extension of the 'Fantasia' idea,"[10] stylized images of eighteenth-century churches, tombstones, angels, and a procession of saints pass across the screen while the young pianist plays by candlelight on an ever-expanding piano. The scene of abstract baroque Christianity added a unique depth to the film, raising the artistic bar in an unexpected way. Sparky's personal religious interests yet again flowed conspicuously across the screen, but this time it was not directly by his own doing.

When the small studio team of less than a dozen regular artists began work on their first feature film, Bill directed artists Evert Brown, Ed Levitt, and Bernie Gruver to work up the designs for non-strip sequences that would fill out the extended length of the picture. They were given rather wide latitude to develop ideas for their scenes, with Bill respecting their talents just as Sparky respected his. "He gave us a lot of creative freedom on these sequences," described Evert, who had recently joined the relaxed animation team in 1967 after working on the studio's logo design and filling in on a psychedelic ReaLemon concentrate commercial the studio was producing.[11] He and Ed thumbed through books in the studio and at the public library to see what inspiration they might find in the era of Schroeder's beloved Beethoven. Meanwhile, Bernie gravitated toward Linus, imagining what his reaction might be to giving his trusted security blanket to Charlie Brown for good luck. Vivid images filled his mind as he crafted a scene that might push the boundaries of spirituality in a darker direction than some would have expected.

In the film, after Linus gives his blanket to Charlie Brown, he begins to suffer dizzying withdrawals and Lucy tells him to go outside and get some fresh air. He does, meeting up with Snoopy, and eventually boarding a bus to go and retrieve his blanket. On the bus, Snoopy begins to play a twangy Jew's harp[12] in the seat behind a delirious Linus. As the boy stares off, the viewer is then given a five-second swirl of psychedelic colors and a twirl of the bus seat before the scene cuts back to the exterior of the bus. In one of the film's storyboards, however, this psychedelic swirl was just the beginning of the dream sequence that Bernie had developed.

In an original storyboard, after his seat spins, Linus then hallucinates a set of five Charlie Browns, each holding a blanket and sucking a thumb. Linus, who has sprouted a fish tail, swims up to the Charlie Browns, who are merging back into one, and gurgles out the word BLANKET. Charlie Brown, however, transforms into a sharp-toothed fish, complete with a zigzag stripe, and takes a vicious snapping bite at Linus. The camera then goes nose to nose with the Charlie Brown fish as it opens its mouth. Inside is another version of Charlie Brown—a demonic version complete with devil ears and a tail. With a wicked grin and furrowed brow, the evil thief is feeding Linus's blanket into a meat grinder, out of which squeeze demonic beasts, flying and tromping across the grass. Linus, now with his head mounted on top of the long neck of a unicycled ostrich is tormented by Snoopy playing the Jew's harp on his back, his blanket dangled on a stick while the demon birds bear down on them. The scene then becomes visually abstract, with a kaleidoscope of shapes and character faces swirling about the screen before cutting to a sickened Linus staring out the window and then an exterior shot of the bus.

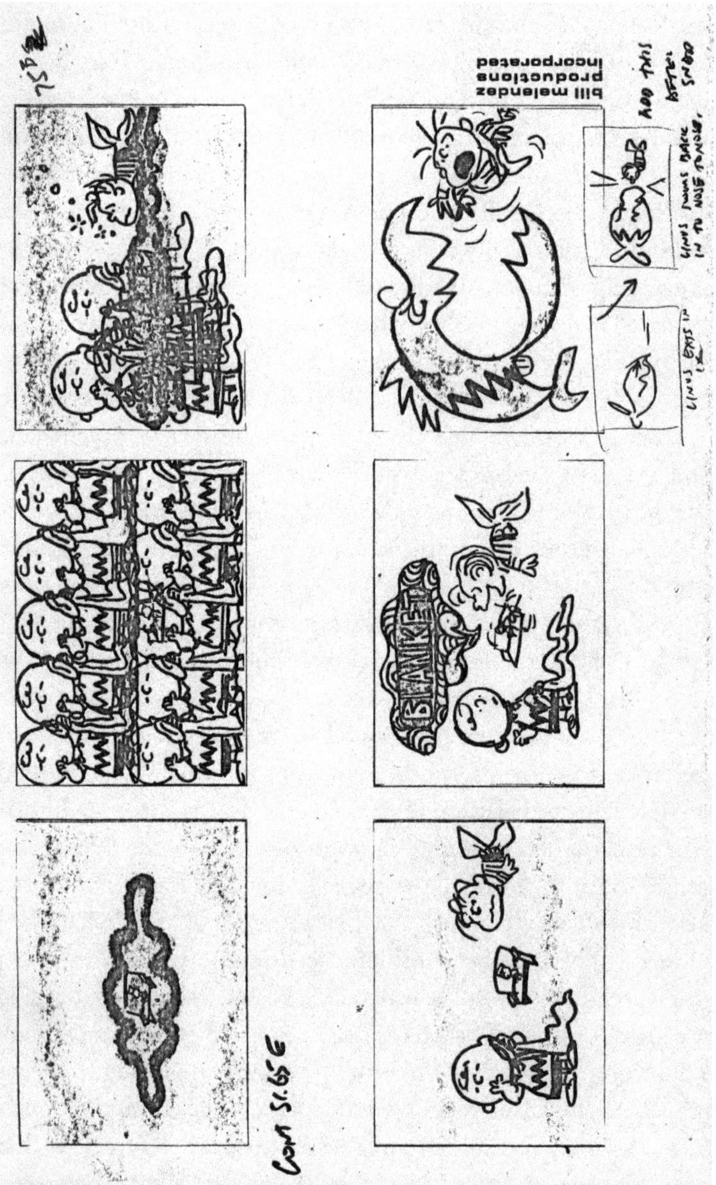

A storyboard scene featuring psychedelic swirls and demonic birds, drawn for 1969's *A Boy Named Charlie Brown*. The scene did not make it into the finalized film release. Courtesy of the Charles M. Schulz Museum and Research Center, Santa Rosa, California, Lee Mendelson Productions, and Bill Melendez Productions, Inc. © Bill Melendez Productions, Inc.

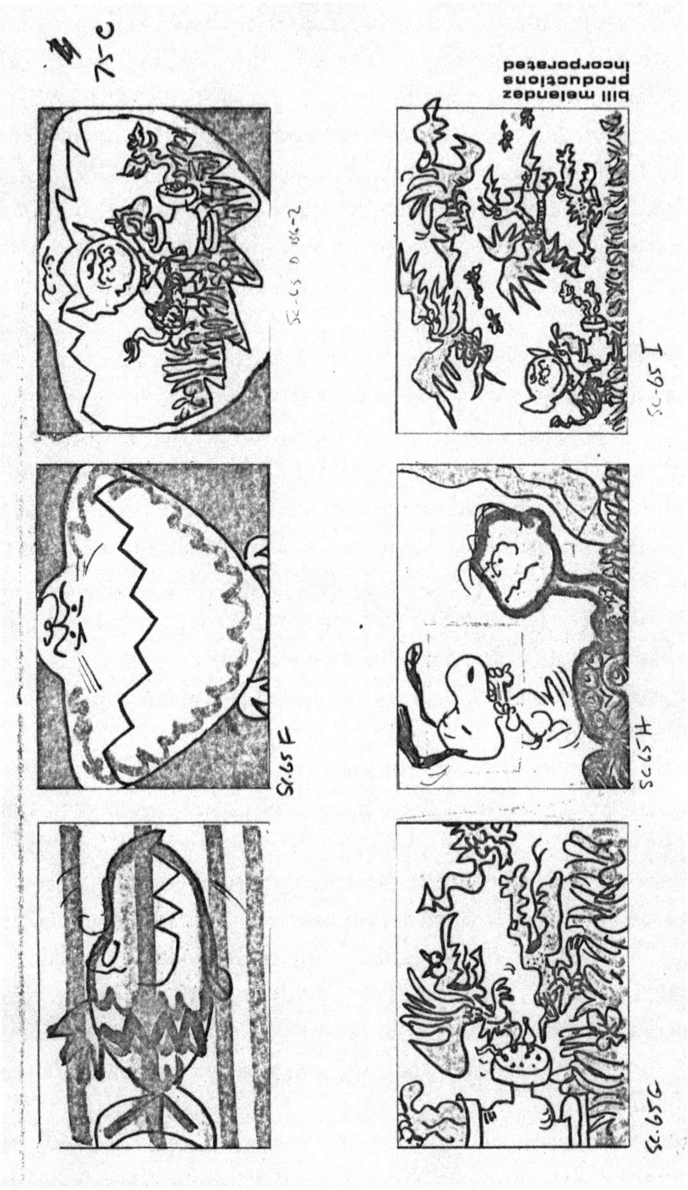

Cut scene from 1969's *A Boy Named Charlie Brown*. Courtesy of the Charles M. Schulz Museum and Research Center, Santa Rosa, California, Lee Mendelson Productions, and Bill Melendez Productions, Inc. © Bill Melendez Productions, Inc.

The scene, drawing heavily on the experimental aesthetic of the late 1960s, was cut from the final animation and production phase of the film. "I have a feeling that Schulz didn't like the radical look of Bernie's design," Evert ventured. "I am sure he wouldn't have liked Charlie with devil ears."[13] At that same time, the animators did manage to briefly show Charlie Brown as a red-horned devil with a pitchfork and tail in 1968's *He's Your Dog, Charlie Brown*, Snoopy imagining his owner that way after Charlie Brown dare hook him to a leash. But while Sparky had made jokes about Linus worrying he was a demon for making the rain stop, picturing one of his characters as a devil grinding out demon birds in an extended sequence for their first feature film was a different matter altogether.

In their theatrical release, the demonic dream sequence was cut back to its narrow edges with just a few swirls of color making it onto the screen. This cut may have been for time, though that is questionable, given that the storyboard sent to Vince Guaraldi containing the full scene did not contain either the *Sonata Pathétique* or the *Stars and Stripes* musical numbers. It is more likely that Sparky or perhaps even Bill in his role as director decided against its tone or pacing, and instead the film featured the extended musical sequence that Evert and Ed had developed around the music of Beethoven.

The scene, complete with its scrolling saints and cathedrals, was not Sparky's idea, but that of the studio artists. Evert and Ed took their inspiration directly from the images they found in the literature on Beethoven, tracing some of the images of churches, angels, and statues right out of their library books, drawing others with felt-tip markers on paper, and then cutting out these images and using them directly in the animation shots. "It was a very loose kind of way of doing it," Evert described. "It became very organic." Their final product was artistically stirring and perhaps more consistent with Sparky's own taste, leaving reviewers with a moving experience in their cinema seats—a different type of emotional response than the provocative demon birds would have elicited.

While the success of *A Boy Named Charlie Brown* was only moderate, many more animated specials would follow, though only one more with CCF. Across over a half-century's run, a total of seventy-five animated *Peanuts* titles have been produced (the seventy-sixth being the 2015 3-D computer animated feature from Fox's Blue Sky Studios).[14] This includes animated television programs, theatrical features, direct-to-video releases, episodes from a television miniseries, and individual titles from a Saturday morning cartoon show. Throughout these programs, religious references are pervasive and diverse, even if most are not richly developed. Only thirteen of the seventy-five titles are absent noticeable religious or spiritual content.[15] For the other sixty-two, the range of references resist classification, drawing on the breadth of Sparky's religious voice and the creative work of his animation team.

The creative canvas for the television specials was much larger than that of the daily strips, requiring new visual elements not previously needed in the world of *Peanuts*. Landscapes were one such element, with a cityscape or country vista needed to contextualize a neighborhood scene or to provide a backdrop to one of Snoopy's fanciful escapades. After Bernie, Ed, or Evert finished the layouts for a scene, they sent their materials to Dean Spille, one of the studio's artists living in Europe during the production of many of the specials. From their layouts, he painted inviting backgrounds, sometimes only in simple watercolor because of the rushed deadlines. "They would be filtered through my personal style—which seemed agreeable to everyone," he described. "I tried to keep them more as colored drawings than paintings, to be compatible with the strips."[16] Received at the studio by postal mail, his landscapes, occasionally filled with a church or graveyard, were placed in sequence with his backgrounds and the animators' character drawings, completing the picture for the screen.

As Woodstock flies overhead in 1977's *It's Your First Kiss, Charlie Brown*, he can see the parade passing a steepled church. In 1980's *Life is a Circus, Charlie Brown*, Snoopy and Fifi wait to run off together at a bus stop near a church and bell tower. In 1983's *What Have We Learned, Charlie Brown*, one of the specials most important to Schulz in its statement on the pains of war, rotoscopic images of soldiers are seen falling on the beach and Linus looks on at a collage of animated cross tombstone grave markers while the voice of President Eisenhower, reflecting on D-Day, echoes. While one of the more transient religious references across the specials, these churches and religious grave markers were purposeful parts of the animation process, providing a visual context that was a good fit for the diverse verbal religious references and for Sparky's own personal interests.[17]

The animators worked to stay true to Schulz's minimalist style, a challenge they faced on every aspect of the animation. "He was so protective of his drawing," noted Phil Roman, an accomplished animator who did early work on *A Boy Named Charlie Brown* and who eventually directed several other *Peanuts* specials, including *A Charlie Brown Thanksgiving* and *It's the Easter Beagle, Charlie Brown.* Roman, like others on the team, joined *Peanuts* in the middle of an outstanding career in animation—he had drawn for other animated classics like Disney's *Sleeping Beauty*, Dr. Seuss's *How the Grinch Stole Christmas!* and Rankin/Bass's animated version of J. R. R. Tolkien's *The Lord of the Rings*, directed a variety of programs (including a wealth of *Garfield* episodes), and eventually produced many other projects (including 159 episodes of *The Simpsons*). "You have to stay on character," Roman said of his work with Schulz. "I mean, those are his kids, those are his babies, so you have to treat them with respect."[18] While Schulz did not particularly care for the cast being referred to as his children (they were his characters, not his children; he had five of his own children), he was insistent that the animated adaptations of all his art stay faithful to his own style, based on the model sheets he provided to Bill Melendez and the animation team.

The relationship between Schulz and the rest of the production team was balanced by respect. They were able to do their work because they understood Schulz's vision and had a sense of fidelity to the source product. In 1984, Schulz commented, "When we first began I think I made a couple of rough drawings to show them the way I thought the characters should be drawn, but since then I just trust it to Bill Melendez. I really should go down to Hollywood more often to see what's going on, but drawing the daily comic strip is still the basis and foundation for the whole thing and I feel this studio is where I belong."[19] This reluctant trust was possible because of Sparky's respect for Bill and for Bill's work. Bill, after all, was his own accomplished craftsman outside of the work he did with Snoopy.

Originally born in Mexico, José Cuauhtémoc "Bill" Melendez was trained at the California Chouinard Art Institute (later called "CalArts") and, in 1938, was hired by Walt Disney, where he worked as an animator on *Fantasia*, *Pinocchio*, *Bambi*, and Mickey Mouse cartoons, among other projects. After being part of the Disney strike in 1941 led by top animator Art Babbitt,[20] Bill signed with Leon Schlesinger Cartoons. That company became Warner Bros. Cartoons, where Bill animated Bugs Bunny, Daffy Duck, and other classic works. He went on to direct industrial films and over 1,000 television productions, being recognized at international film festivals like Cannes and Edinburg—all before joining the *Peanuts* team.

When he was working as a television commercial animator (without owning a television set himself), Bill was asked by the J. Walter Thompson advertising agency to "audition" for the comic strip artist Charles Schulz before animating the precious *Peanuts* gang for Ford Falcon television commercials. It was odd to request that an animator audition, but Bill obliged, visiting Sparky's home in northern California and sufficiently satisfying him with his "unobjectionable" sample reels. "I was introduced to him as a Mexican, see, not as a Hollywoodian," smirked Melendez as he remembered their first meeting. "If I'd been introduced to him as one from Hollywood, he'd have said 'Out! Out, out, out!' But he didn't, and so we became good friends." As their success and friendship grew, it became easier for Sparky to trust his own work in someone else's hands.

That trust was also necessary out of practical limitations of the increasingly busy Charles Schulz, as he described in 1988:

> I wish that I could live right in Hollywood and work in Bill's studio and not have to do all these other things, but be right there when all these shows are done, and be there every day—work with the animators, and look at every scene, and have absolute tight control over them. But I can't. I believe the strip is still the most important thing, so a lot of the things get away from me. He has a good group of animators, and I like them all; we get along well, but I still watch over things.[21]

The animated programs were important to him, but there was a team that could and would bring the vision to life, and he would trust them to do their work while he did his own—trust, but verify.[22] His primary focus was and always would be the drawing of his daily and Sunday comic strips, and that took plenty of his time.

Schulz's primary contribution to the animation enterprise was always the writing of both plot and dialogue. This was especially true of the biblical lines the characters would occasionally utter. As Lee succinctly described, "That area was 100 percent Charles Schulz."[23] While viewers would see or hear about churches in one of every five animated *Peanuts* titles, sometimes from the hand of Dean Spille, there were biblical quotations or references to biblical characters in one of every three, and virtually all were the direct product of Sparky's scriptural knowledge. The animated specials contain a diversity of references, from Genesis to the Gospel of John, sometimes formulated as a direct citation, sometimes merely as an embedded phrase noticeable only to scripturally literate viewers.

As was the case with the comic strips, the majority of the scriptural references in the animated titles tended to be much more particular than one might expect in a mainstream property, and many were explicitly cited in the dialogue. In 1992's *It's Christmastime Again, Charlie Brown*, for example, Sally tries to help her big brother sell wreathes door-to-door by telling the kid at the door that they were made from the forests of Lebanon. "You can read about them in the second chapter of the second book of Chronicles," she says, adding, "If you buy two, we'll throw in an autographed photo of King Solomon." Later in that same special, after trying to read Luke 2 to the distracted Sally, Linus quotes from First Samuel in order to explain to her about the partridge in a pear tree. She asks, "What in the world is a *calming* bird?" "A *calling* bird is a kind of partridge," he explains.[24] "In First Samuel, 26:20 it says, 'For the King of Israel has come out to seek my life, just as though he were hunting the calling bird.' There's a play on words here, you see. David was standing on a mountain calling, and he compared himself to a partridge being hunted. Isn't that fascinating?" After a pause, Sally answers, "If I get socks again for Christmas I'll go even more crazy!"

As in his strips, albeit to a lesser degree, in his animated work Schulz utilized a wide host of biblical characters and phrases drawn from Scriptures or his time in Christian circles. "Count your blessings," Lucy is told;[25] "Ashes to ashes and dust to dust," Linus recites.[26] Woven into their national broadcast television dialogue are nods to Mary, Gabriel, the shepherds, the wise men, Goliath, the Apostles, King Solomon, David, Moses, Luke, and Jezebel, not to mention the references to

Lebanon, Bethlehem, Gilead, the biblical names Lydia, Rachel, and Rebekah, or the innkeeper's wife who may have had naturally curly hair. This is in addition to references to monks, saints, prophets, the devil, powers of darkness, and God.

After ruining her only line in the school play in *It's Christmastime Again, Charlie Brown* (she had been practicing to say "Hark!" before Harold Angel would then walk in, but instead she said, "Hockey stick!"), a distraught Sally wails, "I ruined the whole Christmas play. Everybody hates me—Moses hates me, Luke hates me, the Apostles hate me! All fifty of 'em!" In 1983's full-length television special *It's an Adventure, Charlie Brown*, Charlie Brown wears a paper sack over his head after anxiety causes his head to look like a baseball. Unexpectedly, the bag causes his fellow campers to treat him with respect; he is their de facto leader, "Mr. Sack." Looking out at the stars one evening, he shows a younger cabin mate which star is the North Star. "That's amazing!" the kid says. "Being with you, Mr. Sack, has been the greatest experience of my life." Not used to hearing this sort of praise, the bag-ridden leader sighs through Christ's words in Matthew 13:57, "A prophet is not without honor, save in his own country."

The particularity of these diverse biblical references, not simply drawn from a stock of Sunday school Noah and Jonah flannelgraphs, was a trademark for Schulz in both strip and animation media. Other similar properties would occasionally make generic religious references, such as in a *Merry Melodies* short in which Bugs Bunny (in disguise) and Yosemite Sam almost get married in a nondescript chapel by an off-screen minister, but references to Ruth or the forests of Lebanon were by comparison rather specific for a network program. Though he had been successful with such references in the comic strips, televising these lines again held the possibility of turning off viewers less familiar with the passages and characters being discussed. Worse yet, viewers who interpreted the passages differently or did not believe at all might be offended; that was why the "Bible thing" scared the television executives in the first place.

On one occasion, Sparky made a significant, even if unnoticed, change to a biblical reference for the television screen. In 1985's *Snoopy's Getting Married*, Linus has been asked to perform Snoopy's wedding ceremony to the poodle Genevieve. "I think I'll quote the first verse of the second chapter of John," he decides. The story was an extension of Snoopy's engagement series from August 1977. In the television show, the verse Linus chose but never gets a chance to read aloud simply states, "And the third day there was a marriage in Cana of Galilee; and the mother of Jesus was there." In the comic strip version, however, Linus had declared that the sermon would be based on Genesis 34:9, simply mentioning the chapter and verse number. Readers who looked up the reference would find it reading, "And make ye marriages with us, and give your daughters unto us, and take our daughters unto you." This passage in Genesis is an offer from Hamor the Hivite to the Israelite Jacob, Hamor hoping that his tribe might intermarry with the Israelites and enjoy the benefits of their land. Hamor made this offer after his son Shechem raped Jacob's daughter Dinah. Schechem had fallen in love with Dinah and wanted to marry her as part of the deal. Jacob and his sons found revenge by agreeing to the deal only if Hamor's tribe agreed to be circumcised. They agreed, and as verse twenty-five reads, "when they were sore" from the procedure, Dinah's brothers Simeon and Levi attacked and killed the males of Hamor's tribe.

The change to such a sordid Scripture reference for television likely prevented Sparky from receiving certain critical responses. It also reflected a feeling that he had developed as he worked on more and more specials—that he had more freedom to exercise his voice in the strips than he did on television. Keeping such religious references less provocative for television allowed Schulz to craft mainstream content that evaded the label of "too religious" by viewers or the industry's all-important advertising sponsors. His religious voice on the screen was not inauthentic, but at times it cut shallower than the strips. When Genevieve leaves Snoopy at the altar and runs off with a golden retriever, Linus laments, "What about my sermon?!"

"I really think that our ability to laugh at ourselves has helped mankind to survive," Schulz wrote in 1982. Most of the salient religious references in the animated specials did just that: they used terminology, phrasing, and anecdotes from Scripture to create laughter, not theological debate. One interviewer went so far as to ask Schulz what Charlie Brown might write as an epitaph for Schulz, to which the artist tellingly responded, "Just, 'He made us happy'—which I think is what it's all about."[27] Even with this broader intention of bringing delight, though,

"I'D LIKE TO BE A GREAT THEOLOGIAN, REVEREND HALL, IF IT DIDN'T MEAN THAT I'D HAVE TO BE TOO RELIGIOUS."

Young Pillars. January 6, 1963. © 1989 Warner Press, Inc., Anderson, Indiana. Used with permission.

Schulz's non-confrontational animated religious humor did not tend to be formulaic or convenient humor (save, perhaps, for when Sally drew two cows on the chalkboard for her class, one with an angelic halo and one with a scowl. "A man and a truck drove to the zoo," she explains. "He said to the zookeeper, 'I have got some good gnus for you, and some bad gnus for you").[28] Instead, his humorous use of religious references in the animated programs tended to have the authentic voice of a writer familiar with and respectful of the source material. It was not particularly deep humor, but it was clever, not cheap, and it was certainly not crass.

Free from antagonism, this humorous brevity allowed the broader themes and tropes to remain most salient for viewers, keeping the animated programs from being cast as "evangelical" in the way that other animated features (such as Phil Vischer's *VeggieTales*) have been. The witty approach in *Peanuts* differs significantly from other religious gags in animation, such as those in the wildly popular television show *The*

Simpsons. Broadcast since 1989, Matt Groening's long-running *The Simpsons* has been called "the most 'religious television show' currently being aired."[29] With upwards of 70 percent of episodes containing at least one religious reference, the series is behind the 82 percent of *Peanuts* titles containing a religious reference, but more than 10 percent of *The Simpsons* episodes actually fix the central plot on a specific religious issue. This is a qualitative and quantitative difference between the two programs. While Lucy may momentarily tell Charlie Brown at the pitcher's mound that she thinks what their baseball team really needs is to pray (causing the rest of the team to pray "please not to me, please not to me . . ."[30]), entire episodes of *The Simpsons* revolve around characters engaging in religious dilemmas—from Homer battling with their pastor, Reverend Lovejoy, over the role of deacon,[31] to Lisa struggling to find her own religious identity in Buddhism.[32]

Groening's star on the Hollywood Walk of Fame is only a dozen feet from Schulz's, but their approaches to religious humor at times seem miles apart. One may see Groening's animated uncouth family sitcom as presenting "a mixed but ultimately respectful attitude toward religion and its important role in human development," as media analyst Todd Lewis does, but the show engages religion from a harsher subversive and satirical angle that at times would be foreign to the *Peanuts* animated universe. The show approaches religious issues, from prayer to church leadership, from a burlesque point of view, exposing the often-flawed American attitudes toward religion by poking a stick at the limits of appropriateness. The wily humor is mostly harmless, but usually goes beyond the limits of what Schulz's more tactful creative boundaries would allow. As one of the first to regularly introduce religion into animated programs, though, Schulz's work helped open up the space for serious topics in animated programs like *The Simpsons*. This included space for the religiously profane in the other shows that would follow. The insightful wit of *Peanuts* and the pointed sarcasm of *The Simpsons* would eventually be joined by the provocative mockery of Seth MacFarlane's *Family Guy* on Fox and the blatant sacrilege of Trey Parker and Matt Stone's *South Park* on Comedy Central.

Sparky himself was not a fan of cheaply crass humor, never using blue humor or cursing in his personal life. Debuting at the turn of the millennium, a much later date than Sparky's initial foray into animation, shows like *Family Guy* and *South Park* benefited from an increasingly open television landscape with creative writers and studio executives well aware of the market potential of post-Al Bundy irreverent comedy. While the market loosened its moral grip, Schulz's own personality drifted further and further from his comparatively cruel and sarcastic early creative years. The arrival of grandchildren and his jubilant relationship with his energetic new wife, Jeannie, had also softened the edges of his quick tongue just a bit, something he had been working on for years. "As you get older," he said, "you learn not to be so sarcastic, and to temper yourself."[33]

His work had inadvertently opened the market for less tempered and more blatant criticism of religion in other cartoons, but Sparky certainly would not be competing for it. "I am a little bit disturbed, of course," he said, "the way in our culture that movies, television shows, and everything are becoming more and more outrageous, and in some cases absolutely vulgar. It's become almost intolerable; I think this sort of writing has been released from the box and I don't think it can ever be put back in again."[34] Despite that lament, Sparky kept his focus on his own work. When asked once about *South Park* and its brand of satire, Sparky simply said, "Lee Mendelson and I keep saying we don't care what those other people do, we can still do something that is decent, and we have beaten every one of them."[35]

With an array of identifiable religious content in the programs, even if it was typically brief and not as provocative as that of some of his later peers, Sparky's animated programming was still something of an aberration on the small screen. From the medium's earliest days, a secularizing trend has been consistent across wide spans of television. Reaching back to the Christmas programs of the 1960s, only 8.6 percent of shows contained substantive religious plot direction.[36] In 1990, only a total of 5.6 percent of all characters on network television were found engaging in religious practice or belief. Mainstream studios have "fictionally 'de-legitimized' religious institutions and traditions by symbolically eliminating them from our most pervasive form of popular culture," the research team of Skill, Robinson, Lyons, and Larson described in their study.[37] Again in 2005, only 5.8 percent of prime-time characters were identifiably religious on the then seven broadcast networks, as media scholar Scott Clarke found. Of that 5.8 percent, only 2 percent were

"WHEN YOU LOOK AT MOVIE ADVERTISEMENTS, DOES IT EVER OCCUR TO YOU THAT THOSE PEOPLE AREN'T INTERESTED IN OUR SPIRITUAL DEVELOPMENT?"

Young Pillars. September 18, 1960. © 1989 Warner Press, Inc., Anderson, Indiana. Used with permission.

ever viewed actually engaging in religious behavior, with the other 3.8 percent being merely nominally religious through verbal or visual attribution.[38] The pervasive religious references, then, in animated programs like Schulz's did the relatively rare work of keeping religious content present in mainstream television.

Working against the delegitimizing force of omission, the inclusion of explicit non-hostile spiritual content can allow viewers more freedom in considering their own religious interests as "normal" or "acceptable" in public spaces. The inclusion of cited biblical references in a conversation between siblings, an extended scene featuring religious iconography, or a joke featuring the name of a biblical character has the potential to cultivate in viewers a stronger perception that their religious interests are not out of the ordinary. As Polish argumentation philosopher Chaïm Perelman has described, when a thing is made visible within a sphere of choice, its mere presence acts on one's sensibilities, making it more acceptable.[39] It can prime audiences, as media theorists Berkowitz and Rogers explain, to continue noticing and engaging similar ideas.[40] While the inclusion of a church building on screen would hardly be sufficient to cause a viewer to immediately agree with a particular ideology, pervasive and generally positive religious references from beloved characters have a way of making religion seem a little less taboo, maybe even a little more attractive.

The *Peanuts* characters developed such endearing bonds with readers and viewers over the years that Charles Schulz had more social capital at his disposal than he probably ever realized. His religious risk in *A Charlie Brown Christmas* cashed in on his influence, as did the themes in a number of his comic strips. Only a select few occasions, however, tested the limits of his influence in his animated programs by expanding their themes beyond their introspectively meaningful but expected brand themes. When it was announced that the *Peanuts* franchise would release an Easter special in 1974, some may have expected a message similar to the Christmas special. Sparky chose instead to produce something of a Great Pumpkin duplicate in *It's the Easter Beagle, Charlie Brown*, with Linus believing that the Easter Beagle will deliver Easter eggs to the good little boys and girls Easter morning, letting Snoopy dance with the bunny-wunnies rather than attempting to make a religious statement. "For a long while, I wouldn't do anything on Easter," Sparky described. "I'm very sensitive to not offending anybody and I thought I shouldn't do anything with Easter. But then I thought, 'Oh, the heck with it. It's fun—the Easter Beagle,' so I did it anyway."[41]

That the special is an Easter Beagle special and not a Passover Beagle special certainly demonstrated the Christian predisposition of Schulz and the television industry (which has historically resisted religion, with non-Christian religions being the most infrequently aired).[42] Other than in name, however, the Easter show was devoid of any religious content. Sparky wrote the show in the early 1970s, a period of difficult choices in his personal and church life. At any other period, though, a religious Easter special would still require scriptural authenticity, as this was Sparky's modus operandi. To attempt to integrate the *Peanuts* characters into a discussion of Christ's crucifixion and resurrection would likely have been simply too strong an evangelical statement for the hedged artist.[43]

In his Bible study, Sparky had asked the question, "What new blessing did this past Easter bring you?" Easter had been meaningful to his beliefs, of course, since it was the climax of Jesus's biblical story. The sorrow Jesus felt when crying in the Garden of Gethsemane shortly before He would be crucified had an impact on Sparky. It was "sorrow at seeing His ministry come to a disaster," Schulz wrote, "this hatred turned against His love."[44] Sparky gratefully acknowledged the role of Christ in his own life, referring to Jesus as the means by which to "fellowship with God,"[45] "to see God and to understand His feelings toward us."[46] There was a "real humanity to Jesus' earthly life," full of heartache and trials, he wrote in his Bible. Like Mary, sister of Martha, sitting at the feet of her redeemer, though, it was the teachings of Christ that Charles Schulz was most drawn to in his work. A resistance to quarrel and a predisposition for sameness over difference caused Sparky to prefer discussing Christ's words, not his death. That was the good portion he had chosen.

Brief steeples and atypical biblical quotations would certainly not be sufficient to provoke significant religious pondering in the minds of all television and film audiences. His integration of brief religious moments was pervasive, but very few of his animated moments contained the same theological significance that Schulz had imported into his strips. Charlie Brown did not ask Lucy if she thought God was pleased with her, nor did he discuss with Linus the merits of the scriptural lesson that the rain falls on the just and on the unjust. The medium itself was part of the reason for this difference. In 1980, Sparky noted that "in television it is difficult even to carry on a conversation, let alone philosophize." Pint-sized philosophizing had undergirded much of the comic strip—insecure, introspective, humorous, and humanizing philosophizing about a range of topics from the sacred to the mundane. While he had a resistance to evangelizing, Sparky did not have a resistance to challenging inquiry. In fact, he rather thrived on it, but "all too little of this kind of low-key poetry finds its way into the [television] script," he lamented.[47]

"Television is a tyrannical kind of medium," Sparky described. "You don't have a captive audience the way you do in a movie or play. In TV, you're at the mercy of some guy in a chair."[48] As home video became popular, fans could keep coming back to their favorite *Peanuts* specials time and time again, but that also meant that the anticipation of the seasonal-only *Peanuts* broadcast was no longer enough of a draw to keep viewers hooked to their sets. The number of channels on the television dial also grew as cable technology spread across the country, and Schulz's ability to infuse his specials with his subtle insights became much more difficult, requiring that action become the substitute for introspection or inquiry—"a boat race, a figure-skating competition, a spelling bee, complete with conventional bad guys. That's fine except the story tends to fall into cliché," he said. "In television we tend to settle for the easy way out."

Brief religious references peppered the shows, but Schulz expressed very little serious religious thought outside the dualism of belief and doubt in the Christmas and Halloween specials and Evert Brown's artistic expression of religious weight in *A Boy Named Charlie Brown*. After these, Sparky's most explicit religious pondering in animation came in a short from 1983's *It's an Adventure, Charlie Brown*, a special comprised of a series of small segments based very closely on comic strip series (much like *The Charlie Brown and Snoopy Show*, a Saturday morning, strip-based cartoon series which ended after only two seasons largely due to too much demand on the animators' schedules). Though no singular statement is made in this short from *It's an Adventure, Charlie Brown*, simply called, "Butterfly" and based on a strip series from 1981, Sparky's religious pondering comes forth in rich form for engaged viewers.

In the short, while Peppermint Patty and Marcie are out on the lawn, a butterfly lands on Peppermint Patty's nose. Peppermint Patty asks Marcie, "Do you think it's an omen?" She soon falls asleep. While Peppermint Patty is sleeping, Marcie sends the butterfly fluttering away. Peppermint Patty awakens and says, "Marcie—the butterfly is gone! What happened?!" Marcie explains to her, "A miracle, sir! While you were asleep it turned into an angel." Peppermint Patty then tells Charlie Brown that a butterfly turned into an angel and chose her, saying, "Doesn't that make you shiver all over? I'm trying to stay humble, Chuck." She tells Sally it was a miracle and that she thinks she was chosen to bring a message to the world, saying, "Why else would a butterfly land on my nose and then turn into an angel?"

According to Linus, "the world could certainly use a message," which, according to Peppermint Patty, the angel has said is: "How about—if a foul ball is hit behind third base it's the short stop's play." She even goes to a televangelist's office and tells his receptionist, "I'd like to speak to the preacher please. The one I see on TV all the time. I thought he'd be interested in a miracle that I personally know of." The preacher is busy, so the secretary gives her the Sunday school paper instead. Later, Peppermint Patty rests against a tree and Marcie tells her that she looks tired. "I am exhausted, Marcie," Peppermint Patty says. "I've been to three tabernacles, 14 churches, and two temples." Marcie asks, "No one wanted to hear about your miracle?" Peppermint Patty replies, "All I got was a bunch of tracts and this," holding out a paper that Marcie reads aloud: "Want to receive a blessing? Donate to our new lawn sprinkler system."

Peppermint Patty then phones the *Joe Mel Talk Show* but is hung up on and called "just another nut." She decides to tell Snoopy about her miracle because Snoopy has a big nose too; that explanation irritates the dog, so he turns away. She decides to tell Schroeder her message. He says to her, "That's a very disturbing message." "I expect to be persecuted," she acknowledges. After then telling Sally the message about the third base play, Peppermint Patty says, "That's the message I feel the angel told me to give to the world. There also may be a few earthquakes and some floods." Sally says, "Boy, that's frightening!" to which Peppermint Patty responds, "Thank you."

Finally, sitting on the lawn again, Peppermint Patty and Marcie see the butterfly once more. Marcie, who has been trying this whole time to explain to the oblivious Peppermint Patty that she made the whole thing up, tries another tactic and says that maybe the butterfly is not an angel anymore. Peppermint Patty concludes the short, saying, "That's too bad. Back to the minor leagues."

In this short from the Peabody Award-winning and Emmy-nominated CBS special, viewers were treated to classic Schulzian socio-theological pondering. While Schulz primarily used his religious knowledge to make the *Peanuts* animation humorous, his humor did sometimes explore larger issues of religious thought. It could not help but do so—such was the nature of his creativity. In "Butterfly," if the viewer is willing to think through the issue with the scene, an invitation is extended to consider one's relationship to miracles. The scene asks one to question why it is that some are so wonderfully quick to believe that a miracle has happened to them even when the "real" explanation is being repeated over and over. Yet the viewer is also prompted to consider why others, who are purportedly in the business of miracles (i.e., the churches, tabernacles, and temples), are so wrapped up with the tedious business of Sunday school papers and sprinkler systems that they lose the ability to listen to news of the miraculous. Schulz's work does not offer spoon-fed answers, but instead opens up the provocative field of inquiry for internal engagement, even if driven by witty humor.

"Butterfly" stands as one of the few moments in which Sparky's more poetic religious voice survived translation. Even with a creative mind and decades of strips to draw from, it was at times a challenge to find material for the films, direct-to-video releases, Saturday morning strip cartoons, and seasonal television specials that did not take the easy way out. The challenge resulted in a pervasive array of brief religious references across the franchise. Spoken in typically small samples of Sparky's authentic voice, religious interest, practice, and inquiry were at least marginally present. In a few salient and powerful moments, Sparky's deeper spiritual insights were brought forth for more poetic consideration. Rarely did Schulz give solutions to the questions being considered, almost never making direct evangelical claims. Yet the fact that he was willing to fill the screen with any variety of religious consideration at all was itself a provocative statement. Spoken by beloved characters in titles like *A Boy Named Charlie Brown*, *A Charlie Brown Christmas*, and *It's an Adventure, Charlie Brown's* "Butterfly," these moments had little realistic possibility of provoking defensive retaliation, given their openness, humor, and artistry.

When Paramount Home Video began releasing videotape copies of the *Peanuts* specials, they included an introductory commercial inviting viewers to collect all of the titles. "You'll laugh. (Ho, ho, ho)," the home viewer was told. "You'll cry. (Augh!) You'll get up and dance!" Perhaps the commercial narrator should have added, "You might even sit back and think; you might even consider some deeper philosophizing from one of America's foremost comic humorists." Sparky's animated work was not usually as provocative as his strips, and not as inflammatory as some of its later competition, but when the introspective spiritual thinker did enunciate his religious inquiry, laughing and crying were only the beginning.

7

SHORE TO SHORE

"Little things that we say and do in Christ's name are like pebbles thrown in the water. The ripples spread out in circles, and influence people we may know only slightly and sometimes not at all."

—CHARLES M. SCHULZ

WITH HANDS RAISED OFF THE TABLE AND EYES SQUINTED IN DELIGHT, President Reagan reeled back in laughter at the words of Queen Elizabeth II. Deadpan, she had made the most simple of jokes—one about the weather—to the gleeful amusement of the president and their shared guests. "I knew before we came that we had exported many of our traditions to the United States," the queen said. "But I had not realized before that weather was one of them."[1] The weather had been unseasonably stormy during the queen and Prince Philip's visit to California, a week-long stop during her world tour on her royal yacht *Britannia,* then the largest ship of its kind in the world, but that did not turn away the jubilant crowd from enjoying a dinner hosted by the Reagans in honor of the visiting English royalty.

The dinner was held at the De Young Art Museum in San Francisco on March 3, 1983. It was one of the last official events the queen and Prince Phillip would enjoy before retreating to a relaxing stay in snowy Yosemite National Park. Though many points in the histories of the two nations were surely solemn, evidenced by the 7,000 protesters demonstrating outside the museum in Golden Gate Park, the event inside was a joyous one. It was a "glittering affair," remarked dinner guest and economist Milton Friedman, "attended by the leading citizens of California and many from the rest of the country."[2] Among those leading

Californians were Sparky and Jeannie, attending at the request of the Reagans. Making their way through the reception line to greet the Reagans, Prince Philip, and the queen, a line which Sparky noted "moved so fast we did not feel that we had the time to express any kind of pleasantries," Jeannie and Sparky abided by the directive to not touch the queen and to be sure that the women curtsied. The president and Sparky greeted each other warmly, and Sparky and the queen shared formal acknowledgments, though she did not recognize the prolific cartoonist. When Sparky had gone a few steps further, the president leaned in and whispered to the queen, "that's the man who draws Snoopy!" With her iconic English vocal drawl, the queen piqued, "Oh reeaally," and Jeannie and Sparky took their seats for dinner.

The two took delight in their evening mixing with the elite crowd, full of industry magnates, political leaders, and cultural movers, though the bustle of such a gathering of distinguished strangers could be difficult to navigate, even awkward at times. While they had been waiting, Sparky had spotted from across the room the familiar face of a man whose work he had thoroughly respected. Making his way through the sea of people, Sparky took the opportunity to greet none other than the Reverend Billy Graham. The evangelist was also a friend of the Reagans and was no stranger to the English shores, having spread his famous crusades over to the United Kingdom many years before. Writing to Nancy Reagan days later, Sparky would remark that he and Jeannie "had a thoroughly enjoyable evening."[3]

As the queen had noted in her witty speech at the dinner, England shared a common vision of freedom with the United States, and it was that ideal that Lee Mendelson hoped would produce the *Peanuts* franchise's next great animated feature. Pitching to Sparky and Bill the idea of a theatrical film in which the characters would visit historical sites in the U.S., much as they had done in Europe in *Bon Voyage Charlie Brown (And Don't Come Back!)* and *What Have We Learned, Charlie Brown?*, Lee took on the responsibility of conducting the research for the program, traveling to Williamsburg where he would learn of the wig maker's tool called a "blockhead," and even contacting the White House in 1984 to inquire about shooting a scene for the film with President Reagan over which they would animate the *Peanuts* characters. Despite Lee's enthusiasm for the project, though, his feature-length idea never gained traction, and the team devoted their efforts to their other animated endeavors.

Several years later, Lee would find a new outlet for his patriotic project, but only after CBS, which was losing the ratings war, informed him that they would no longer be purchasing any new animated *Peanuts* specials. "Our ratings had finally dropped off to what I considered a dangerous level," Lee said of their own mid-1980s contributions to the network. Called into the office of Kim LeMasters, the new president of the network who had to his credit the development of many hits, including *Dallas*, *Knots Landing*, *Designing Women*, and *Murphy Brown*, Lee was told that their animation run had come to an end.

Looking out LeMasters's office window, Lee noticed a large American flag flying and was struck with inspiration for changing the tone of the conversation. "You know," he told the television boss, "I've been doing some research for a possible movie we have been considering, where we take the kids back into the most dramatic events in our history. But as we're sitting here, I am thinking maybe it would be a better television series of specials. We could do the first animated miniseries!" Kim stared back at Lee for a moment before making a quick phone call and announcing that one of their programming executives thought it was a fabulous idea. "How many shows do you think?" he asked Lee. "Maybe eight," Lee blurted back to him. "We have a deal," Kim said. "Hollywood always has been a gut-reaction town," Lee would remark years later, "but that has to be one of the fastest."[4]

For the eight-part miniseries, they would leave behind Lee's idea of live-action filming, which they would use in 1988's *It's the Girl in the Red Truck, Charlie Brown*, a hybridized TV movie written by Sparky and his son Monte, in which an animated Spike befriends the would-be dancer Jenny, played by Monte's younger sister, Jill. In *This is America, Charlie Brown*, the animators instead recreated historic scenes and settings, placing the *Peanuts* gang at the heart of celebrated national moments, often superimposing the characters over artistically rendered archival images to add authenticity and depth.[5] Because Lee had taken the lead on research, Sparky took a step back from directly writing each episode. While he reviewed the programs before they were finalized and was given writing co-credit for the first four, he was grateful to have Lee and Bill to take the reigns. "Sparky was so busy and had so many other things," noted Jeannie, "that he was happy to have it done."[6]

The miniseries episodes, each twenty-four minutes in length, include a surprising array of references as they bounce through national historical highlights, such as Linus learning about the variety of influences that inspired the telephone from inventors Alexander Graham Bell[7] and Thomas Watson in "The Great Inventors" (including African tribal drums and the challenges faced by deaf children). In "The Building of the Transcontinental Railroad," Snoopy stands in as a surveyor as Charlie Brown narrates the labored task undertaken by Chinese workers laying train tracks across the west. In "The Smithsonian and the Presidency," the characters tour the museum's exhibits of the First Ladies' inaugural gowns and the Apollo 10 lunar module. Peppermint Patty even notices the comic strip exhibit featuring the October 4, 1964, *Peanuts* football episode comic.

Perhaps the most successful of the eight episodes was "The Mayflower Voyagers," directed by Evert Brown and made popular through its connection to the successful *A Charlie Brown Thanksgiving*. In the episode, the *Peanuts* cast joins the party of strangers, servants, and Pilgrims traveling to the New World aboard the historic *Mayflower*. The episode is sobering at times. The ship's crew and passengers struggle with sickness and storms on their long voyage and are then unprepared for the harsh realities of the American wilderness. "By the end of February, two and a half months after landing at Plymouth, no Indians have been seen," Charlie Brown narrates, "but the combination of a terrible winter and lack of nutritious food and necessary medical supplies has been devastating," Charlie Brown continues as the camera pans over adults quietly hauling a stretcher carrying a covered body to a freshly made graveyard marked with crosses: "Half of the original 102 passengers have died. Only twenty adults and thirty children have survived."

A "miracle" saves the settlers from being forced to return to England as native Samoset peacefully greets Linus and Charlie Brown, introducing them to Squanto, another English-speaking native who spent years in forced servitude in Spain before returning home. Squanto teaches the settlers of the "heritage of his fathers," including planting maize, and ushering in a treaty of friendship between the tribal and settler peoples.

Ninety of the tribe join the fifty settlers for a feast of thanksgiving, re-enacting the historical event that 1973's Emmy-winning holiday special, *A Charlie Brown Thanksgiving*, celebrated. The linking of the two animated stories, for researcher and producer Lee Mendelson, was "one of my favorite moments in our 50 years of production."[8]

Along with connecting the historical thread across the specials, the re-enactment also highlighted the tradition of prayer that Schulz had already written into the original holiday special. "Are we going to have a prayer?" Peppermint Patty asks in *A Charlie Brown Thanksgiving* as they all sit down for a makeshift meal of popcorn and toast. "It's Thanksgiving, you know. Before we're served shouldn't we say grace?" Some of the other characters appear caught off guard, even dejected at not having a prayer in order. Linus responds by framing a prayer within a little speech about the history of Thanksgiving, saying, "Elder William Brewster said a prayer that went a little something like this . . ." after which Peppermint Patty says a convincing "Amen." In "The Mayflower Voyagers," the characters have no need to pause; prayer is a natural part of their lives and they have no shame in being public about it. As the feast is about to begin, Charlie Brown prays with folded hands, "We thank the Lord for our bountiful harvest." "We give thanks for our new home and our good health," Linus then declares, with Lucy then adding, "Thank you for giving us Samoset and Squanto and the great Chief Massasoit."

Early in the episode, the passengers and crew are also performing their religious faith, bowing in corporate prayer aboard the tiny *Mayflower*. Their "belief in God, their desire for freedom from religious persecution, and their dreams of creating a new world for future generations all make their life-threatening journey a risk worth taking" Charlie Brown's voice-over describes. Later in the episode, before the settlers are rescued by the miraculous arrival of Squanto, Captain Miles Standish is even seen holding a Bible marked with a cross[9] as Charlie Brown explains that "the strong faith of the surviving Pilgrims is just about all they have left."

Brief acknowledgments of the national and social importance of faith throughout various American eras are peppered throughout *This is America, Charlie Brown*. In "The Birth of the Constitution," for example, also directed by Evert Brown, Linus explains to his friends that

Peppermint Patty is seen amongst the passengers aboard the Mayflower in 1988's "The Mayflower Voyagers," bowing in corporate prayer as their faith gives them strength during the difficult journey. Courtesy of Lee Mendelson Productions.

the arduous work of drafting the Constitution, performed by the delegates at the Constitutional Convention that the characters had been tending to for months, was really only the beginning. The task of convincing each state to ratify it may take months or even years. After they pass by the wig maker's shop, Sally and Charlie Brown retire to their own home. Before they close the door, Sally tells Linus, "I'll say a little prayer for our people, Linus." In "The Smithsonian and the Presidency," instead of meeting with a live Ronald Reagan as Lee had originally envisioned, the animation team brought Charlie Brown and Linus onto the animated train carrying Abraham Lincoln to Gettysburg to deliver his famous address at the dedication for the national cemetery lined with cross grave markers. As the train sets to leave, the two must depart, but Charlie Brown's narration continues to explain how Abraham Lincoln labored over his Gettysburg address, describing how the president "debated about whether he would use the words 'under God'"[10] and that "he thought of the words of Patrick Henry, of Daniel Webster, of Henry Clay, and he thought deeply about the Scriptures."

The episodes aired on CBS in late 1988 and early 1989. Though LeMasters had originally told Lee that CBS was ending their run of new *Peanuts* programs, the miniseries would provide a timely rescue for the network. In March 1988, the Writers Guild of America, the labor union of film and television writers, went on strike. The strike, which lasted for five months, centered on the scale of residuals payments for reruns and greater creative control by the writers. To fill in the programming gaps left by series episodes that could not be completed without the scriptwriters, the networks drew on sports programs, newsmagazines like *48 Hours*, and unscripted reality programming like *COPS* to complete their schedules. CBS also drew from their backlog of movies and miniseries, increasing their planned number from twenty-five that season to a total of fifty. This would include the *Peanuts* miniseries. Because original programming was sparse, *This is America, Charlie Brown* would be promoted with even more excitement by the network, billed as Lee had suggested as "the first animated miniseries."

As "The Mayflower Voyagers" airdate approached, CBS sent advance scripts to local stations, which disseminated them to local schools. Receiving a copy of the advance script, the Concerned American Indian Parents group from Sparky's hometown of Minneapolis complained to CBS. The group feared that the episode stereotyped the native peoples, even portraying Squanto as a "grateful slave" who had learned English after being captured and taken to Europe. Revising the word "savages" out of the program, CBS's vice president of program practices for CBS, Carol Altieri, was confident in their final product and kept the broadcast on schedule. "We're not stereotyping Indians or Native Americans here," she said, "as much as we are telling the story of a man (Squanto) who, through extreme adverse experiences in his life brought those experiences to bear in becoming the salvation of people who landed in this strange land."[11]

For family programming, the miniseries admittedly referenced a considerable number of serious issues, from slavery to poverty, even if only briefly. The program's overriding tone was nonetheless one of optimism, consistent with Schulz's view of America. While he had his own critiques of American sociopolitics, chiding those who created needless divisions and cautioning those who were quick to go to war, Sparky also had a strong love for his country. "He was from that World War II generation and thought that if there was anything the world needed, America could do it," Jeannie described, admitting that "it was a very idealistic look, but I think it was typical of his generation too."

Sparky avoided broaching issues of national politics in his strips, save perhaps for the topic of war. War carried a heavy burden, he knew, and he briefly alluded to such in a few select strips—Franklin's father off fighting in the distant Vietnam War,[12] Snoopy being hit over the head by a supper dish thrown by rioting antiwar dogs at the Daisy Hill Puppy Farm,[13] and Snoopy then trudging through the surf at Omaha Beach as the World Famous GI in a memorial strip honoring the anniversary of D-Day.[14] "I would have given anything in the world to have met General Eisenhower," Sparky said. "What an honor. What a tremendous feat he had commanding D-Day. The decisions he had to make were just unbelievable."[15] Sparky had met President Reagan, who he thought was likewise a thoughtful leader, and would meet Presidents Jimmy Carter, George H. W. Bush, and Bill Clinton as well. Amongst the many correspondences he had with college students who were engrossed in his strips during the 1960s, Sparky had even sent a young Hillary Clinton a personal note signed with a beagle paw in 1968 to congratulate her on becoming the Wellesley College government president. Clinton treasured her note from Sparky, hanging it on the wall in her office at the White House during her husband's presidency.

Outside of his strip, Sparky's personal approach to politics was nuanced. "Was Dad a Republican or Democrat?" wondered his son Monte. "Well, certainly he was a Republican during the Eisenhower years, but he endorsed many liberal virtues, being no fan of the war in Vietnam, nor persecutions of any sort, and considered Martin Luther King Jr. to be one of American history's greatest figures."[16] Sparky was a supporter of women's equality and opportunity, especially in sports, and had pressed back against some editors' criticisms in the 1960s over having an African American character attend school with the white characters. "He confessed to me once," Monte also remembered, "that had he the opportunity to do it over again, he would have voted for Kennedy in 1960 instead of Nixon." Later, in the 1990s, Sparky supported the Republican senator later dubbed a "maverick," John McCain, during one of McCain's runs for office. Though his voting record tended to be conservative, pigeonholes and stereotypes would simply not suffice in explaining Sparky's approach to politics.

Sparky lived a "conservative" personal lifestyle—no drinking, smoking, or crude language—but identified his social outlook as "liberal"—an accepting one in which respect and generosity were important. Politically, he was not in favor of big government. It was his "only argument with Clinton's whole philosophy," he said. "He just thinks that government can do everything." Communism had "proven to be a disaster," noted Sparky, and socialism "simply doesn't work." His father, Carl, had been a Republican, and Sparky noted with a laugh that "owning your own business will turn you into a Republican in a hurry."[17] If liberal governmental policies capped and redistributed his wealth, he argued to one liberal contender for California's governorship at a reception for her that he and Jeannie attended, he would not be able to undertake the significant charitable giving he was committed to.

Like Sparky's strips, the *This is America, Charlie Brown* miniseries was not overtly political, but it would carry a select history of America's somber challenges and a message of American optimism to not only family living rooms—"The Mayflower Voyagers" eventually seeing annual re-airings when it was later paired with *A Charlie Brown Thanksgiving*—but also to school classrooms across the country. Released on VHS in 1994 and then promoted as part of what the *Washington Post* called Paramount Home Video's "Back to School Push,"[18] the episodes would be readily available for grade school teachers, providing an educational tool much like the musical program sold to ABC by advertising agency McCaffrey & McCall, *School House Rock*. Some would critique certain episodes of the *Peanuts* program, including "The Mayflower Voyagers" for perpetuating errant myths of the first Thanksgiving,[19] but it was not long before the miniseries was a staple on many educators' lesson plans.

While the 1973 Charlie Brown edition of *The Rainbow Dictionary* by Wendell Wright would teach pint-size scholars that church is "a place where people come together to think about God,"[20] and that God is someone to pray to "because we feel He loves us and takes care of us,"[21] the videotapes of *This is America, Charlie Brown* would be used by countless teachers seeking to share America's historical highlights with young students in an entertaining and engaging way. Those highlights would include the various references to religious faith, something that would often otherwise be avoided in many public schools for fear of crossing the uncertain boundaries between church and state. Because it was historically contextualized and disarmingly presented within the nationally beloved world of *Peanuts*, teachers would face very little pushback on the programs, despite the fact that many teachers were showing such histories in public school districts often wary of broaching religious topics.[22]

The religious content in the miniseries was consistent with Schulz's own understanding of faith's importance in American history. Denying that belief in God was important to historical or contemporary Americans would be naïve, even delusional. Those religions that rotated the equation, however, making their own particular religious faith synonymous with and necessary for patriotism, were a dangerous and misguided breed. "I am very fearful of a church which equates itself with Americanism," Sparky once said. "This is a frightening trend—people who regard Christianity and Americanism as being virtually the same thing."[23]

Statistically, the American populace has always had spiritual interests and beliefs that run both deep and wide. In 1988, when the miniseries began airing, 85 percent of American adults identified religion as fairly or very important in their lives (54 percent answering that it was very important), and 84 percent of American adults self-identified as Christian.[24] Yet Schulz knew, of course, that not everyone in the country shared a uniform Christian perspective. He had always believed that one should be free to explore the mysteries of faith on a personal level, even if others around disagreed. It was one of his own children, though, not the entertainment industry, that would put that perspective to the test.

Soon after they moved to California, Joyce had no longer felt obligated to continue attending church with Sparky, and the prospective chore of getting five children who were not interested in attending church dressed up to drive across town did not persuade her otherwise. Thus, after only a short period when they were very young, and save for a brief period in high school when Monte and Meredith were required to attend out of their mother's hopes of balancing the culture's bad influences, the children did not spend time in religious studies. "It was a lot of fuss to get us ready!" recalled Jill, the youngest of the five who would remember very little of her experience with church.[25]

Sparky's father, Carl, who had become a Lutheran usher in his final years, had never been a religious leader of the family while Sparky was growing up, opting instead to spend his Sundays taking his wife and child to visit relatives or carving out time for a little fishing. In his own way, Sparky seemed to be following in his father's footsteps. Not particularly inclined to urge others to follow his own way of thinking on personal matters, Sparky never insisted his own family join him at church. At home, he was rather silent about religion. Joyce was familiar with the Scriptures, but neither she nor Sparky prompted family devotion or study time at home, explaining it away by saying their children were too young. "But we admire those who do it even with our age children," Joyce once remarked, a few years before she stopped attending church altogether.[26] Though Sparky played an active role in his children's young lives, the self-studier who had read the Bible several times from cover to cover did not actively discuss the sacred text with his children, let alone teach them it as definitive Truth. They knew he studied the Bible, often seeing him in his yellow armchair with a stack of books, but he was not in the habit of exploring his religious readings or thoughts with his wife or with his kids throughout their childhoods.

"If God is there, why can't I see Him?" a very young Meredith once asked her mother while they were all still relatively active in the Minnesota church. Joyce recalled explaining simply to her that "He is there even though she can't see Him and that He does take care of people."[27] In California, Sparky was even given inspiration for a comic strip when Jill came running across the dark Coffee Grounds yard one night after visiting their own Coca-Cola machine. Spooked by the nighttime yard, the idea of prayer came to her mind, but by the time she finished the short trip back to the house, her idea had become a silly one. "If you hold your hands upside down, you get the opposite of what you pray for!" she told her father who would then give the line to Linus in a strip as the boy's own "new theological discovery."[28] But as young children, the Schulzes were not clamoring for spiritual knowledge from their father. As they grew, their personalities naturally began to bring about unique passions and skills in other things. Some of their father's affinities, like a love for spending time on the ice, rubbed off on most of them, but the personal study of the Scriptures did not. In each of their unique interests, Charles Schulz engaged his children with sincerity and support, and each of the children found passions that commanded a significant amount of their time. Much like their father's devotion to his comic work, the kids' interests at times had a singular focus. "We tend to do one thing . . . and do it a lot," Jill said. "Maybe we inherited that."

Literature, for example, quickly became a focus of Monte's attention. The eldest of the two sons, Monte would eventually write his own novels, drawing on names from family history for his key characters. Growing up, Monte's interest in the precious art of reading was buoyed by his father's eclectic and broad field of literary vision. Sparky did not give his son illustrated versions of the Bible stories he knew so well, though, but instead passed along books like *Treasure Island* and *Driscoll's Book of Pirates*. Later in life, his father's interest in studying theology would rub off, though Monte would not believe the theology of the Bible or any other religious text to be true in the ways that his father may have believed. The two would at times discuss matters of theology, though rarely from the same perspective, but that made their connection no less rich or sincere.

While Monte and Sparky would connect over the written word, it was skating that started Sparky and daughter Amy down an unexpected path of special connection. Like her brothers and her younger sister Jill, Amy developed a love for the ice, taking lessons from an early age at the Redwood Empire Ice Arena that Joyce and Sparky had built for the community. The two younger sisters had been dressed alike from childhood, often lumped together as "Jill-n-Amy," a single title for the pair. Sparky loved skating himself, enjoying not only playing hockey but also watching figure skating during his morning breakfast routine at his regular table in the Warm Puppy Café inside the ice arena, the ritual that enabled him to meet Jeannie.

Both girls were accomplished skaters; Jill even earned enough points for a gold medal from the U.S. Figure Skating Association. Much like their father's correspondence course training in which he practiced his pen lines over and over, they would practice their compulsory figures for hours on end, an exercise in which the skater must repeatedly carve specific figure-eight patterns into the perfectly smoothed ice, pushing off only once at the top of the figure and attempting to glide on one foot without straying from the exact line the blade left on the last pass. Amy was a highly lyrical skater, listening to the movements in the music and gracefully choreographing her own routines to match the ebb and flow of the score. With her skills at their peak, Sparky had Amy perform part of a skating routine for Lee Mendelson, who used the footage to animate Peppermint Patty in *She's a Good Skate, Charlie Brown*.[29] He also had her skate in the televised ice special, *Snoopy's Musical on Ice*, in a lineup that included Olympic champion Peggy Fleming—one of the world's finest skaters and a master of the figures. Amy skated to a compilation of hymns that Sparky had chosen personally. "The hymns didn't mean anything to me," said Amy, though, "except that I was doing it for my dad."[30]

Though she would not follow her younger sister to travel internationally with *Ice Follies*, the ice rink would usher in a new change for Amy and her father, as one of Amy's skating friendships caused her to meet Brad Lowder, a boy from a local clean-cut family. Amy had a natural rapport with Brad and his family, having inherited her father's almost genetic predisposition against drinking, smoking, and cursing, and the two were soon engaged. The Lowders were not simply a socially conservative family, though, they were members of the Church of Jesus Christ of Latter-day Saints (LDS)—the Mormon Church.

While Brad was away fulfilling a common LDS call to the mission field in 1976, Amy spent time with his family, taking part in their Monday night "Family Home Evening," a weekly gathering similar to other denominations' weekly Bible studies in which the family comes together to read materials provided by the church and to pray. These at-home scriptural lessons were unlike anything she had experienced before, even with her own Scripture-proficient father. The Lowder home was a safe and welcoming space, though, and Amy was encouraged to join in, even taking turns in leading the Mormon lessons.

The process of religious study was new to Amy, who had initially been simply drawn to the comfort of the Mormon community. "I just remember thinking, 'What? No way?! Nobody in your church drinks? That's unbelievable!'" said Amy. "I always thought I wasn't going to be able to get married because I wouldn't marry anybody that drank." She was being confronted with more than a lifestyle, however; she was being confronted with questions of theology and organized religion. "I had no interest in religion," she said, not having ever explored it seriously before this point. "Dad, you should have taught me something about religion!" she would lament to herself. He had taught her to lick the bowl when she was done with her ice cream, but not what it meant to believe in a Heavenly Father.

Sparky had enjoyed the open supportive environment that Carl and Dena had provided him during his own childhood. His parents had given him the freedom to develop his own passions, and he wanted to maintain that same non-intrusive stance with his own children. For Monte, this had allowed him to go in a different analytical direction than his father, passionately but respectfully disagreeing while pondering through their own theological conversations without such disagreements hindering their relationship. But looking back, Amy wanted Sparky to have taught her. Had he done so, perhaps her response to Mormonism may have been different. Sparky had wanted his children to come to religion on their own, if they would at all, and Amy had.

Though her relationship with Brad would eventually come to an end, Amy had begun taking formal lessons at the LDS church, and in the spring of 1979, she was baptized into the church and confirmed by the laying on of hands. Later that year, she would tell the *Deseret News*, a newspaper owned by the LDS Church, "I wish I had learned all of this before when I was growing up. One significant change that I have made is my belief in God and Jesus Christ. I understand Them better now and that makes me happy."[31]

As a well-studied reader of the Scriptures, Charles Schulz disagreed with his daughter's new Mormon beliefs. Before he left on his mission, Brad shared a copy of *The Book of Mormon* and the LDS *Doctrine and Covenants* with Sparky, which Sparky read. "I didn't share them with any great expectation that he would have some spiritual epiphany and convert to Mormonism, it was just out of love," said Brad, wanting Sparky to better understand what was so sacred to him.[32] Sparky found the claim that Joseph Smith was directed by an angel to special tablets from which he received the *Book of Mormon* to be "an outrageous statement."[33] "It's either a hoax, or it's the truth," Sparky told Amy, "and I think it's a hoax."

Just two years before Amy was baptized into the church, Schulz told Peter France of the BBC that spiritual expression is not accomplished by "dropping money in the collection plate, which is nice of course; it's not building temples." "Perhaps," Schulz continued, "the church has gotten too big."[34] The LDS church was just the sort of large, highly organized approach to religion that Sparky resisted. Sermons delivered across Mormon churches followed prescribed parameters, uniformly spreading around the world with few deviating sects, and LDS rhetoric referred to the order as "the only true Church."[35] More than a decade before Amy found her way to Mormonism, Sparky had told the *Christian Herald*,

> We are surrounded by scribes and Pharisees who insist upon worshipping on certain days, upon having certain ceremonies and holidays and that people go to certain rituals. We find certain groups among us declaring that they are the true church. You could think of six separate groups right now without putting your mind to it, each of which declares that it has the complete truth and has absolutely no tolerance for anything that any other group is teaching. This is to me the most frightening aspect of what is going on in Christianity today. While we are trying desperately to draw near to each other, there are groups doing exactly the opposite. They are not simply groups to which we can't pay any attention but ones that are gaining ground amazingly each day, gaining adherents.[36]

Schulz may very well have been thinking explicitly of the Mormon Church when speaking to the *Christian Herald*. Believing that the relational architecture of Christ's "one true church" was restored through Joseph Smith, the ever-expanding LDS church had been structured on a system of elders, apostles, and a living prophet (not wholly dissimilar to the prophetic beliefs of Judaism or the structures of bishops, cardinals, and the pope in Catholicism). Doctrine would disseminate from the centralized council, duplicated verbatim throughout the organization. Such comparative inflexibility and depersonalization of spiritual inquiry inherent in such highly organized denominationalism were non-starters for Charles Schulz. For him, theological investigation should be earnest and personal, never bureaucratic. Studied belief was best produced by small groups of individuals operating simply with a few moderate commentaries, not from mimeographed doctrine handed down through structured hierarchy.

Like with each of his children, Sparky had a special, unique relationship with Amy, a sensitive daughter whom he often called Amos. On her fourteenth birthday, Sparky had given her a dozen roses, telling her, "I want to be the first person in your life to give you a dozen roses."[37] Amy knew enough about her father's beliefs to know that he did not agree with Mormon theology. Her brother, Monte, had spent his own time with her explaining why he disagreed with its tenets, but lecturing Amy on Mormonism's hermeneutic shortcomings was simply not a consideration for their father.

With the Mormon church, Amy had found a home in a welcoming community, not unlike what her father had found upon returning from the war. Thus, despite theologically disbelieving LDS doctrine, and despite his general distaste for religious dogmatism, Charles Schulz became generally supportive of Amy, even when she decided to travel on her own Mormon mission. "Once he realized that the Mormon lifestyle fit her well, he just wanted her to be happy," Jill explained.[38] Amy was aware that her father disagreed with her beliefs, but his approach in telling her so was soft and his criticism only momentary. He even agreed to speak at her sendoff ceremony. "You know there's no such thing as the Melchizedek priesthood[39] anymore," he said to her, almost as a rib, before Amy's "setting apart" ritual in which through the laying on of hands Amy was "set apart by the power of the Melchizedek priesthood" to carry out her duties as a Mormon missionary. She was much too new to thinking about theology for herself to untangle such beliefs with her father, but she was nonetheless excited to be striking out on an adventure, crafting an identity that was her own, and fulfilling a call to spread the good news of the Mormon church.

In 1981, after receiving her letter from the central LDS offices revealing where she was to witness for the next year and a half, Amy traveled to the West Midlands, England, roughly 100 miles northwest of central London. It was a rather cold locale in comparison to her comfortable home in warm northern California, and there Amy would experience the highs and lows of missionary work. Waking up at dawn each morning, she and her LDS companions would ready themselves for a full day of "tracting," going door-to-door handing out religious pamphlets. Amy was earnest in her desire to witness and enjoyed the anonymity of the foreign landscape, having made this decision for herself, unrelated

TRUTH
"YOU'VE GIVEN ME ONE OF YOUR TRACTS, SIR, AND I'VE GIVEN YOU ONE OF MINE. NOW, WHERE DO WE STAND?"

Young Pillars. December 23, 1962. © 1989 Warner Press, Inc., Anderson, Indiana. Used with permission.

to any of her father's successes. "I get to be equal; I get to be normal" she thought,[40] which happened to include facing more literal slammed doors than she had ever expected. "I thought that was just an expression!" she joked, surprised that she was not having more success with her door-to-door evangelism.

Closed doors and strong allegiances to the Church of England aside, for Amy, "it was exciting to care about something in my heart and want to share it with people." While in England she also met Johnny Johnson, the zone leader for the Coventry area. Well-versed in LDS theology, Johnny was to be a comfort and guide for the region's missionaries. He and Amy would soon find delight in each other's company, and upon their return home, the two would be married. Sparky would later immortalize his daughter's efforts abroad in a series of comic strips in which Linus tries in vain to hand out tracts sharing the message of the Great Pumpkin. "To Johnny and Amy, who know what it's like," Schulz signed on one of the originals,[41] to be hung on the wall of Amy's Utah home after the passing of her father.

As is the case with most missionary work, Amy not only experienced the excitement of the adventure but also the hardships of the calling—the rejections, the occasional loneliness, and even the unfamiliar weather. She wrote home regularly during the one day a week that she and her companions were allowed to do so, sharing her joys and her struggles with her father by postal mail. In her father's responses, she found not only comfort, but also a spiritual bond that neither she nor Sparky had expected.

Though Sparky had a special relationship with Amy, the only one of his children he would regularly wish a happy birthday to in his strips, guidance was not something she expected to receive. "He would never tell you what to do—almost to the point of being annoying," Amy said. In one letter, Sparky wrote, "In your last letter, you asked if I had any advice. Sure—See your dentist twice a year—Don't go on the ice with your guards on—and don't eat too many doughnuts with your pizza."[42] While Sparky would typically shy away from insisting on his own advice, the letters he would send his daughter provided not only a comfort that she would cherish, but for the first time would also give her a very direct view of the enduringly personal spiritual faith of her father.

"I love your wonderful letters," Sparky told Amy. He enjoyed hearing about his daughter's investment in her new work. On March 22, 1982, upon returning from a pro-am golf tournament in Las Vegas, Sparky wrote back after receiving a particularly sorrowful letter from his daughter. "Please think of this as completely natural," he wrote. "The apostle Paul became confused often and of course even Jesus knew that He could not keep up the work among people without sometimes getting away and being alone. Above all, do not feel guilty. God knows your heart. He knows your feelings and always understands."[43]

Nine days later, he wrote her a lengthier letter, telling her,

> Remember also that any suffering you are going through such as loneliness, etc. is making you into a better person. Steel is no good until it is refined in fire. We are worthless as human beings until we have been refined by troubles and suffering. You will be of enormous value to other people, your friends and your own children some day because you will have ex-

> perienced the problems that they will come to you with. This is how our Heavenly Father can use us as we live in His world, and this is what faith is. You know that He understands your doubts, your fears and even your desires. Don't let guilt about desires bother you either. God understands your needs before you even think about them. No one else around you may understand, but He knows your heart, and this is your faith.[44]

While he had disagreed with certain fundamental elements of Amy's new faith, writing to his missionary daughter gave Charles Schulz an opportunity to do something he had not been able to do before—openly connect with a family member on his spiritual beliefs. He and Monte had discussed theology from an academic standpoint over the years, but they had never spoken from the same perspective of belief. Amy was still relatively new to her faith, but it was important to her, and it provided Sparky with the chance to share just how important faith was to him.

"I am more pleased than you know," he wrote to her, "to have a daughter who is working as a missionary, and that you are learning the scriptures. I love you, Amos."[45] "I have spent the last twenty five years praying for you; for your safety, for your happiness . . . and thanking God for having you as my daughter."[46] When she shared with him that her own faith was growing, he reached back, letting her know specifically what this meant to him. With a felt-tipped marker on a legal pad, he wrote to her, "Dear Amos, I got your letter today with its strong statement of your faith, and it pleased me very much. I pray for you, too, and it is always for His will to be done."[47] Referencing the Apostle Paul's hardships of shipwrecks and imprisonment, he assured her that the difficulties of tracting would become more tolerable, even if only because the weather would eventually warm up.

One letter filled with personal thoughts from Amy even brought tears to Sparky's eyes, and he wrote to his daughter that they were "tears of gratitude that you and I are being brought closer together each day by our experiences and love for God. This is more important than anything that has ever happened to the two of us."[48]

Despite not agreeing with Mormonism in particular, Sparky was proud of the work his daughter was doing, and told her so explicitly. "Keep working hard. God is with you, and I pray for your well-being and the success of your work," he wrote at the end of one letter to her.[49]

He even bragged to Mormon golfer Johnny Miller that his daughter was on her mission. He let a reminder of his distaste for Mormonism slip in one of his letters addressing her concerns that Johnny Johnson may be called away from the Midlands. "This is one of the problems of being not free in your kind of work," Sparky said. "It is hard to be at the mercy of someone else's authority and there is no answer to it except extraordinary patience."[50] Later, he would assure her, though, that he was more interested in their spiritual commonalities than their differences. "Please don't worry about my criticism of the church," he wrote her. "That doesn't change at all my joy for the work you are doing."[51]

On a rare international trip to England that included plans to do site research for *What Have We Learned, Charlie Brown?*, and to attend the Wimbledon tennis tournament where Sparky's dear friend, tennis legend Billie Jean King, was in her penultimate competitive appearance, Sparky visited Amy halfway through her anticipated eighteen-month stay. The trip to England was already being planned aside from the possibility of visiting with Amy, and Sparky had written her at Christmas, telling her not to miss him. "Let us not be sad because we are apart at Christmas time," he wrote. "Let us instead rejoice that we love Him and He loves us and we love each other. I am glad you are with friends and doing a good work."[52] Nevertheless, some in the family would remember the trip as also providing Sparky with an opportunity to try and "rescue" his daughter from her mission. Sparky was worried about the inflexibility of LDS service, but from Amy's perspective, no rescue was needed. They had a tender visit, taking time for a photo in England's Sherwood Forest, and Sparky would then return home to his studio, while Amy set out for another day of sharing her beliefs.

Later that year, months before the scheduled end of her mission, Amy made the difficult decision to come home early. She had been proud of her time in England, and it broke her heart to cut it short, but an exciting new life with Johnny awaited her back home in the protective Mormon shelter of Greater Salt Lake City. Once back in the U.S., her marriage to Johnny posed another religiously inspired challenge for Sparky and the family. As members of the Mormon Church baptized under priesthood authority, Amy and Johnny were eligible to be married in the temple. Being married in the temple, according to Mormon doctrine, is a sacred and special opportunity that allows one's marriage

Craig and Amy stand with Sparky in front of the Major Oak in Sherwood Forest while visiting Amy during her LDS mission to England (1982). According to legend, the tree served as shelter for Robin Hood and his merry men. Courtesy Amy Johnson.

to be sealed for eternity as a "celestial marriage." While they could have married outside of the temple, their marriage would not be sealed past their life on earth in the eyes of the church. They chose to marry in the temple, but this meant that Sparky could not be a part of his daughter's wedding ceremony as he was not part of the Mormon Church. Sparky waited in the parking lot of the temple while Amy and Johnny committed their lives to each other before God.

After the wedding ceremony, Amy and Johnny Johnson held a reception in which Sparky and the rest of the family were able to celebrate with them. She and Johnny would have nine children, nestled in the supportive Utah Mormon community. Amy committed to providing for her children a religiously vibrant home that explicitly nurtured their Mormon beliefs. It was an opportunity for religious teaching and cultivation that her religiously knowledgeable father had not sponsored during Amy's childhood. The Johnsons would enjoy their own weekly Family Home Evenings, and some of Amy's nine children would even go on their own missions. When others of the nine decided to leave the church, Amy would then strive to draw on what Sparky did provide

Sparky and Jeannie stand around newlyweds Amy and Johnny Johnson outside the Oakland California Temple. October 30, 1982. Courtesy Amy Johnson.

her—a level of understanding and support even when the parent and child differed on theological belief. If her father could give her that, she could endeavor to do the same, difficult though it would be.

Through a series of experiences much different from those of her younger sister, Meredith too would develop her own deeply felt Christian faith later in life. When her first husband, Gary Fredricksen, drowned in a tragic swimming accident, Meredith, toughened by years of hard lessons, began to see that there were new personal choices she had to make to be happier, healthier, and safer. For her, faith was a key part of the process. She began to see the hand of God at work in her life, bringing her out of her wilder days as a youth briefly experimenting with ideas of witchcraft while abroad in Switzerland and leading her

Amy dances with her father at her wedding reception held at the Yulupa Avenue Mormon Church in Santa Rosa, California. October 30, 1982. Courtesy Amy Johnson.

to become an adult who would profess faith in Christ. Even in tragedy she began to see where God would show her—"Yes, I am here. Yes, I am here." Life on Earth is no Garden of Eden, she would describe, but rather it is "God school," preparing people's spirits to go to be with God in Heaven. "It's the most complicated, intrinsically successful school that could ever be, because of the way He teaches us."[53]

Perhaps one might see Meredith as a demonstration of Proverbs 22:6: "Train up a child in the way he should go, and when he is old, he will not depart from it." Meredith was the only child to have had a rather regular presence in Sunday school, taking her small white leather Bible with her in which her father had inscribed from Mark 5:19, "Go home to your friends, and tell them how much the Lord has done for you." Being the oldest, she had naturally been in church the longest. "You get that initial introduction, and then you go off in this world of many things, and then you find your own way back . . . if you're going to be coming back," she explained. "And I think it's really important that people realize that, yeah, God loves you and He's there." The relationship she had with Sparky on such matters, though, was markedly different from Monte's or Amy's. "We didn't talk religion on the phone," she said, thinking of her father and wondering if he ever even realized how much religious faith she had developed after moving away to Colorado, devoting herself to innovatively effective techniques to improve the posture of equine companions. Her father's influence was not lost on her, though, even if he did not know it. "He made an indelible mark," she said.

Sparky may never have been fully aware of the impact he made on Meredith. In the safe space of transatlantic letters to Amy, though, he had been able to offer the comfort of a concerned father and the hope of a studied believer. With a certain level of irony in never fully knowing what impact his own faith would have not just on *Peanuts* fans but also on his own family, Sparky wrote to Amy on November 4, 1981:

> Many people are not able to see the spiritual truths and gifts that God presents to us, and are robbed of wonderful blessings. I think you should always remember that your influence in the Kingdom of God cannot always be seen immediately so do not despair or become discouraged. Sometimes our lives affect people in small ways that can't show up for years. Little things that we say and do in Christ's name are like pebbles thrown in the water. The ripples spread out in circles, and influence people we may know only slightly and sometimes not at all.

The historical content in *This is America, Charlie Brown* had recognized the important ripples of religious faith in the nation's past. Sparky's own faith would connect him in diverse ways with his own children after they were grown—sincere and meaningful connections that he could not have expected, especially having been silent on religion at home for much of their childhoods. Through the lives of his children and grandchildren, and through his work on the page and on the screen, these ripples would continue for generations to come.

8

SECULAR HUMANIST

"The church is composed of Christians who turn toward Christ and then operate within this church to accomplish things of a Christian nature, but I think the Kingdom of God is much larger."

—CHARLES M. SCHULZ

WHEN RAY BRADBURY TOOK THE FLOOR EACH YEAR AT BARNABY CONRAD'S Santa Barbara Writers Conference, Charles Schulz made sure to be in the audience, listening with great interest to the legendary author share insights from his successes and failures in the literary arts. The writer of *Fahrenheit 451* was one of many great writers that Schulz enjoyed being in the presence of at the conference, a week-long gathering that drew in the likes of Jonathan Winters, Gore Vidal, and Alex Haley. Schulz never considered himself skilled enough to write an epic novel, though he did have Snoopy try his hand at writing the next great American classic—perhaps *Small Women*[1] . . . or *Crime and Peace*[2] . . . or *Long John Beagle*[3] . . . or *The Maltese Beagle*[4] . . . or maybe the biblical classic, *John the Beagle.*[5] Each was met with the same rejection slip, but the hound would have moderate success with *It Was a Dark and Stormy Night.*[6] Outside his comic panel, Sparky enjoyed being in the company of those whose grand works had moved readers worldwide, authors whose works Sparky himself had enjoyed reading.

Conrad, a prolific author best known for his 1952 novel *El Matador* and his Hollywood A-lister club of the same name (Conrad had some bullfighting experience and was non-fatally gored by a bull during a charity bullfight in Spain), began the conference in 1972. Thanks to the significant work of his wife, Mary, Conrad was able to offer a vibrant week of workshops at the Miramar hotel that brought together agents, publishers, and budding writers by promising the opportunity to mix with some of the day's literary greats. Thanks to Conrad, Sparky was given an annual opportunity to become part of their scene as well. Several years earlier, in 1967, Conrad had interviewed Sparky at Coffee Grounds for the *New York Times Magazine*, quoting Schulz as saying that the artist was only a "fairly" sort of person, who only wrote "fairly well." "If you wrote *really* well," Sparky had said, "you'd be writing books."[7] But Conrad saw through the humility, knowing full well of Sparky's talents and success, and invited him to be part of the 1973 conference.

A true admirer of literature, Sparky obliged, and found himself hooked, returning annually and regularly giving talks himself. As Monte[8] described, "The conference became part of his life, his yearly getaway, much as was the Bing Crosby Pro-Am [golf tournament]: something to look forward to, a break from his own enforced routine, a chance to step out of his own life and indulge one of his passions."[9] Many of those in attendance relished the chance to meet Charles Schulz and to hear him give his Saturday evening address, but Schulz too enjoyed being in the presence of writers he admired. He would play tennis with his literary friends, catch an occasional speech, and genuinely enjoy himself.

Of course, Charles Schulz was no great metropolitan socialite like the charming Barnaby Conrad, who had a "talent for dwelling at epicenters of rarified, exclusive realms."[10] Stepping out to circulate in the exciting gatherings of the Writers Conference, the National Cartoonists Society gatherings, or the pro-am golf tournaments was always something of an exception for Sparky's normally reserved demeanor, but he enjoyed the company of his friends, often lamenting that people did not just "hang out" enough. Living in northern California and not prone to enjoying travel, Schulz could reconnect with many of his friends at the annual conference, most of the 350 annual attendees being returnees. More often, though, he would catch up with his friends through a quick letter, phone call, or cup of hot chocolate at his ice arena.

Sparky was at times shy, but he had one trick at his disposal that could keep him socially connected without fail. When he wanted to speak with someone, the cartoonist simply had to have a member of the *Peanuts* cast mention that person's name in a strip, and invariably Sparky's phone would ring or a letter would arrive a short six to ten weeks later when the strip appeared in the paper. "I receive more fan mail when Dr. Seuss is mentioned by Schulz[11] than I do when Dr. Seuss is mentioned by Dr. Seuss," Dr. Seuss himself (Theodor Geisel) had once written to Sparky, inviting him to visit.[12] The name-dropping trick allowed Sparky to reach out to new acquaintances on his own terms, and it also let his friends know they were on his mind, even if they had not chatted in some time. "When I would read *Peanuts* on the road, I would just have a chuckle to start the day with. It just started the day right, ya know?" remembered Sparky's friend, tennis legend Billie Jean King. He was not in the habit of calling her too often. Instead, the name "Billie Jean King" would miraculously appear in the athlete's newspaper while she sipped her coffee en route to the next tournament. "I knew when he mentioned my name [in the comic] that it was time to call him," she said, remembering following up the morning funnies with a call to the artist—"Hi Sparky, I've been thinking about you!"[13]

One of the many friends with whom Sparky enjoyed an occasional phone call over the years was best-selling author Joanne Greenberg, writer of *I Never Promised You a Rose Garden*. The two shared a wit that allowed them to easily connect, first meeting after Greenberg's publishers (Holt, Rinehart and Winston) cheekily suggested she thank the comic strip artist for his unknowing hand in the publication of her first book, 1963's *The King's Person*. Like many publishers in that era, Holt had a career-author model, and brought Joanne to their offices to introduce her to the team when she signed her first contract. Upon arriving, the publishing agents explained to the eager writer who had been rejected by eight other publishers, "You owe your thanks to Charles Schulz." Remembering the conversation with a little of her own colorful self-deprecation, Greenberg humorously recalled being told that "[Schulz] is making money hand-over-fist and we are then free to publish twits like you! You ought to call him up and thank him." She took the idea seriously, and wrote to Sparky, thanking him. He wrote back personally, as he was accustomed to doing in those days, adding his own waggery to the exchange, and a new friendship was formed.

The two exchanged occasional letters over the years, and Greenberg enjoyed visiting Sparky in Santa Rosa. They would talk on the phone from time to time, and she told him how *Peanuts* characters had lined the classroom of the tutoring center that helped her get her GED. "It was a terrific lift to me," she remembered telling him, but Sparky often downplayed such compliments from the wry Joanne, simply responding, "Isn't that great." She ribbed him in her magazine book reviews, coyly criticizing Snoopy for things like his distaste for cats as a way to jab at another writer in her own field without being crassly direct. Sparky in turn published a collection of Snoopy's writings, including the polar epic *"Toodle-oo, Caribou!": A Tale of the Frozen North* under the title *I Never Promised You an Apple Orchard*, with the dedication, "For Joanne Greenberg, of course."

Over the course of two decades, up until the late 1980s when they simply fell out of touch, Sparky and Joanne would chat about their lives, Sparky once telling her that the honor of having Snoopy go to space was almost too overwhelming to be enjoyed. Ceremonially singled out by the space agency in naming the Apollo 10 modules, Sparky worried, "What if something went wrong?!" He shared with Joanne the pain and concern he felt when Amy decided to join such a single-voiced religious group like the Mormon Church, and Joanne shared with Sparky about her own religious life as a practicing Jew—a "paradox Jew" she would call herself, observing the Sabbath but not keeping kosher. Sparky, never one for meaningless, disconnected small talk, enjoyed such conversations. Joanne was not only a clever writerly friend who could match his quickness, she was also someone who could reflect on his spiritual thoughts with a level of openness and understanding.

In the course of one of their conversations, Sparky had shared with Joanne some of the nuances of his own religious beliefs, beliefs that had developed new contours over the years. Listening to his thoughts on the limits of denominational theology and on the need for caring for others regardless of faith background, Joanne offered him a term that seemed to sum up for her the perspectives Sparky was embodying. Perhaps his thinking reflected something of "secular humanism," she suggested to the religious self-studier. "She asked me what I believed in," Sparky remembered. "I said what I thought I believed in, and she said, 'You're a secular humanist, that's what you are,' and I said, 'I am?' and she said, 'Yeah, that's what I think you are.'"[14]

Humanism was not a term Sparky had full command over at the time, but once the confident Joanne offered it to him he

"HI! I'VE JUST BEEN TOLD THAT
I AM ONE OF GOD'S CHILDREN....
WHO ARE YOU?"

Two by Fours. 1965. © 1989 Warner Press, Inc., Anderson, Indiana. Used with permission.

found himself occasionally invoking the term in interviews. One of his earliest public uses of the term came in 1985 at the end of a press preview for a thirty-fifth anniversary exhibit of his work at the Oakland Museum. When a young reporter asked him about "being religious," Schulz answered quickly with a deflecting tone that belied the nuances in the answer itself, saying, "I think the best theology is no theology. That's pretty radical. I'm becoming more and more of a humanist."[15]

For an interviewer to explore the nuances in Schulz's perspective, he or she would occasionally have to do extra labor. Sparky was reserved, but he was also competitive; he was humble, but he was also proud of his innovations. The task of the interviewer would be to ask the follow-up questions (sometimes multiple times) in order to create the space for Sparky to explore his ideas out loud. In the case of religious topics, Sparky simply did not expect most interviewers to ever reflect his own thoughts accurately. "I do not find it easy to discuss with an interviewer things of a spiritual nature . . . there are too many 'howevers' that need to be spoken when discussing subjects this sensitive," Schulz wrote in

1975, "and they simply do not come out well in the average magazine or newspaper interview."[16]

When he was quoted in Rheta Grimsley Johnson's 1989 biography as saying, "I guess you might say I've come around to secular humanism," Sparky nearly indelibly linked himself to the system of thought simply by using such a specific term. He would repeat his invocation of the term over the next decade, and it would be repeated exponentially more once the Internet allowed for fans to self-publish their thoughts and lay histories through message boards and wiki entries. Often repeated in posts like "Schultz [*sic*] himself claimed later in life to be a secular humanist,"[17] attributions of the philosophy to Schulz would typically lack any further explanation from Schulz himself or any explanation of what "secular humanism" might mean. The term would simply stand in for something set in opposition to his earlier Christian beliefs. He was now seen by some simply as "secular," a "humanist," and perhaps even an atheist. Because of the easily quoted line, he would even end up with his own entry on CelebAtheist.com.

Those who believed he had turned to atheism were not without unintended support from Sparky himself. He had laid the groundwork for readers to believe he had undergone a radical loss of faith, writing in 1975 that "my own theological views have changed considerably over the past twenty-five years." In a 1977 *Newsday* interview, he added that "the only true theology is that there is no theology,"[18] repeating it again in 1981 for an *Atlanta Weekly* article,[19] and again to the reporter at the Oakland Museum in 1985. Just as there were diverse Christian denominations across the country in the '50s and '60s ready to see Sparky as their own, the personal connection individuals had with Schulz's highly malleable artwork made those resistant to theistic faith or religious practice likewise ready to see him as their own. These phrases, amplifying the hints some had divined in the Great Pumpkin strips, now gave them permission. In a 2006 online video[20] that the *New York Times* called an "incendiary hit"[21] with millions of views and reportedly an award for "Excellence in Humanist Communications" from the Harvard University Humanist Chaplaincy, Vancouver Film School student Zachary Kroger used Schulz as one example (among others) of a celebrity "atheist" who was not "vile," as the Psalmist had warned, but was in fact doing good.

Charles Schulz's theology had perceptively changed; his own statements attested to such explicitly. That change, however, was not one towards atheism. Charles Schulz was not an atheist. The developments in his views were perhaps not even toward secular humanism, despite his use of the term. Instead, in the years after he had stopped attending church, Sparky's interview answers began to adjust the focus of his faith—a faith that he had always understood as complex, even if newspaper write-ups did not have the page space to consider it complexly. Though he called it "secular humanism" on occasion, Schulz's statements reflected something more like a biblical humanism—merely a loosening of the already open, thoughtful faith that he had held since before leaving Minnesota. It was not a reversal of his faith, nor was it a signal of a personal religious crisis.

When he wrote to his army buddy Frank Dieffenwierth in 1948, Sparky admitted to worrying that while he believed in God, religion might not be able to give him answers. As he became more active in the Church of God, his Bible studies rescued him from much of that fear, and he wrote to his friend, "I am right where I belong. I am a firm believer in Jesus Christ."[22] As he continued to study the Bible, he nonetheless found that understanding God was immensely complex—that there was still a mystery to much of it. His belief in Jesus Christ was the meaningful way by which he had come to God, but he also maintained an awareness that his belief was a personal one and that others might not share the exact same experience. In 1967, only two years after insisting that *A Charlie Brown Christmas* contain the story of the birth of Christ, Sparky attempted to explain this perspective when asked, "For you, is religion something that happens primarily inside a church or something that happens primarily outside?"

> I think it's a perfect combination of the two. Religion happens first inside the person. I think that at some time in everybody's life he feels some sort of calling by the Holy Spirit or whatever we wish to call it—I am certainly more flexible along these lines in my thinking than some might be. Some would say you have to be called by the Holy Spirit and put it just that way. I would want to qualify it more than that. I don't know theologically what it is or who it is that speaks to us, but I think we'll have a time when we become aware of something and it is at this point that some react by what

Jesus called being born again. Now, being born again may be going to the altar at a Sunday evening service and it may merely be a turning around spiritually in your life, just facing toward more mature things. It doesn't matter what you call it, but there is some kind of experience which happens to those who then decide that they want to do something for God or want to be closer to Him.[23]

Charles Schulz was not a Christian exclusivist. Even in 1967, while leading his Sunday school class at the Methodist church, he believed that one could be something other than a Protestant or a Catholic and still be part of the Kingdom of God:

I try to be very flexible. I hate to use the world "tolerant," and I don't really know what word to use to talk about these things. But I want to leave it open enough not to give the impression of excluding anyone from the Kingdom of God. I think the Kingdom of God is a very broad Kingdom. The church is more narrow. The church is composed of Christians who turn toward Christ and then operate within this church to accomplish things of a Christian nature, but I think the Kingdom of God is much larger. But the more I talk about it the more difficult it gets for me to express it and it just simply gets away from me![24]

Ten years later, he was better prepared to describe what he meant by a broader Kingdom of God. In a 1977 interview with the BBC's Peter France, Sparky pulled his Bible out from under his chair when the interviewer asked him about his faith. Schulz turned to a passage in the New Testament he had outlined in a ragged blue rectangle. With the Scriptures in hand, he was able to more substantively explain how he understood the ways in which one might be reconciled to God. That reconciliation might happen, Sparky believed, and the person might never even know it:

I think we merely have to live with the faith that God understands our heart and that Jesus knows we love Him, and with that faith, simply carry on through life. . . . In the Book of Acts it says the Lord added to the church daily such as were being saved; those people are in the church and they are part of the Kingdom of God, but I think there are people who are outside the Christian church who *have* to be part of the Kingdom of God, and this is much more important. I am sure that these friends that I'm talking about, and I know they are good people, and they are doing good things for others—I have a host of doctor friends, and they're marvelous people, and I am convinced they are part of God's kingdom. [*"Can you be part of the Kingdom of God without knowing it?" asked Peter France*] Oh yes. In fact, you may be better off [*Sparky laughed*]. . . .

In the 25th chapter of Matthew in the 34th verse, Jesus is telling them [*reading from his Bible*], "Then shall the King say unto them on his right hand, come ye blessed of my father, inherit the kingdom prepared for you from the foundation of the world. For I was and hungered and ye gave me meat, I was thirsty and ye gave me drink, I was a stranger and ye took me in. Naked and ye clothed me, I was sick and ye visited me, I was in prison and ye came unto me." Now here's the point—"Then shall the righteous answer him, saying 'Lord, when saw we thee hungered and fed thee or thirsty and gave thee drink? When saw we thee a stranger and took thee in, or naked and clothed thee? Or when saw we thee sick or in prison and came unto thee?'" See, these people did all of these things just because this is what you should do for your fellow man. [*Reading*] "And the King shall answer and say unto them, 'Verily I say unto you, inasmuch as you have done it unto one of the least of these my brethren, you have done it unto me.'" And that to me is pure worship. There's no other way of worship. When it talks about worshipping in spirit and in truth, this is what it is.[25]

Jesus had led Charles Schulz to the Kingdom of God through the Church of God gatherings, and Schulz spoke about Jesus in a fashion that reflected Jesus's divine role, but the well-read cartoonist believed that there were others who were part of that Kingdom without even knowing it, without believing in Jesus. They were worshipping God through their heart attitudes and their merciful actions, regardless of their theological beliefs. One did not need to profess faith in the biblical God in order to be merciful toward one's neighbor. Just as with the workers in Matthew 25, one should desire to do good irrespective of one's theism. This was the sort of humanistic sentiment that Joanne Greenberg had keyed in on. Sparky rooted his perspective not in secularized enlightenment, though, but in his understanding of the Kingdom of God through the language of the Scriptures. While he called for the same neighborly goodwill of the secular humanist, many of Schulz's own descriptions of his changing theology were not actually secular in nature. He was, after all, quoting from Matthew. Of course, his interpretations were not those of conventional Christian dogma either.

This development in Schulz's thinking was a definite departure from those espoused by mainline denominations. "He was a heretic," his close friend, Catholic priest Father Gary Lombardi, half-joked.[26] Sparky had even sidestepped the guidance of his trusted *The Interpreter's Bible*, which emphasized and celebrated the compassionate ethic in Christ's parable in Matthew 25 but which had added, "Then does it matter nothing what a man believes? It matters everything; for love springs from faith—the faith that men are worth loving, and the faith that God loves and bids us love. Besides, Christ is on the throne. Judgment and love are both clearly understood only in him."[27] Schulz was not particularly disagreeing with the messages of Christ's redemptive work taught from mainstream pulpits across the country, but he was not intellectually and spiritually content with the exclusivity by which those doctrines were maintained. Matthew 25 suggested to him that God operated differently.

John 14:6 records Jesus saying to his disciple Thomas, "I am the way, and the truth, and the life; no one comes to the Father, but by me." Without noting the reason, Sparky underlined the first half of the verse, stopping before Christ said "no one comes to the Father, but by me." For Sparky, Jesus was someone who allowed individuals "to see God and to understand His feelings toward us."[28] His *The Interpreter's Bible* explained that "charity, springing from the love made known in Christ, is an essential act without which faith languishes and dies." Coming to the Father through Christ, though, did not necessarily mean making a proclamation of faith in Christ, according to Sparky. The Father, after all, knows the hearts of strangers, even if they do not know Him. Perhaps Christ's sacrificial death alone, not one's statement of belief in it, was sufficient for one to come unto God through Christ. This is how Robert Short characterized his friend's belief, describing Sparky in 1998 as a "Christian universalist." "He believed," Short explained in *Peanuts* metaphor, "as I do also, that finally all people are going to be rounded up by Christ the sheep dog. He believed that because the Red Baron has already fallen from heaven, that ultimately all people would replace the

Peanuts © Peanuts Worldwide LLC. Used with permission. April 13, 1984.

Red Baron, or Satan, in heaven. The direction of Sparky Schulz's theology is from 'security blanket' to 'blanket security.'"[29] Though "universalism" is laden with its own baggage, and may not capture the nuances of the heart attitude Sparky spoke of God knowing, Sparky's descriptions of his own theology seem to fit better with the term Short suggested than the one Greenberg offered. Reducing the mystery of faith down to just one simplistic term, though, was just the sort of thing that had made Schulz personally and theologically uncomfortable to begin with.

The view that Christ's work had atoned for all mankind's sin, regardless of their religious affiliation, and that God knew the heart of each man and woman sufficient to determine if they were part of His kingdom, seems consistent with Sparky's various comments on his faith. Certainly Sparky did not know how to fully untangle all the theological equations involved. Perhaps he never fully reconciled in his own mind the Bible's recounting of Christ's sacrifice with Christ's teachings in John 14 and Matthew 25. Sparky had already embraced the truth that the Bible itself was full of mystery, and he did not see himself as an expert theologian responsible or equipped for delineating absolute understanding to anyone—not to his Bible class, not to his children, and not to his strip readers. "If people are going to look to me for religious guidance, then I think they're looking in the wrong place," he said.[30]

Not counting himself an expert and not trusting in authoritarian religious superstructures, Schulz nonetheless did believe that some faiths were simply ill-conceived. He had little interest in soothsayers or astrologers, for instance, beyond what inspiration they might provide him for a one-off Snoopy gag in his strip. When the hippie movement rose to prominence in the 1960s, he questioned whether their spirituality was coherent. "The hippies talk a lot about religion, but I have my doubts," he said. "Do you remember James's definition of religion? 'Pure religion is this, to visit the fatherless and widows in their affliction. . . .' He was talking about an active form of love. The hippie cult seems to preach a kind of self-love."[31] As his daughter Amy knew all too well, he was also uneasy about the extra-biblical teachings of the Latter-day Saints, believing such teachings to be potential fabrications with a superstructure that commanded too much conformity. Sparky had simply encountered too many questions in his own studies to think that any group could explain the mysteries of the Bible and the truths of God with rigid authority.

In 1981, he explained,

> I defy anybody to prove to me that their denomination has all the truth. I don't pretend to be able to discuss profound theological problems, but I do think that the only true theology is no theology at all. I think the only theology that exists is that God exists as a spirit, and that we live in His world, and the minute we begin to form some sort of theology, we begin to drift away from the truth.[32]

Truth was not an illusion according to Sparky, who had maintained a belief in God—but gripping theological details too tightly would ultimately fail. It was God, not man, who was equipped for full understanding, he told Amy in 1982. Actively trusting in Him may not be fully necessary, but it was sufficient. "God knows your heart,"[33] he wrote. "No one else around you may understand, but He knows your heart, and this is your faith."[34]

In Joanne Greenberg's conversations with Sparky, it seemed clear to her that he did have some semblance of a "God sense," which she described as being "like a set of overtones" that one does or does not hear. She wondered if perhaps Sparky might also have some resistance to hearing more of it, but their talks gave her the sense that he did want to hear the tones. When he explained to her his ideas of the neighborly good coming from outside the church as much as from within, it seemed to her that "secular humanism" might be a somewhat fitting term for her friend. While for many secular humanism may be about the denial of the need for religion, Greenberg saw the term operating on a second level. It was also, she described as she searched for the right words years later, about "saying, 'those folks' [outside the church] are as good as us [in the church]," adding that "even to say that is not right, not what I want to say . . . 'as good as' means that I'm judging, looking out."[35] In this way, she and Sparky seemed to be on the same page, even if the broader use of the term proved to be a bit of a misnomer for Sparky, who still believed that God knows your heart.

Perhaps like in his squabbles with ophthalmologists and optometrists over the proper medical venue and ocular treatments Schulz referenced in late 1965 amblyopia strips, secular humanism may have been a term that Schulz only understood within the limits of his intended usage. He had been reading Bible commentaries for decades, with over eighty volumes on the sacred text in his personal library, but he had no books devoted to this new label he had been given. Like a borrowed suit jacket that fit in the shoulders but not in the arms, secular humanism simply seemed good enough, even if the lack of tailoring could be a little misleading. He could not have known how it would be misshapen over the years to categorize him as an atheist.[36]

"I don't even know what secular humanism is," Sparky joked with Gary Groth in 1992, but the use of the term had allowed him to shift away from describing himself in classic Christian terminology, with which he had grown uncomfortable over the years. When Peter France asked him, "In what way would your life be different if there were no God?" Sparky answered in a way that still affirmed a belief in the divine but that also distanced himself from typical labels:

> Oh, I wouldn't have any idea. Now you're—that's beyond me. I don't know. Who can say? . . . I just have a feeling that the church has taken much away from us. It's a very difficult thing to define what a "believing Christian" is because the minute I say I'm a believing Christian, then these definitions leap to mind that others might have, and I don't know what that belief would be. Isn't it a pity that a religion which is supposed to draw all of us together simply drives us apart? This is the thing that bothers me so much.

What Schulz may not have realized was that his new term would be no less loaded than the Christian-ese he resisted for its tendency to pigeonhole. At its most basic level, secular humanism is a belief structure that has no reference to a transcendental divine figure (i.e., no God is necessary for the belief; it is thus often a viewpoint espoused by atheists and agnostics) and that instead focuses through reason on the pains and pleasures of the existing human condition (e.g., reducing suffering, increasing comfort). Throughout political and religious circles in 1980s American culture, though, the term's connotation was being fiercely debated. Pundits used the term "secular humanism" to refer to a godless hedonism, atheism, and at times even the evils of communism.[37] Prominent proponents of the worldview formed the Council for Democratic and Secular Humanism to oppose and distinguish themselves from communistic humanisms, and conservative groups like the Moral Majority used the term in the ongoing culture wars, calling for the Supreme Court to officially rule secular humanism a religion in order to prevent public schools from teaching it to the youth.[38] Given the climate for the term, it is not surprising that Schulz's use gained historical traction.

Schulz did not comment on any of such conspiracies, debates, or squabbles over secular humanism, perhaps because he was unaware of them, or perhaps simply because he was not invested in the nuances of the paradigm (let alone its politics). His invocations of the term were not accompanied by any renunciations of his previously pronounced Christian faith, nor did he chide himself for having served the church. Instead, "secular humanism," in Sparky's minimalist use of the term, came to describe merely one portion of his beliefs—that one should be doing good in the world. The 1980s biography had explained as much, but the statement would be truncated by other journalists, bloggers, and critics over the years, leaving out the key component that explained Schulz's use of the term as he and Joanne had seen it. Often repeated simply as "I guess you might say I've come around to secular humanism," Johnson's treatment records Sparky as explaining, "I do not go to church anymore, because I could not be an active part of things. I guess you might say I've come around to secular humanism, an obligation I believe all humans have to others and the world we live in."[39]

This obligation was not at all antithetical to his previous statements of his faith, and it was one that Sparky had lived out in his own personal life. He had allowed his wealth to provide a more than comfortable material life for himself and his family (though his kids would routinely remember that "we were raised not to care about material things"), and he allowed it to improve the lives of others as well. From the beginning, Sparky had generously directed significant monetary and intellectual resources toward helping others. From the early days of mailing original comic strips to fans and granting copyright permission to high-school yearbook staffs, to building an ice rink for the community and later offering educational programs through the museum, the Schulzian life was one imbued with giving.

On August 1, 1959, Linus told Charlie Brown, "When I get big, I want to be a great philanthropist!" "You have to have a lot of money to be a great philanthropist," noted Charlie Brown. After pausing to think, Linus responded in amendment, "I want to be a great philanthropist with someone else's money!" Across the arc of his whole career, by contrast, Sparky had been giving generously with his own money. As early as 1955, he had explained that "religion that is pure and undefiled before God and the Father is this: to visit orphans and widows in their affliction, and to keep oneself unstained from the world."[40] Not desiring to publicize his acts, he simply gave because he believed it the right thing to do. When, for example, the public school called the Schulz home at Coffee Grounds to report to parents that the school bus route would be discontinued because there was not enough money to replace the hazardous set of bus tires, Sparky quietly stepped in. "When the driver went to school the next day, he had all new tires," Craig recalled.[41] Though Sparky often drove his own children and two neighbor kids to school, the difficulty others would face was too solvable for him to ignore.

In 1997, at the other end of his career, Sparky took on a more high-profile role in raising needed capital, serving as the chairman of the fundraising campaign for the National D-Day Memorial in Bedford, Virginia. He donated $1 million himself, and was joined by other large donors like film giant Steven Spielberg, who also contributed toward the $25 million site. Schulz commented, "I am proud to help in any way I can to make the long overdue National D-Day Memorial to the valor, fidelity and sacrifice of the Allied forces a reality as quickly as possible."[42]

Sparky did not usually like to talk publicly about his generous giving. "He loved to give without recognition," recalled his friend Eugene Sterner, a minister in the Church of God. "It was typical for him to remain in the background."[43] Sparky's reticence toward credit for his generosity was one that fulfilled Christ's cautioning in Matthew 6:1—"Beware of practicing your piety before men in order to be seen by them." Schulz had underlined that line in his Bible, noting in the margins that it was a question of "motive," and that "no one! must know!" The passage continues that "your Father who sees in secret will reward you," and Sparky noted that "we have to presuppose that God is omnipotent." He knows your heart, and He knows your hands.

Sparky had done his best to limit recognition for a gift he gave to Anderson University midway through his career. In 1978, at the prodding of then-president of the university, Sparky's friend Bob Reardon, Sparky donated a generous amount of money for the construction of a new fine arts building at the university campus. Visiting Sparky at the ice arena in Santa Rosa, Reardon laid out his request for Sparky, who had called his business manager, Ron Nelson, into the office for financial suggestions. After a short tête-à-tête with Nelson, who was resistant to any requests for donations (which could at times seem unending), Reardon was able to describe the opportunity to an "amused" Sparky. The interested comic strip artist agreed, donating a significant amount of money to fund the new building project. Sparky would not, however, allow them to name the new art building after himself. Instead, he took Reardon's suggestion and used the gift to honor Sparky's former pastor, Brother Marvin Forbes.

Sparky joined Reardon and Forbes in April 1979 for the dedication and ribbon-cutting ceremony for the new Marvin L. Forbes Art Building on campus. Jeannie accompanied him, and the two stayed at the university's presidential residence, the Boyes House, with President Reardon and his wife, Jerry. Demonstrating the personal affinity he had for this particular gathering, Sparky brought even more gifts along for his friends. "At breakfast the four of us were joined by Rev. Marvin and [his wife] Ruth Forbes," Reardon remembered. "After coffee Sparky surprised both Jerry and Ruth with beautiful gifts, a Cartier gold Snoopy and chain for each as a memento of the occasion."[44] The extra gift was not one of obligation, of course, Sparky having already donated significantly toward the school. Instead, the gift was more an indication that his friends from church were ever-meaningful to him, regardless of the evolution in how Sparky described his own theology.

While in Anderson for the dedication of the Forbes Art Building, part of the Krannert Fine Arts Center, Sparky also joined Marvin and Ruth Forbes at the university campus's adjoining Park Place Church of God. April 1979. Courtesy of Anderson University & Church of God Archives.

At the ceremony, Sparky took the opportunity to visit with other friends from his Church of God tenure, including Bernetta and Wally Nelson. Bernetta had supported Sparky by singing at the funeral of both of Sparky's parents, and Sparky continued to return the friend's favor by sending money and clothes from California to the young girl the Nelsons had taken under their wing, Linda. "We didn't adopt her, she adopted us," Bernetta recalled of the informal but precious relationship they had struck with the young girl from a rough situation. "He was very attentive to my little Linda," she said. "Sparky would really help."[45]

The successful comic strip artist had financially helped many of his Church of God friends over the years—giving pastor Cliff Thor and his wife a bond once a month while they struggled to make ends meet after Cliff finished seminary, building a home for Marvin and Ruth Forbes when they retired from full-time ministry (Sparky had always been uncomfortable with the meager living space the church had been able to provide), and paying for Walt Ortman to complete a master's degree from the University of Minnesota so that he could pursue a career as

Sparky visits with Church of God friend Bernetta Nelson at the dedication of the Forbes Building at Anderson University. 1979. Courtesy Bernetta Nelson.

a social worker. "Don't you dare drop out," Sparky told his friend who had made it through college on the GI Bill after serving in the air force. Walt's family was blessed even further by Sparky's extended generosity when Walt's daughter Nancy received an assistance dog from the Canine Companions for Independence program that Sparky and especially Jeannie actively nurtured. Visiting Sparky in California with his wife, Lois, Walt tried to repay Sparky with at least a kind gesture by buying him lunch at the ice arena's the Warm Puppy Café. When he offered, Sparky looked at Walt and reminded the old friend, "Walt, I own the place!"[46]

More important to the close group than his financial gifts, though, was their friendship. "I feel my life was enriched knowing him," Walt Ortman said, choking up slightly as he remembered the close friendship Sparky had enjoyed with their group. When Avis Kriebel and her family would visit Sparky in California, the stays were "bittersweet"—full of warmth and enjoyment, but with an inevitable goodbye as they parted ways. Sparky could keep things light, though, once telling Avis

Sparky visits with Wally Nelson and Brother Marvin Forbes at the dedication of the Forbes Building at Anderson University. 1979. Courtesy Bernetta Nelson.

as she stopped to snap a picture of the group, "Make me look as young as Wally Nelson!"

In June 1982, Sparky wrote to another of his older friends, Reverend Marvin Hartman, telling him he wished he could join him at a church convention. "I have a craving to hear some good preaching," he confessed.[47] The two had connected in the late '50s through mutual Church of God friends, and Sparky reconnected with Marv and his wife, Madelyn, upon returning to receive his honorary degree, remaining good friends for many years. While Sparky would not join for the 1982 conference, they planned to have the Hartmans stay in Santa Rosa later that summer. Marv visited as often as he could while traveling as president of the Board of Church Extension. "Sparky was always gracious and welcoming in spite of a heavy work load," Madelyn reminisced. "The first question he would ask was, 'Marv, what new books about theology are being written today?' Or, 'What have you been reading lately?'"[48] He may have been talking humanism with interviewers, but he continued to discuss biblical theology with his friends. He continued to do so with his readers as well. Throughout his career, the frequency of religious references grew. In 1985, Lucy kneeled by her bedside, praying for greater patience and understanding. She quit, though, she explained to Linus, because, "I was afraid I might get it!"[49]

In September 1985, one year before Marv died suddenly of a blood clot, Marv sent Sparky a selection of books by Cambridge theologian H. A. Williams, including a collection of Williams's sermons and the book *True Resurrection*, Williams's attempt to rediscover "a theology of the self"—how one might internally experience Christian resurrection instead of viewing it as an activity of Christ's ancient past or the Christian's distant future. "'True Resurrection' was slightly over my head," Sparky admitted to Marv, "but the collection of his sermons did much for me. I especially like the one concerning saints."[50] In his sermon on the saints, Williams had attempted to humanize those placed on a pedestal by the church. "In general, our views of what a saint is like are totally unrealistic," Williams preached. The saints were "touchy, quarrelsome, wanting the approval of others, sometimes breaking their principles to get it."[51] This acknowledgment of the struggles of even the most venerated of believers was important to Williams, for whom belief was personal and lived, not merely decreed by the church. "That is what saintliness is: something of Christ revealed in a person," wrote the Anglican monk.[52] These thoughts were meaningful to Schulz who had already been moving away from simplistic trappings of common church thinking, but for whom belief was still personally important.

Charles Schulz was of course no lofty saint, having been divorced under the shadow of an affair from a wife who was no longer interested in him, having struggled against recurring burdens of lonesomeness, insecurity, and agoraphobia, and having rather disliked ever signing autographs for his adoring fans. But internal struggles were a natural, perhaps even inherent, part of the life of any believer—even the most revered. Mother Teresa, the "Saint of Calcutta," wrote during certain seasons of her own service, service that she zealously embraced, that "within me—nothing but darkness, conflict, loneliness so terrible." Knowing the impacts her work was making, she added with a sense of maturity and grace that, "I am perfectly happy to be like this to the end of life."[53] And hers was a life that revealed something of Christ, to borrow from Williams, through the works of love that she undertook.

Charles Schulz, for his own meaningful part, desired that good be done in the world. "He was a nice man," Greenberg recalled. "He wanted to be nicer than he was."[54] Though he had his own deep emotional suffering over the years, he did not believe suffering or reluctant obligatory charity was the way to holiness. "Remember that Jesus said God desired mercy, not sacrifice," he explained in 1967. "I think all God really requires of us is that we love one another. But this is hard to do. It is much easier to burn a sacrifice to God than to love someone. We take the easy way out by turning to formal religions and adding their customs to our theology. We find modern substitutes for sacrifices instead of just loving one another."[55] In 1977, he explained:

> To me, God does not want to be worshipped, and this is the key to the whole thing. The minute you attempt to worship God in some manner, the minute you approach the altar, the minute you bring Him a gift, the minute you do anything like that, you are substituting love for your fellow man, which is the only way in my way of thinking that God can be worshipped. He can be worshipped only by the love that we show for other creatures. He cannot be worshipped by singing him a song, by writing him a poem, by listening to a preacher preach. This is a substitute. The minute this happens, you are slipping backwards.[56]

Many of his Church of God friends, like Bob Reardon and Gene Sterner had also broadened their descriptive theological views over the course of their lives, a natural development for many coming out of the mid-century Church of God. "The Church of God did not have this whole 'theological scheme' lined out," described Ken Hall, explaining the comparative openness that local study-rich congregations would espouse.[57] Sparky, like a few others in his circle, had come to believe that God knew the hearts of people regardless of one's church affiliation or even vocal statement of belief. God would be the one to separate the sheep from the goats, those who had done works in His name or not . . . even if they were not aware of it.

Deflecting in 1997, Schulz distanced himself from his own religious advocacy in one interview, saying, "I don't really care what anyone believes as long as they behave well."[58] But Charles Schulz had not denounced his own beliefs in the biblical God or the importance of

"HOW CAN YOU BE A
GOOD CHRISTIAN
WHEN YOUR
STOMACH HURTS?"

Young Pillars. February 21, 1965. © 1989 Warner Press, Inc., Anderson, Indiana. Used with permission.

Christ—not in public statements or to his closest friends. He simply could find no personal interest or theological ground from which to question others—at least not those who were (knowingly or not) honoring God by fulfilling Christ's instruction to "love thy neighbor."[59] This was not only Schulz's preferred point of departure, but his studies had also led him to believe that this was the singular way by which God could be worshiped.

As his relationship to the church and Christian terminology evolved over the years, Sparky's use of the provocative terminology of humanism may have obscured how some would understand the artist's descriptions of his own spiritual beliefs. In his art, he had expert control over his lines. He developed an ability to angle Woodstock's eyes just right to capture the perfect curiosity, squiggling Charlie Brown's frown in a way that portrayed the perfect amount of worry. In his theology, though, singular terms could only capture so much. The suggestion of humanism that he had gotten from Joanne Greenberg reflected part of his beliefs, but not the whole. A note Sparky made at the back of his Bible may more wholly sum up the core of his beliefs, consistent across Schulz's spiritual history. Marked with Scripture references just one page before the back cover where he had taped a picture of Jesus, Charles Schulz wrote:[60]

What we are not—Judges.
What we are—Keepers, Neighbors, Servants.

9

SWEET HOUR OF PRAYER

"I just did the best I could."

—CHARLES M. SCHULZ

SPARKY TOOK HIS SEAT IN ONE OF THE CREAM AND YELLOW ZIGZAG CHAIRS that enjoyed the light of the large glass doors in the house he and Jeannie called home. Across from him in the matching chair was Patty, his faithful cousin, while his daughter Amy sat close by on the deep floral sofa. Filling the room with pleasant tones and rhythms as she had done many times, teenager Stephanie Johnson sat on the thickly tufted bench of the room's piano, reading the sheet music before her and bringing melodies from the keys, much to Sparky's content. To Stephanie, though, Charles Schulz was not a famous artist. He was not even a close friend named Sparky. To her, he was simply "grampa."

Muffled by the room's carpet and cushioned furniture, the music was, as ever, familiar to Sparky. Rummaging through the church hymnals her grandfather had kept, Stephanie found songs she and Sparky both knew, her proud Mormon mother Amy finding more to play as she sat dwarfed by the oversized sofa cushions. As her mother had become, Stephanie was committed to her LDS beliefs and service to the church. Her Mormon hymnal was a little different from her grandpa's *Hymnal of the Church of God*, but the two found more than enough in common, songs and otherwise, for the two to deeply enjoy their time together. He cherished many of these songs, from "How Great Thou Art" to "Blessed Assurance." As the sun dipped lower in the afternoon sky, Stephanie played the hymns with well-practiced hands for her grandpa, a man for whom pleasure had become harder to find. It was Christmas 1999, and

Sparky's granddaughter Stephanie (Johnson) Revelli plays hymns on the piano while her mother Amy, Sparky, and Sparky's cousin Patty listen at the Schulz home in Santa Rosa, California. December 1999. Courtesy Amy Johnson.

Sparky had requested that he just sit there and listen to Stephanie play hymns—an event that he had not requested quite like this before. Amy and Johnny had taken their kids up to see Sparky, leaving their Christmas presents behind to be opened later. Just weeks before, Sparky had been diagnosed with terminal colon cancer, a diagnosis that meant he might not have many more Christmases to hear these hymns. While she could, Stephanie would continue to play.

For Stephanie, visiting her grandparents in Santa Rosa was the defining part of her early life. "It seems like my whole childhood was going there," she remembered.[1] During the rest of the year in Utah, she would look forward to receiving the occasional letter from Sparky, adorned with an original Snoopy sketch. The value in these to Stephanie, her

eight brothers and sisters, and her many cousins, though, was not their exchange rate on the collectibles market, but rather the sentimental value they held—the notes were drawn by her grandpa, not some famous artist. On one letter he sent in late 1990, Sparky drew a large Snoopy sitting at his faithful typewriter, typing out hearts. "Dear Stephanie, I like your letters," he wrote to this very special seven-year-old. "Love, Grampa." Stephanie decided the letter could be even better with her own embellishments, adding stickers to it—"Love one another" and "I am a Child of God."

As the oldest of her siblings, Stephanie had the privilege of spending the most time with Sparky. The two enjoyed a special bond, different from the unique relationships that he shared with the others. Sparky sealed the deal on their closeness when he gave his young granddaughter the complete plush set of Snoopy, his brothers, and Belle during one of their family visits from Utah to see Grandpa Schulz and Grandma

Jeannie, who had been the only Schulz grandma Amy's kids ever really knew. When they would visit, they would pile into the basement of Sparky and Jeannie's, arranging as many as nine children as best they could across pull-out couches and comfy sections of floor. Though he was not one who loved traveling (despite doing it relatively often for various events), Sparky even made his way out to Utah on occasion to visit with Amy, Johnny, and the kids.

Craig had flown his father out to visit with Amy in 1996 when the Mount Timpanogas Temple in American Fork, Utah, near Salt Lake City was to be opened. Sparky made the trip and took the temple tour with his daughter, despite the burden of travel and his known attitude toward Mormon theology, endeavoring to carve out at least a little window to spend with his faraway family. When he would visit, he would pull grandkids in wagons and draw Snoopys on scratch paper, which the children would color right over with their crayons. Laying on the floor with his little grandson Chuck, Sparky joked to Amy, "I like this place! I could live here!" even though he was a little antsy to get back in the jet and return to the comfort of home. He taught his granddaughter Missy to draw Woodstock with sidewalk chalk, and he was even there to pick up his grandson Brian on the boy's first day of junior high. For a young artist who had shared many sketching sessions with his grandpa while visiting California, the special escort was a more than welcome addition to the inaugural school day's end. Sparky made his grandchildren feel special, as was his privilege as grandpa.

Sparky had a knack for making visits with almost anyone seem special. His grandchildren had a unique pull on his heartstrings, but others could feel his magnetism quickly as well. "He was captivating," Joan Secchia, the wife of the U.S. ambassador to Italy, said of her visit with Sparky in 1992.[2] He was "fairly shy," she remembered, and he did not at all seem absorbed with his own fame, even though the two were meeting at a special luncheon in Rome to celebrate an Italian exhibit of Snoopy fashion. Instead of basking in his own accomplishments, Sparky had a way of including the person he was talking with in the conversation, making sure to ask them as much (if not more) about them than they were asking about him.

When contemporary Christian music phenom Sandi Patty likewise had the pleasure of meeting with the comic strip legend in the early '90s, this was just the sort of warm treatment she received as well. Carolyn Gill, a friend of Sandi's who was pastoring a church near Santa Rosa had enjoyed an occasional chat with Sparky at the Warm Puppy. "I love sitting and talking with her about things," Sparky said.[3] When Sandi was in town, Carolyn took her along to meet the famous cartoonist. Sandi herself, of course, was likewise famous in her own right. Often hailed simply as "The Voice," with hits like the Grammy-winning songs "More Than Wonderful" (1984) and "Was it a Morning Like This" (1987), Sandi had contributed significantly to the new wave of sacred music that was taking music stores and radio stations by storm. She was part of a rising movement that added more contemporary rhythms (which some fundamentalist groups were deeply concerned about) to the sacred tradition of gospel music—a tradition that Schulz deeply enjoyed.

Sparky had delighted in listening to music for many years. When he was in the army, he was "always one of the staunchest opponents of classical music,"[4] but he gave in to the temptation shortly after he returned, much to the credit of his educated Art Instruction colleague friends. Soon, he owned most of Beethoven's symphonies and a collection of Haydn, Mozart, Brahms, and others to play on a huge Zenith combination with a built-in long-playing record attachment. His time with the Twin Cities Church of God group then opened up his knowledge of and love for sacred hymns, a love that would stick with Schulz throughout the rest of his life. "You'll be stunned to discover that the tape I've been listening to the last three days is Andy Griffith singing gospel songs," he joked with Gary Groth in 1997, noting that Griffith was not quite as good as Tennessee Ernie Ford, who Schulz had known from their early animation work. "Ernie Ford had a wonderful, rich voice. He used to sing those gospel songs so beautifully."[5]

As a fellow member of the Church of God, growing up in the denomination that was headquartered in her college town of Anderson, Indiana, Sandi Patty could identify with Schulz's love for the gospel music, and the two had a lovely talk while looking on at the ice rink. Rather than just talk about their mutual love for hymn music, though, Sparky focused the conversation toward the more salient troubles in Sandi's life. They talked for a time about Sparky's love for his grandkids, but he then turned the conversation toward Sandi and the struggles she was going through as she lived out a rather public divorce—something particularly difficult for a public persona living as an icon in the Christian community. Sparky was concerned about how Sandi's kids were handling it and how she was handling it. Their love for sacred music may have given them room to connect, but it was Sparky's way of expressing concern about Sandi's personal pain that made them bond in that moment—just as his strip allowed millions of readers to personally connect through the pain felt by Charlie Brown or Peppermint Patty.

In 1995, as news was breaking in Christian circles that Sandi had an affair prior to her divorce, Sparky then reached out to her through that very medium that was most personal to him—his strip. On September 12, 1995, in a single-panel strip (Sparky had been breaking the four-panel format since the late 1980s), Charlie Brown stands beside a disheveled Linus, who seemed to have crashed into a nearby fence as the two attempted to inline skate. Head spinning, Linus explains his fall, saying, "As I rounded the corner, Sandi Patti hit a high note . ." Seeing the strip, Sandi's heart was warmed as she was otherwise reliving the pain of her past. "For this lil' gal in Indiana that was hurting badly that weekend, he just kind of said 'I see you,'" Sandi remembered. "'I see you, it's okay.' It was so sweet."[6]

Just a few years earlier, Sparky had insisted that his new network television special include a hymn in what was surely one of his most emotionally charged shows, *Why, Charlie Brown, Why?* Singing the song would be Becky Reardon, the daughter of Sparky's Church of God friend Bob Reardon, but this was only possible after Schulz insisted that the song must be included and that he had the right voice for it—a voice he had come to enjoy for over two decades. In 1971, Lee Mendelson was working on a documentary celebrating the national park system, *From Yellowstone to Tomorrow*. In the program, Emmy Award-winning actor George C. Scott would narrate the centennial celebration, complete with music from Grammy-winning *The 5th Dimension* (of "Age of Aquarius" fame) and with a guest appearance by comedian Jonathan Winters. Bob Reardon's daughter, Becky, was trying to make it as a folk singer in the San Francisco Bay Area at the time. Sparky and Bob were good friends, so Sparky was happy to pass along his daughter's name to Lee who graciously agreed to include her in the lineup. Her folk singing would pair nicely with the theme of the program anyway.

Sparky particularly enjoyed Becky's singing, and when he was putting together his skating show in 1978, *Snoopy's Musical on Ice*, he again wanted to include her. She would sing the medley of hymns that Sparky's own daughter Amy would skate to. Though the hymns meant little to Amy at the time, another chance to perform on television was meaningful for Becky, and the songs themselves were meaningful for Sparky. He had always dreamed of doing an entire ice show made up only of sacred hymns, writing to Amy about the wild possibility while she was on her mission, but he was certain that the idea would be resisted too strongly for him to ever have the nerve to suggest it. The medley would have to suffice. Becky would be joined by *Peanuts* vocal alum Larry Finlayson, and Amy would delicately skate to the medley of "Sweet Hour of Prayer," "I Come to the Garden Alone," and "My Soul Is Satisfied" on national television. She recorded again for Sparky in 1981, singing "(When I Feel Most) Alone" for the animated special *Someday You'll Find Her, Charlie Brown*.

Music had been an important part of the animation projects from the early years of Vince Guaraldi's jazz scores. Sparky likewise brought music to his strips through Schroeder's classical devotion, and he also integrated an occasional sacred musical reference within the panels across his work. One small character in *Two by Fours* says from atop a stack of books, "One more songbook, and I think I'll almost be able to see the preacher . . ." In the *Peanuts* strips, Snoopy once scolds Woodstock for singing "Shall We Gather at the River" near the golf course water hazard;[7] Sally complains that she doesn't know what a sheave is, but if she sees one she'll bring it in;[8] and Marcie gets trapped in her theater seat while standing for the "Hallelujah" chorus in the Tiny Tots production of Handel's "Messiah."[9]

Schulz and his creative team made room for occasional sacred music throughout certain television specials, each time in a respectful way. In the *This is America, Charlie Brown* miniseries entry "The Building of the Transcontinental Railroad," Franklin has added prominence as the program features the gospel spirituals "Get on Board Little Children" and "This Train is Bound for Glory," as well as Christian American standards "Battle Hymn of the Republic," "America the Beautiful," and the eschatological folk tune "She'll be Coming 'Round the Mountain." In

"ONE MORE SONGBOOK, AND I THINK I'LL ALMOST BE ABLE TO SEE THE PREACHER...."

Two by Fours. 1965. © 1989 Warner Press, Inc., Anderson, Indiana. Used with permission.

"The Music and Heroes of America," viewers could hear "When the Saints Go Marching In," and fans had of course been listening to "Hark! The Herald Angels Sing" since the 1965 debut of *A Charlie Brown Christmas*. When network editors trimmed the sacred carol from the yearly airing in order to allow for more commercial breaks, enough fan criticism came by mail that the song would be returned to later annual airings of the Christmas classic.

In 1990, Sparky and Lee brought Becky back to lend her flowing voice to the rather unique *Why, Charlie Brown, Why*? It was an atypical program for the *Peanuts* cast in which the gang struggles to cope with a friend's sudden illness. Janice, a character introduced only in this special, had been bruising easily and felt rather sick at school, so she goes to see the school nurse and then a doctor. When Linus and Charlie Brown visit her in her hospital room, they are surprised and scared by what she tells them. "It wasn't just a fever," Janice explains. "I have cancer." "Are you going to die?" blurts Charlie Brown. Janice has leukemia, but the doctors are confident that with chemotherapy treatment she will get well, the girl tells her friends, though it proves to be a lot for them to consider.

As Janice explains the diagnosis process, from blood samples and bone marrow tests to X-Rays and IVs, Charlie Brown and Linus begin to understand, as was the goal of the whole program—to help young viewers understand. The program was the idea of Sylvia Cook, a nurse at Stanford Memorial hospital who wrote to Schulz in 1985 in the hope that he might one day put together a short *Peanuts* video for children and families to view in hospitals. With the help of the American Cancer Society and the promise of supporting revenue from network advertisers, Schulz developed the idea into a full broadcast program for CBS. "If someone writes and tells you they want to do something for children with cancer, how can you ignore it?" he said. Producer Lee Mendelson added, "We're not just an entertainment show every time."

Secondary scenes were drawn from Schulz's comics, with Sally complaining about going to school and Snoopy roaming the halls as a world-famous surgeon, but the bulk of the program was centered on Janice, written in collaboration with Helen Crothers of the American Cancer Society and with Sylvia Cook. "This is the greatest opportunity we've ever had to get the message across about childhood cancer," Crothers said as the show was about to go to air. "I just hope it helps," said Schulz.[10]

Walking away from the hospital after their visit, Linus continues to wrestle with the pain his friend is going through. "Why, Charlie Brown, why?" he asks. As Linus walks down the sidewalk, autumn leaves blowing in the wind and a tear falling from his eye, Becky Reardon's lyrical sway fills the scene with the chorus of the southern gospel song once recorded by Schulz's favorite Tennessee Ernie Ford, "Farther Along":

> Farther along, we'll know all about it;
> Farther along, we'll understand why.
> Cheer up my brother; walk in the sunlight.
> We'll understand it, all by and by.
> We'll understand it, all by and by.

When Becky was asked to sing on the special, she had the impression that Sparky had once again faced some opposition for suggesting the religious hymn be included in the mainstream program. "He loved and felt very, very deeply about the traditional hymns of the church," Becky recalled, and Sparky ultimately convinced any concerned voices that the chorus was a worthy match for their efforts in the program. He certainly had the support of Becky's parents, both being well-versed in the hymn tradition, something they shared with Sparky. "That love of music," Becky said of her parents' relationship with the artist, "that connection through the music of the church was very deep for them." When it came time to record Becky's vocal track with producer Judy Munsen, Sparky had made his choice of hymn without foreknowledge of the studio musicians. None knew the song except for Sparky and the Reardons, but with Becky's mother, Geraldine, on hand, there was a solution to Sparky's dilemma. "There wasn't a pianist who knew the songs off the top of her head, so my mom stepped in and without any nervousness at all laid down the tracks for me to record the vocals to," Becky remembered.[11] Later, the studio had an orchestra lay down the full background accompaniment, and the song was able to add its depth to the special.

When the snowplows are finished clearing the winter roads, Linus is excited to see Janice crossing the street to join them at the bus stop. Her long blond hair is gone, and she wears a pink ball cap and a wide smile. She was beginning to feel pretty good, she tells her friends. Arriving at school, Janice's troubles are not over, though, as a bully taunts her for her hat. Knocking it off her head, he erupts into laughter, yelling, "Hey, look at this, a baldy!" bringing Janice to tears. Linus, at his angriest in any of the entire franchise, takes the bully by his green turtleneck, and growls, "You blockhead! What's the matter with you?! Janice has got leukemia, cement head. That's cancer. Have you ever heard of cancer?! She's been in the hospital and she's had chemotherapy to help her get better, and it makes her hair fall out. Does that make you happy?! Would you like to go through what she's gone through? Think about it! Or don't you ever think about anything?" "I'm sorry," the boy says, apologetically.

Janice's own sisters had some understanding to gain as well, struggling with the extra attention their sister had received and the extra caution that they had to take around her, but by spring, Janice is back with the gang. As Linus pushes her on the swings, her pink cap flies off, her blond hair flows in the wind, and the credits roll as she giggles in delight.

The show was nominated for an Emmy, but its most potent impact may have been with the viewers who had an emotional response to the program, many of them very young. "I liked your video. I have a sister that has leukemia and she had an IV," wrote a young Massachusetts girl to Lee Mendelson. "Next year she won't be sick anymore. She has already went threw [*sic*] a year of leukemia. Sometimes I felt like Janice's sisters."

Released on video and in book form, the work was then able to reach those affected by illness around the globe. "It's remarkable, it's been a long time until I have found a book that reflects my thoughts regarding how my patients are treated in the world they live in, with their laughs, their sorrows, their jealousy and love. . . . In fact, as real as life itself and as real as the life of a child," an oncologist from Madrid wrote to the team when the book was finally translated into Spanish.[12] Charles Schulz had witnessed his mother and his aunt Marion endure the struggle of cancer; both received a terminal diagnoses. To imagine a child going through such an ordeal would be too much. He worried enough about what would happen to Amy's large brood of nine children if something were to befall their parents. And while some would find the grace to learn through the unbearable, Sparky did not believe that God would ever orchestrate such a tragedy to befall one person in order to enlighten another. "That would be the highest form of egotism. . . . God does not cause little kids to die to teach their parents a lesson," he said. "Never!"[13] With the hardships of cancer weighing heavily, Sparky was proud of the story they put together in *Why, Charlie Brown, Why?* and he hoped that it might help the very real patients who lived with the disease. He had no way of knowing, of course, that the life of a cancer patient would be his own by the decade's end.

In 1981, after a tightness in his chest had convinced him to see a doctor, Schulz underwent quadruple bypass surgery to free up complete blockage in one vessel and significant blockage in the others. He would be among the first patients to undergo open-heart surgery at Santa Rosa Memorial Hospital, which had been delayed for some time in receiving the necessary licensing by the State Department of Health Services due

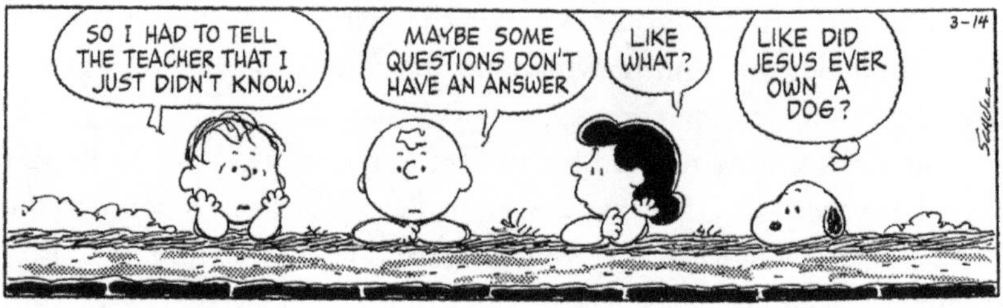

Peanuts © Peanuts Worldwide LLC. Used with permission. March 14, 1995.

to "puzzling interpretations of the law." The new head cardiac surgeon, Dr. Theodore L. Folkerth, a skilled physician and Vietnam veteran who was formerly at San Jose's Good Samaritan Hospital, was to be Sparky's surgeon. "[Bypass] lets the patients carry on their lives doing the things they want to do, enjoying life," Folkerth said of the procedure,[14] and that was exactly what Sparky wanted to do—carry on with his life. "The idea of surgery terrified him, but the medications he'd been taking had left him so debilitated that surgery became the option he was forced to consider," Monte said.[15] "Just pray for me," Sparky wrote to Amy as he approached the surgery, adding from James 5:16: "The prayer of a righteous man availeth much."[16]

Pleased with his doctor's qualifications, the reluctant patient underwent the vital procedure successfully. While resting afterward, trying to regain steadiness in a shaky post-surgery hand, Sparky enjoyed a phone call from his longtime friend, President Ronald Reagan. The first lady had sent a lovely bouquet of anthurium to the artist's hospital bedside, and the president wished him a speedy recovery.

Sparky's recovery was reasonably quick, and other than a three-week bout with giardia, a nasty intestinal parasite, in 1985, Schulz's health stayed in relatively good shape for the next decade. To his dismay, though, the aging artist never regained the steady pen line of his youth, a prospect that had bothered him even before he underwent bypass surgery. He found a way to brace his hand while drawing, and his wavering line became an endearing trait of his work, but Charles Schulz simply did not want to get old. It was already a "gloomy thought" for him in 1980,[17] and in 1996, his friend and fellow cartoonist Lynn Johnston described him as being "bitter about getting old."[18] In 1997, Schulz put it succinctly—"I'm fighting it."[19]

Getting old put Schulz at odds with the philosophy of "maturity" that he had been vocalizing for years. "My own private theological theory," he described in 1967, "is that when Jesus said: 'Be ye perfect, even as your Father in Heaven is perfect,' He was talking about maturity."[20] To Schulz, perfection did not mean never making a mistake—making mistakes was inevitable with so much mystery in the world. Perfection meant a broader foundation of understanding, of acceptance, of mercy, and of responsibility.

This maturity comes with an openness toward one's experience and with the passing of time. With maturity, one sees more than just the surface of a scenario and responds with more than knee-jerk reactions. "[It] is absolutely necessary for each one of us to strive to gain emotional maturity," he said. "Unless a person becomes mature in all things, he will always have fears and anxieties plaguing him."[21] Charles Schulz could never master this emotional maturity, battling anxiety and self-diagnosed agoraphobia throughout his adult life.

Schulz's *Peanuts* strips had worked so well in part because the mature themes of grief and hope were packaged in such pint-size characters. The disjuncture allowed the themes to resonate much more clearly than if an adult character had voiced them. He used constant and creative variations on his classic themes throughout his fifty-year career—a steady and committed approach that required its own maturity. "The ability to create ideas improves as you yourself mature," he said in 1973.[22] In the mid-'90s, his strip ideas continued to explore variations on simple and profound theological ideas, such as when Charlie Brown wondered, "Did Jesus ever own a dog?"[23]

As the strips taught Charlie Brown on a daily basis, maturity also meant accepting that not all of life would be easy. No one was promised a rose garden . . . or an apple orchard. "Dad seemed to equate maturity with the acceptance and fulfillment of responsibility," Monte described. "When we grow up (mature), we do certain things because they need to be done by us, without reluctance or complaint or excuse. He accepted his own responsibility to art, work, family and friends, often without enthusiasm but always with that certain pride that goes along with the recognition that one has matured enough to see and do what must be done."[24] Growing old had made it harder for Schulz to take care of his responsibilities, but as he had also said, "It is also immature not to be able to realize that things that are going to happen in the future are quite often inevitable."[25] The inevitability of getting old, of not being able to do as much, of having struggles challenge his ability to engage even the simple joys and responsibilities . . . it was simply setting in too early. He was not ready, and he wanted to fight it.

Already wanting to be younger and healthier than he was, Charles Schulz was broken when he learned there was little he could do to fight what would be his final battle—a battle more cruel than mere old age. In November 1999, Schulz was rushed to Santa Rosa Memorial Hospital after collapsing in his studio. During emergency surgery to clear a blocked abdominal aorta, Schulz suffered several small strokes, and the doctors discovered cancer throughout his colon. Diagnosed with Stage IV colon cancer, Schulz was given at best a year or two to live.

"The universe boggles us," he had written in 1980. "In the larger scheme, we suddenly realize, we amount to very little. It's frightening. Only a certain maturity will make us able to cope. The minute we abandon the quest for it we leave ourselves open to tragic results."[26] Schulz struggled to find just how he could cope with his cancer beyond undergoing the pains of chemotherapy. He had never gotten over his own mother's battle, and his doctors did not have the encouraging words that added comfort to *Why, Charlie Brown, Why?* It had been hard enough for him to cope with the loss of his wire-haired fox terrier Andy a few years earlier. After they put Andy to sleep, Sparky smashed his driveway sign that read, "Please drive slowly. Small dog does not see or hear well"—a sign that could not save the dog from its own internal sickness.

Realizing what his own diagnosis meant for his work, the seventy-seven-year-old Schulz was devastated. "I never dreamed that this is what would happen to me," he told Al Roker in a final, heart-wrenching interview. "I always had the feeling that I would probably, I'd stay with the strip, maybe, oh, 'til I was maybe early eighties or something like that, and all of a sudden, it's gone! It's been taken away from me."[27] Schulz could no longer trust his wrists to command a golf club, his hand to hold a pen, or his eyes not to cry. In late 1999, with his global readership surpassing 300 million, he announced his retirement from the strip.

Sparky's family returned to Santa Rosa as often as they could in his final months. It meant everything to him, he told cartoonist friend Cathy

Guisewite, that they had dropped everything to be with him. His vast array of close and distant friends reached out to him, outmatched only by the force of the fan letters that had poured in after Sparky announced the end of his comic. Father Gary Lombardi, one of Sparky's closest friends in the later years of his life, spent time with him on good and bad days, reading Scriptures with his friend at Sparky's request. "I don't have any friends," Sparky would occasionally say, a slightly witty expression of deep feelings of loneliness. "But I've found a friend in a place I never expected to find it—the Roman Catholic Church!"[28] In fact, in 1997 Sparky had actually referred to the priest as "the best friend that I have now,"[29] a friend with whom he enjoyed many conversations about religious ideas.

Sparky and Lombardi had met through a mutual friend in the late 1980s and were soon part of a weekly golfing foursome. Sparky liked to rib Lombardi on the course, once warning as the priest teed up that up ahead were two water traps, and one was filled with holy water. "We tease him unmercifully," Sparky joked.[30] Sparky even invited him to join their trip to Rome to celebrate Schulz's Italian "Award of Merit" and the Snoopy fashion exhibit. Largely because his Catholic friend was along, Sparky included a tour of the Vatican during their stay, and they also visited Assisi, home of St. Francis. "There was a young Franciscan monk who was showing us around," Lombardi remembered, "and we had a lovely tour; Sparky was very much touched by it." During their lunch, though, the monk began describing what Lombardi called an exclusionary "pre-Vatican II view of the Catholic Church." "I just remember Sparky's eyes hooding over," Lombardi said. "He would not accept that God was limited to any one denomination."

Sparky had embraced his faith with openness, gratitude, and mystery for over half of a century. The sacred Bible passages, though, could now offer only a partial comfort to him as Lombardi read them by his bedside. Their message of hope was a struggle for the man who so desperately wanted to be well again but who had been given a terminal diagnosis. Prayer in particular was a challenge for the lay scholar. Schulz had always regarded prayer as very personal, rejecting the rote prayers of liturgical denominations. "I believe in prayer," Lombardi remembered him once saying, "but I do not believe in *a* prayer." Prayer should not be routine, should not be a mere list of requests, and by itself could never be a true act of worship, which was only accomplished through acts of love.

Sparky did not favor the belief that prayer would result in spontaneous alterations in everyday life either. "He did not believe in a God of magic," Father Lombardi explained. Even if such requests might be fulfilled, Sparky questioned whether or not leaving such decisions up to man would make for a good existence. In the book of James, the Scripture writer reminds that Elijah "prayed fervently that it might not rain, and for three years and six months it did not rain on the earth."[31] Sparky had joked in one of his strips that God did not have an investment in the outcome of golf tournaments,[32] and in the margins of the verse in James he wrote, "Do we really want our world of nature controlled by prayer?" In 1977, he then made clear that he did not believe prayer was ever intended for dependent pleading:

> I think God wants us to be able to stand on our own two feet and not continually pray for his help and his security and every time we venture out of the house we pray God keep me safe. He wants us to go out and live in His world—the world He has given us—and not to hang on to his apron strings.[33]

Prayer was an opportunity to give spiritual voice to one's thoughts, directing them with hope toward God. Sparky had once rather atypically directed his family to offer a prayer of thanks after Jeannie's daughter survived a near-fatal car accident, but he would admit that "I find it very difficult to know how to pray sometimes. I really, I just don't know what to say."[34] Sparky's characters demonstrated better and worse versions of prayer throughout the strip. "Sometimes I lie awake at night," Charlie Brown said on February 7, 1994, "and I ask, 'Why am I here?' Then a voice answers, 'Why? Where do you want to be?'" Lucy and the rest of the baseball team once broke into prayer that the ball not get hit to any of them;[35] Peppermint Patty had on occasion prayed at the chalkboard for divine intervention;[36] and standing outside of the principal's office, Charlie Brown, who had offered some of the most earnest prayers of any of the characters, invoked the Psalmist's sober appeal, "'Plead my cause, O Lord, with them that strive with me: Fight against them that fight against me . . . Deliver me from the hand of them that persecute me . .'[37] My stomach hurts!"[38]

Brother Forbes had described prayer as a tunnel of faith one would naturally wrestle with. "As with prayer so it is with other matters of faith," the pastor said. "They are like tunnels. If you go half way in all will be dark, but if you push on through you will come out into the light, because tunnels have light at both ends."[39] But that light could be hard to see.

It was understandably hard for Sparky to find hope in his prayers after his diagnosis, though he knew prayers for him were abundant. "Do you realize how many millions and millions of people are praying for you?" Chuck Bartley said to Sparky during one of his last visits, hoping to reassure his close friend. In fact, unbeknownst to Bartley, the Family Christian bookstore headquarters had even set up a giant card for customers to sign in order to let Sparky know just how strongly the Christian community was praying for him, their beloved cartoonist. Stricken with grief, though, Sparky struggled to understand how that might be of any comfort. When told that millions were praying for him, he looked up at his friend and responded in agony, "Why then, am I dying?"[40]

Though his grief was natural and at times difficult to reconcile with certain hopeful theologies, Sparky gave no indication that he had truly lost his faith in his final months. While visiting at Christmas, Amy remembered her father enjoying his day, listening to hymns, during which he asked her, "What sort of thing do you think you'd ask Jesus when you meet him?" Caught off guard by the question, Amy fumbled for a response, but was later comforted by the memory. "He *must* have been thinking about Heaven," she figured.[41] He had, after all, sent her a sermon from Brother Forbes while Amy was in England in which Sparky's former pastor described his tunnels of faith, including the tunnel that connects the present life to the next. "Remember, a tunnel has light at both ends, and we have our Lord's word for it that at the other end of the tunnel of death he waits to greet his friends," Forbes encouraged.[42] Sparky had been given a year or two to live at most, but he told his friends he was planning to recover. With his diagnosis in mind, though, asking his daughter about what one might say at the other end of the tunnel was no leap for the insightful artist.

Jeannie had a more fluid, perhaps even cosmopolitan view on spirituality, a topic she did not turn to as frequently as Sparky, so the two did not talk about Heaven or an afterlife at length, before or after the diagnosis. Sparky had not actually made clear in interviews or in conversations with close family or friends what his specific systematic beliefs on the afterlife were, largely because he had a hard time being dogmatic about such mysterious and uncertain issues. "I'm a firm believer in the Kingdom of God," he said in 1995, "but I don't know about the afterlife—that baffles me. I think life is a total mystery. I have no idea why we're here, where it all came from or where we're all going, and I don't think anybody knows."[43]

This did not mean that Charles Schulz was without any belief that he would reach a blessed shore. "I'm a firm believer in the Kingdom of God," he insisted. And he could maintain hope, which is perhaps the singular gift of his well-worn Bible. For Charles Schulz, this hope was perhaps best expressed in his January 26, 1985, strip. Looking at her brother inquisitively, Sally asked Charlie Brown, "When we die, will we go to Heaven?" "I like to think so," Charlie Brown said. This was not indecision on the part of Sally's big brother; this was honesty and the willingness to have hope. This was the nature of Charles Schulz's faith, which was often reflected in the funny sketches he made for newspapers. Charlie Brown could not say for sure if Heaven literally existed, nor could Charles Schulz. If Sparky's question to Amy and his semi-autobiographical strips were any indication, though, perhaps they both liked to think so.

Before they went into repeats, Sparky's last religious *Peanuts* strip ran on December 12, 1999. It was a Christmas story, like his first explicit and his most famous uses of his well-worn biblical familiarity. In the strip, Peppermint Patty meets up with Marcie, excited about that year's Christmas play. Peppermint Patty was going to play Jesus's mother, Mary, and wasn't quite sure what to wear. Much to Peppermint Patty's disappointment, Marcie tells her friend that there is not going to be a Christmas play. There was one the year before, but not this year. Sunken on the couch, Peppermint Patty has to accept the news that she will not have the chance to again share her talents with the world. When Sparky announced his own professional retirement, he was ahead enough in his work that his strips would continue to run for many more weeks, but he had wished he could have shared more with the world. He had wanted to continue his work much longer, to continue the work that he so deeply felt that he was meant to do. He could not give his readers all of the answers they wanted, but he could make them laugh, and perhaps occasionally make them think. "I just did the best I could," he told Al Roker, choking back tears in his final interview.

With help from his creative director, Schulz put together his final *Peanuts* strip. With cutout images from classic strips, including Linus with his blanket, Lucy holding the football, and Charlie Brown leaning on the brick wall, Snoopy typed:

> Dear Friends,
>
> I have been fortunate to draw Charlie Brown and his friends for almost 50 years. It has been the fulfillment of my childhood ambition.
>
> Unfortunately, I am no longer able to maintain the schedule demanded by a daily comic strip. My family does not wish Peanuts to be continued by anyone else, therefore I am announcing my retirement.
>
> I have been grateful over the years for the loyalty of our editors and the wonderful support and love expressed to me by fans of the comic strip. Charlie Brown, Snoopy, Linus, Lucy . . . how can I ever forget them . . .
>
> Charles M. Schulz

Following the strips he had completed before his health deteriorated, that final panel was scheduled to run on Sunday, February 13. As newspapers across the country were bound up for delivery the night of Saturday, February 12, Charles Schulz crawled into bed, exhausted. Jeannie spent time with him before letting him pull the covers up to his chin. "I'm tired. I'm going to go to sleep," he said. "Ok, I'll go wash up the dishes," she told him, as he closed his eyes. There would be no more lying awake and wondering for Charles M. Schulz. That night, complications from the cancer took their final toll, likely producing a pulmonary embolism, and Sparky died in his sleep.

The next morning, Sparky's final strip, his last Sunday in which he said goodbye to his faithful readers, ran on schedule, now imbued with another layer of meaning that none could have predicted, nor written more poetically. As news of his death swept over the world, letters of sympathy and support came pouring in once more. Regina Hotchkiss's fifth-grade class at the Temple-Tifiereth Israel school planted a tree in Sparky's honor for Tu B'Shevat, the Jewish arboreal New Year. The Sisters of the Order of Notre Dame wrote that their love for Charlie Brown had always been love for Charles Schulz. The manager of Santa Rosa's local Family Christian bookstore finally sent in the large greeting card, only just completed on February 12. The manager wrote to Jeannie and the family: "After many tears I realized God's answer was what was best for Charles. The unexpected and untimely departure of Charles to be with the Lord, though hard for everyone to understand, we can rest assured that it was part of the master plan, like everything else in his life."[44] Though the manager did not reference the date of the last strip's printing, there were many that had found the timing divinely inspired. Jeannie wrote back: "You know, all our prayers *were* answered. Sparky died at peace, knowing he was loved, knowing he did the best he could with what he was given."[45]

On February 16, the family gathered under rainy northern California skies for a private funeral at the Pleasant Hills Cemetery in Sebastopol. Programs had been printed for the secluded service conducted by Father Lombardi. On the outside was the picture of Jesus[46] that Sparky had hanging in his studio. The family would use a picture of Sparky golfing for the public service. This intimate laying to rest was a somber gathering. Monte shared a passage from Thomas Wolfe's *You Can't Go Home Again*, and Stephanie played hymns.

At the graveside, the family stood in black with their large umbrellas protecting them from the rain. Sparky had loved drawing the rain in his strips. They each laid a white lily on the casket. "It felt like a movie," remembered Stephanie, who was sixteen at the time. As the casket lowered, it got caught, and the attendants were forced to raise it back up to make clearance. Painful as though this may have been in the moment of grieving, some of the family would later chuckle as one of them imagined Sparky quipping, "What—resurrected already?" At his grave, a stone bench carved with *Peanuts* characters was added to memorialize the work he had done. A military grave marker was added to honor the service he had given. On the grave marker, a cross signified the faith he had held.

A military grave marker marked with a cross honors Schulz's service and faith. Family, friends, and fans line it with flowers, a flag, and *Peanuts* collectibles. 2012. Photo by author.

On February 23, the family began the public move from grieving to memorializing and celebration. Santa Rosa's Luther Burbank Center[47] was filled to its 1,600-person capacity while a camera crew broadcasted a public memorial service to the local television and radio networks and the hundreds of attendees who poured into the parking lot to watch the service on overflow screens. During the service, an array of friends and family spoke—Monte read selections of his own writing that his father had loved, Jill recalled her father calling her his "rare gem," Billie Jean King spoke at length about her time with her dear friend, and *Cathy* cartoonist Cathy Guisewite cracked insightfully wise about the deep reassurance Sparky had given them all. Speakers' comments at the memorial made evident their awareness of Sparky's deeply personal faith. "Sparky, you were always humble, ethical, moral, and God fearing, just like Charlie Brown," eulogized close friend and surgeon/magician Dr. Bob Albo, who commented that Sparky had left this world "for a better job as the Lord's cartoonist." After humorously remembering many good times with his friend and before reading a rendition of "A Golfer's Prayer," Dean James suspected in his eulogy that Sparky was in Heaven, already setting up new golf foursomes.

The service was full of music, aptly opening with "You're a Good Man, Charlie Brown," sung by cast members from the Broadway musical revival including Kristin Chenoweth and Anthony Rapp, followed by a prayer from Amy's husband Johnny, and a soprano rendition of the hymn "Softly and Tenderly" sung by local vocalist Carol Menke. This was one of three hymns Sparky had wanted at his funeral. Menke would sing "I Come to the Garden Alone" later in the service, the third hymn coming in the form of a piano special. When Sparky had mentioned these three favorites, years before he was ill, Jeannie wrote them down and taped them to the bathroom mirror. "She's planning my funeral before I'm even dead!" Sparky had joked with her. Though some of the hymns may have held different theological meaning for Jeannie than for Sparky, the two had shared nearly three happy decades together, and Jeannie made sure that these songs were part of his memorial. Taking the stage, the newly widowed partial-heir to the *Peanuts* legacy shared with the friends and public what their support had meant to her husband:

> While [Sparky] knew well that he had fans, he could not know the extent of the impact he had made. I believe that's what these last months have been about. Twelve days ago, someone asked him about the outpouring of affection, and he said, "I'm glad I'm alive to see it." My comfort comes from knowing that he fully received the love and appreciation that poured out to him.

As Jeannie returned to sit, Sparky's teenage granddaughter Stephanie walked up to the microphone. "My name is Stephanie Johnson," she said. "I would like to dedicate this hymn to my grampa." Stepping up to the piano, she unfurled her sheet music, brushed her long black skirt over the bench, and began softly playing one of Sparky's favorite hymns, "Sweet Hour of Prayer." The stage was much larger than the intimate room in her grandpa's home she had played in just a few weeks before,

Sparky sitting in his zigzag chair. With a video camera four feet away to broadcast the service, but with a calm that she suspected may have been from beyond herself, Stephanie's fingers brought forth musical notes from the grand piano. "It was a privilege," she remembered later, as tears dared well up. She delicately made her way through the arrangement before quietly picking up her music and returning to her seat next to her brother, Brian,[48] amidst earnest clapping from those in attendance. There were no words to accompany her musical tribute, but for those who knew the song, deeper reflection was more than abundant, as was the style of her grandfather's own artistry.

In his February 17, 1974, strip, Charles Schulz included a passage of Scripture from the eighth chapter of Romans that was important to him. One of his favorites, Sparky had connected deeply with it and would often invoke it in spiritual conversations. It was simple and poetic, even musical. Yet it was laden with a deep understanding of the limitations of the faithful servant and the understanding of a Heavenly God. Before the Broadway singers would return to the stage to sing "Just One Person,"[49] before Monte would offer closing words at his father's memorial service, before Carol Menke would movingly sing Fauré's Requiem, and before he would close in his own prayer, Father Lombardi gave voice to this passage from the book of Romans, chapter eight, verse twenty-six—"Likewise the Spirit helps us in our weakness; for we do not know how to pray as we ought, but the Spirit himself intercedes for us with sighs too deep for words."[50]

Sparky's humorous art had never been about answers, nor had his own spiritual beliefs in a Heavenly Father been about absolute certainty and dogma, but both his life and work had been filled with profound sighs. His was not a wishy-washy faith; it was an honest one. It was an open one in which the musical mystery of a sacred text exposed more questions than answers while simultaneously providing a sense of faith and a sense of security. Filled with religious references and provocative spiritual moments, Charles M. Schulz's globally and personally influential work, featuring Charlie Brown, Linus, Lucy, Snoopy, Woodstock, Sally, Schroeder, Peppermint Patty, Marcie, and the rest, was able to do the same.

EPILOGUE

PEANUTS AFTER SPARKY

"It's a balancing act."

—PAIGE BRADDOCK

OVER A DECADE AFTER CHARLES SCHULZ DIED, A GREAT CROWD GATHERS ON a chilly Halloween night. They are a dedicated group filling a Santa Rosa, California field. There is nothing but sincerity as far as the eye can see. Gathered are ghosts and goblins, princesses and pirates, and even a Flying Ace. What those gathered are waiting to see, though, is not each other's festive adornments. They wait to see the Great Pumpkin. Of course, it won't be the Great Pumpkin himself (not even Linus Van Pelt ever had that honor), but instead the group sits on bales of hay in a ball field lined with delicately carved jack-o'-lanterns bearing the faces of Schulz's *Peanuts* characters (Charlie Brown's round head mapping easily onto the orange autumnal squash), waiting for the annual outdoor screening of Schulz's Halloween classic, *It's the Great Pumpkin, Charlie Brown*.

Sparky's younger son, Craig, plays host and MC for the outdoor viewing of his father's harvest classic. Welcoming the crowd and encouraging them to take part in the cocoa and cider, the quiet child of the comic strip genius then leads those willing in a rousing round of pumpkin carols. Perhaps "rousing" is an overstatement, given that the carols never quite caught on after Hallmark introduced them through their Ambassador Cards line around 1967 as part of a mass-merchandizing promotional. Nonetheless, the event remains a success, the crowd cheering as the 1966 television special plays in the ball field situated between the Charles M. Schulz Museum and Research Center and Sparky's old drawing studio. The event is a gift from the ice arena to the community,[1] part of the ongoing legacy of Schulz's work, and is perhaps one of the simplest of the many challenging creative endeavors that Jeannie, Craig, and the other executives in the *Peanuts* franchise continue to navigate as the love for Sparky's creations continues.

When Sparky successfully renegotiated his contract with United Media in 1978 (the year that *What a Nightmare, Charlie Brown* was released) his children insisted that they include a clause guaranteeing that no artist would be able to produce new *Peanuts* comic strips after Sparky died. Over the years, Schulz had by necessity relinquished certain amounts of creative and artistic control over adaptations of his strips (he gave Bill Melendez creative space in animation, for example, and Sasseville, Hale, Pocrnich, and Palmquist drew the early comic books). When Sparky died in 2000, then, his family was comfortable with the franchise producing new goods, so long as no new comic strips were drawn. Balloons would continue to be made for the Macy's Thanksgiving Day Parade, Camp Snoopy would grow across theme parks, and unseen animated features would even be finished and released.

In 2010, their efforts were given new life when *Peanuts* syndicate United Media closed its doors, selling off its properties to the highest bidder. The rights to *Peanuts* were purchased by Peanuts Worldwide, LLC, a newly formed company run by the Schulz family and the New York-based Iconix Brand Group. Holding 20 percent ownership in Peanuts Worldwide, the family may not have gained full legal ownership of Sparky's creation,[2] but the purchase marked a strong corporate reclamation. With the addition of Iconix, a brand management company owned by Neil Cole and his fashion designer brother Kenneth Cole (husband of Maria Cuomo, daughter of former New York governor Mario Cuomo), the Schulzes gained an energetic equity ally. Sold for $175 million, with annual sales estimated at more than $2 billion, the group has actively sought to reignite the once-dominant property's global power, desiring to make *Peanuts* salient and engaging for a whole new generation. "Peanuts now has the best of both worlds—family ownership and the vision and resources of Iconix to perpetuate what my father created throughout the next century with all the goodwill his lovable characters bring," Craig said at the time of the sale.[3]

Those lovable characters came off the page and began filling store shelves when Hungerford Plastics Corporation produced the first polyvinyl figurines in 1958, followed by merchandizing powerhouse Connie Boucher's smash-hit idea of Schulz's booklet *Happiness is a Warm Puppy*. Wanting to maintain control over his own creation, Sparky had insisted on actively approving his merchandise, resulting in a struggle at times between him and the United Media agents, who originally retained licensing authority. He had grown accustomed to approving individual uses of his strips for various groups, but he would occasionally wrestle with what products bore the image of his creations, once telling an interviewer that the way products skewed the franchise towards a kiddy property sometimes frustrated him: "If you have to do something for children, that's fine, but let's not forget that our main reading audience is out there among the college kids, and in the fathers and mothers and grandmothers. . . . I have not been able to close the floodgates. The children's products just keep coming."[4]

After renegotiating his contract, Sparky not only ensured that no other artist would take over the strips, he also gained approval status over all uses of his art, a relinquishing of control that the syndicate officials feared. His monstrous success and his own track record of sound artistic choices, however, made the syndicate unable to resist their most profitable artist. With his new contractual authority, Sparky did not shoot down the licensing, but instead weeded out the outliers, like the Charlie Brown-branded razor blades for sale in Germany that did not fit either Sparky's personal or brand ethos. "Whose idea was that?" an annoyed Sparky asked. "Charlie Brown shouldn't be selling razor blades."[5]

With approval rights at his command, licensing still continued under Sparky's increasingly busy eye, thanks to the help of associates like business managers Warren Lockhart and Ron Nelson who had proven themselves trusted allies through Joyce's ice arena endeavors. In 1970, they formed the Charles M. Schulz Creative Development Corporation to manage the franchise's business operations, with Lockhart named as president and Nelson as manager. Sparky had given a secretary position to one of his Methodist church Sunday school class members, Evelyn Ellison. The licensing would then continue through the business division after Sparky's death (the corporation later renamed Charles M. Schulz Creative Associates), a reality that he never attempted to prevent. His had not been an aspendental dream of great success and wealth that could quietly help others, but such had become his life. "There were a lot of people that were supported by the licensing business of *Peanuts*," one of the artist's close business associates later explained, "and he recognized that; he felt responsible for those people. He was a realist."[6]

Taking over the licensing process a decade after Sparky's passing, the Iconix brand agents went through what Neil Cole described as a "painful time" trying to re-engineer the *Peanuts* business model from the myriad of small deals that Sparky had routinely approved toward larger licensee relationships that would make their business model more streamlined and profitable. A key component in the process of maintaining not only profits but also the essence of Schulz's characters would require relying on the melding of business and art management that Schulz had begun when he established the separate business side of the studio. Established to see to the ever-growing demands of licensing, the team at Creative Associates would make it their mission to continue to leave Sparky's mark on *Peanuts* products, long after he was gone.

Reviewing between 2,000 and 6,000 product requests each month (depending on the season), it has been the task of the dozen members of Creative Associates to work with licensees to produce merchandise artistically and thematically consistent with their understandings of Sparky's ethos. A semi-uniform understanding is guided by their "quick-reference art guide," which reminds the agents and licensees that "it is important to realize that it is not only the visual image that is used in a design that we review for approval, but also the spirit and context in which that image is used."[7] The guide clarifies that art from different decades should not be mixed, line quality should not be altered, and Snoopy should never be given shoes. But with nearly 18,000 comic strips and several canonized television specials as source material, the task of editorial review is not merely algorithmic.

Perhaps more potent than the handbook, this process of maintaining fidelity to Schulz's artwork has been guided since Sparky's death by Creative Associate's vice president and creative director, Paige Braddock. Working with licensees selling products in over forty countries, Braddock, the Eisner Award-nominated creator of the *Jane's World* comic strip, provides the artistic and copy-editing direction for the entire team. The task is one Braddock has taken seriously, having been hired directly by Sparky himself.

She had bumped into him once in a gift shop in the early 1990s, and had her first conversation with him a few years later at a National Cartoonists Society convention. Walking the grounds of the hotel, she saw Sparky, the comic giant himself, playing catch with Jeannie. Paige sat on the steps to admire the scene, and much to everyone's surprise the sprinklers soon came on. Escaping from the insistent irrigation system, Sparky went and sat by Paige, asking to see her sketchbook. Surprising her again, Sparky quickly interjected one of his profound inquiries into the conversation, asking about Paige's thoughts on a tragic shooting recently in the news. "In the absence of a good explanation for these evil acts," she said to Sparky, "does anyone ever consider that evil is a force in the world?"[8] Impressed by the potency of her reply, Sparky pondered the theological and social implications of the question with Paige before returning to the routine of the convention.

Not long after this chance meeting (which Paige retells to anyone who questions whether or not something like "fate" is real), Sparky offered Paige a job. She had been ill-prepared for a conference speech and had decided instead to go on a soapbox-style rant, trying to impress upon the audience the need to eschew superficial concerns about the newest gimmick in favor of instead consciously working to improve one's craft. Impressed by her commitment to craft, Sparky once again approached Paige, later noting that he did so because he knew she would not be afraid to turn him down. "I don't know exactly what you do," he said to her after the speech, "but do you want a job?"[9]

Braddock said yes, and Sparky gave her the position of creative director at Creative Associates, allowing Sparky to continue his work without micromanaging the licensing. Like Jeannie and Craig, and the many other workers in and around the museum, ice arena, and *Peanuts* offices, Paige's personal interaction with Sparky gave her a deep sense of respect for the art and ethos of the characters that Sparky had created. As a former divinity student at Emory's Candler School of Theology, Braddock had been aware of Sparky's religious beliefs and curiosities from their first sprinkler-prompted encounter, a sensitivity she would have to occasionally employ in her position as creative director.

Though Sparky had been inundated early in his career with requests from church groups hoping to use his characters in their publications, religiously related requests have not been particularly numerous for Creative Associates. The market for branded religious products is simply not something most major merchandizers and retailers are attracted to, fearing ostracizing non-religious consumers. "You're not going to see big T-shirt companies doing John 3:16 [on a shirt]," commented one member of Creative Associates. "Walmart or Kmart or Target are not going to buy it, for better or worse. But that's just the reality of global capitalism."[10] Yet significant amounts of religious products are purchased each year, amounting to a $4.6 billion annual industry, with a majority of products purchased through religious stores—twice as many Christian books, for instance, are purchased through Christian retailers than mass merchandisers.[11]

"Christian bookstores," explains sociologist Anne Borden, "and the sale of Christian commercialized material culture survive against a background of secularization."[12] Organizations like the CBA (formerly called the Christian Booksellers Association) attempt to fulfill their mission to "help improve the business conditions for Christian retail"[13] that the secularization of the mass-market challenges, bringing together producers and retailers through global networks facilitated by efforts like the annual International Christian Retail Show. One will not typically find major franchise brands gracing the products at the show, but to the surprise of some, Charlie Brown, Snoopy, and the gang can be found in Christian bookstores.

Hallmark began producing *Peanuts* cards in 1960, and its acquisition of Christian card company DaySpring in 1999 gave it the opportunity to capitalize on its unique relationship with Schulz's brand inside the massive niche market of religious retail. In what Paige calls a "religion-lite" style of licensing, Hallmark produces greeting cards and tchotchkes such as mugs, calendars, and partyware featuring the *Peanuts* characters alongside scriptural verses that are at least superficially related. A 2014 party set napkin, for example, featuring Charlie Brown and Snoopy with the text "Celebrate with great JOY" is captioned with the book and verse "Nehemiah 8:12." While the scriptural text is not present, the chapter and verse label near the text of course implies to the napkin's purchaser and user that the phrase must have a biblical connection.[14]

Similarly, in a 2010 "thinking of you" greeting card, artistically embossed with black felt, Linus says on the front of the card, "It's been shown that elevated levels of stress can result in highly irrational behavior." The large image of Linus is above the rare reprint of one of Schulz's strip panels in which Linus reads to Charlie Brown an abbreviated version of I Kings 19:4: "And Elijah fled into the wilderness, and sat under a broom tree, and said, 'I am no better than my fathers'" (to which Charlie Brown replies, "He was really depressed," and Snoopy thinks, "A wirehaired fox terrier could have cheered him up . ."). Inside, the card continues with, "In your case, I'm prescribing elevated levels of fun immediately!" across from the caption, "A cheerful heart is good medicine. PROVERBS 17:22 NIV." This card is comparatively more substantive, with the verse quoted and the strip panel present, but the product still reflects conspicuous editorial restraint, employing only a broadly applicable, de-contextualized proverb.

In 2014, Hallmark reported that their growing DaySpring line could be found in "more than 2,000 Christian retail stores in the U.S. and in 60 countries around the world." Many of these stores feature large displays of the religion-lite *Peanuts* cards; a 2012 line contained more than forty variations that the card giant adds to each year. As it releases more cards, though, it must abide by the editorial direction of Creative Associates, which requires that the characters are not shown expressing theological statements or reciting Bible verses themselves (unless it is in the rare direct reprint of a strip). Over the years, the greeting card editorializing has tended to run smoothly, given the companies' collaborative origins; Sparky originally drew the art for the Hallmark cards. This congenial relationship notwithstanding, it is no small matter that Snoopy is found dancing across the fold from a Bible verse; it is something consumers will not find Mickey Mouse, Barbie, or GI Joe doing in a Christian bookstore, or any store for that matter.

The Christian content is allowed because of a strong devotion to Schulzian fidelity that most all of the workers associated with *Peanuts* have, many of them knowing Sparky personally. In the art guide they provide to licensees, the team explains, "You may feel we do not understand the market when we reject something, or request a correction. However, our first concern is always the protection of the *Peanuts* characters as created by Charles Schulz."[15] Not all of those working in

The Charles M. Schulz Museum and Research Center in Santa Rosa, California. 2012. Photo by author.

Schulz's vicarious stead have the exact same interpretation of the lay theologian's religious perspective, of course, so certain principles help guide the creative design process. The Creative Associates art guide instructs licensees: "Do not make references to alcohol"; "Do not use Peanuts artwork in morally suggestive designs"; and "Do not mix Peanuts artwork with overtly religious elements." But Paige has no doubts about the property's religious heritage. "You'd be hard pressed to say that *Peanuts* does not come from a Christian background," she says. "It is Sparky—'I grew up in Minnesota, I went to the Church of God.' You don't want to pretend that you don't have that."[16] Hallmark associating the characters with Christian platitudes is thus thematically coherent with Sparky's own religious history, and his pervasive Christian references across the franchise make it difficult to argue against such reasonable use.

Sparky's work had an openness that, when presented in its own right, could strongly connect with diverse audiences. In 2002, under Jeannie's leadership, the Charles M. Schulz Museum and Research Center opened, showcasing the 7,000 original comic strips that remained in

Sparky's estate, a Schulzian biographic timeline, and rotating thematic exhibits. The museum would not typically make explicit statements on Schulz's religious perspectives in the exhibits, though, leaving the set of *The Interpreter's Bible* on display in their permanent recreation of Sparky's studio to speak for itself. Specific requests from licensees, though, require more specific approaches.

"A lot of licensees we've worked with for a long time," the creative director explains. "There's only a few that require a lot of hands-on management. A lot of those are: open it, check it, make sure they didn't use profanity or alcohol."[17] Other editorial decisions, though, are not so simple for Paige and the team at Creative Associates. Holding to an undefined sense of Schulzian fidelity while also protecting and promoting the brand's place in the global marketplace can pose quite the challenge, especially in the context of diverse religious product proposals. "It's a balancing act," Paige says, knowing that the franchise does not want to be known as an evangelical property like *VeggieTales* or *Superbook*. Weighing the profitability of an idea against the brand's conceptual self-identity and a desire to be true to Sparky Schulz results in some ideas being rejected, including ideas that would transgress the religious interests of the brand or Schulz himself.

In various Asian cultures, for instance, such as in the lucrative Japanese market, licensees often want to place popular culture icons in front of tourist attractions on postcards and souvenir merchandise. Many of these attractions, however, include Buddhist temples and shrines. While Sanrio's *Hello Kitty* has obliged,[18] the *Peanuts* executives are more hesitant. "We have some tough editorial conversations about how we can accommodate that without looking like we're trying to be Buddhist," Braddock says. The tacit endorsement of Snoopy at a shrine creates not only a conflict for the brand that would often prefer to be areligious, but also for the desire for Schulzian consistency, given that Sparky did not endorse Buddhism. Chinese licensees likewise offer a salient editorial challenge, as many of the requests involve references to astrological horoscopes that Schulz himself did not care for and poked fun at in strips.[19] "You have to be relevant in some way to a buyer in China," Braddock explains, adding that "every year it's a struggle with how we honor that while still keeping an editorial boundary." The way that struggle would be managed would shift at times. In 2015, one of the licensing artists at Creative Associates noted that they had "loosened up a little in the last couple years," and had worked with a licensee to approve production of a new series of Snoopy figurines to celebrate the festive zodiac animals of the Chinese New Year.

Charles Schulz was not one to actively speak against particular non-Christian religions, but the only sacred religious tradition he ever explicitly endorsed was a biblical one, even when explaining what he meant by "secular humanism." Though Schulz poked fun in short-lived references to non-Christian elements in strips such as Snoopy reaching the alpha state in meditation and trying to divine his way to answers through his Beagle Board, the cartoonist did not produce any recurring strip motifs in which he supported non-biblical religions in *Peanuts*. Readers will not find strips in which Linus expounds upon the historical settings of a Buddhist text, in which Marcie ponders the tenets of Hinduism, or in which Charlie Brown wonders if he would ever reach an Islamic paradise. These were simply outside of Schulz's Christian studies and beliefs. This general Christian backstop has provided an editorial benchmark that the franchise executives have tentatively held on to, despite the short-term financial temptation of a new licensee.

For Paige and others at Creative Associates, the clearest justification, perhaps even requirement, for religious content in product merchandizing presents itself in print adaptations of *A Charlie Brown Christmas*, the animated special that Schulz had insisted contain the biblical telling of Christ's birth. Book publishers wishing to print various book incarnations of the holiday classic are granted almost instant approval to include the passage from the Gospel of Luke, given that it was a part of the original script. Over the years, though, some publishers have sought just the opposite—to omit Linus's recitation of the Scripture in hopes of making the book more broadly appealing to non-Christian buyers. Such was reportedly the case for a board book published in 2007 by Running Press Kidz, adapted by *Pearls Before Swine* cartoonist Stephan Pastis and illustrated by Creative Associate's Justin Thompson. Thumbing through the book during an interview, one member of the team recalled, "the publishers requested that we take this part [Linus's recitation of the Gospel] out, because they wanted to keep it lively and everything, and we fought them on it because it's the soul of the whole piece, it's the point of the whole thing, and we finally got our way."[20] It is a fight that

Schulz himself began in 1965—"If we don't do it, who will?" Sparky had asked when he met resistance over including religion in his holiday classic—and the Creative Associates team knows it. "That's where I draw the line," says Braddock. "That would not be honoring who Schulz was." The biblical Christmas text must remain.

This is not to say that all *Peanuts* Christmas products contain a gospel message, however. A 2010 Hallmark sound recording greeting card contains a shortened version of Linus's speech that still references God but omits the reference to the birth of Christ. Linus is left speaking a generic message of serenity instead of divinity when the reader opens the card: "And suddenly there was with the angel a multitude of the heavenly host, praising God and saying 'glory to God in the highest and on Earth, peace, goodwill toward men.' That's what Christmas is all about, Charlie Brown!"

More provocatively, a 2011 plush Linus doll from Hallmark speaks a poorly abbreviated version of the gospel text that avoids all explicit references to the biblical message, redirecting Schulz's statement of "what Christmas is all about" from the birth of Christ to a secular seasonal greeting: "For behold, I bring you tidings of great joy, which will be to all people. And on Earth, peace, goodwill toward men. That's what Christmas is all about, Charlie Brown."

Sometimes, albeit rarely, products simply slip through the system without consistent editorial corrective, such as a Snoopy greeting card that uses the acronym "P.O.O.P." to refer to a "Person Of Outstanding Pedigree" or a Charlie Brown T-shirt that reads "I'm just one big freaking ray of sunshine aren't I?" Though not particularly vulgar by most twenty-first-century standards, toilet humor and euphemisms were not part of Schulz's personal or artistic vernacular, and would normally be edited out by the appropriate agent at Creative Associates. Other companies, though, also exert influence on the process, at times pushing the editorial balance. Hallmark, for example, has enjoyed success through its DaySpring line, but also has a much larger global footprint than just its religious subdivision. The 2011 Linus plush was marketed in Hallmark's mainstream stores, making a secularizing approach to the product appear commercially attractive. According to Hallmark creative director Peggy Wrightsman-Parolin, the *Peanuts* franchise "knows no religion, nor nationality. This has been the guiding principle for how

As Joseph and Mary, Charlie Brown and Lucy accompany the figure of the baby Jesus in the 2001 "Peanuts Pageant" Hallmark Keepsake Ornament. Photo by author.

Hallmark has used the *Peanuts* characters on products throughout the years."[21] Given the desire to reach global audiences with little overhead, removing religious reference can be attractive for some companies, just as producing potently religious products are for others. Creative Associates is tasked with managing that balance.

The sort of editorial balance that the caretakers of Schulz's work attempt to produce is evident in various nativity displays sold at Christmastime. The *Peanuts* characters can be found acting out the scene of Mary and Joseph by the manger in products such as Christmas ornaments, snow globes, and mantle-top nativity crèche displays. For Braddock, working with licensees to produce appropriate nativity scenes is "a big kind of editorial problem . . . because who's baby Jesus in that scenario?" Some feature a realistic baby, such as the 2001 Hallmark Keepsake ornament that has Charlie Brown (as Joseph) and Lucy (as Mary) looking down upon a smiling face and tuft of hair coming out of a bundle of swaddling cloth.

2007 Lenox crèche, delicately crafted and ornamented with 24 karat gold, titled "The Christmas Pageant." Originally retailed for $179. Photo by author.

The franchise's preferred artistic answer, however, is often to have Woodstock fill in for the Christ child, as in the case of the high-end 2007 Lenox crèche, originally retailing at $179. In this beautifully crafted, hand-painted set of ivory fine China, 24-karat gold accents the white straw of Woodstock's manger bed. The editorial goal is not to defile the sacred image by having Snoopy's ill-flighted friend claim divine rights, but rather to orient the scene as performance, not history—as a holiday custom, not a supernatural truth. Sally, as a shepherd, still has her bow in her hair, wise man Linus carries his blanket, and a modernly decorated Christmas tree completes the set.

Ensuring that the brand's position is clear, the display, like all of the *Peanuts* nativity displays, is labeled as a "pageant." The Lenox set is "The Christmas Pageant," and the Hallmark ornament is "Peanuts Pageant." A 2011 "Mini Figure Set with Fold-Out Christmas Play Stage" by Forever Fun makes the point clear, with a toy sign included in the set that reads "CHRISTMAS PLAY TODAY 4:00 P.M." Snoopy wears a removable sheep costume (though devoted fans know that he can be all the animals in the play), and Sally wears makeshift angel garb, complete with removable wings and a halo made of tinsel. The fabrication choice

Sally Brown figurine from 2007 Forever Fun toy set, featuring removable angel wings and tinsel halo. Photo by author.

is not an economical one—it would be easier, more efficient, and less expensive to produce Sally from one plastic mold. The mixed-media parts, though, are purposefully chosen, and dramatically emphasize that Sally is taking part in a holiday tradition—a children's Christmas pageant—not asserting the historical accuracy of the biblical tale.

While the subtleties of this choice may not be apparent to all consumers when they purchase the $20 Forever Fun set from their local store, the difference is important for the *Peanuts* executives, affording them a mechanism to balance their desires for fidelity and franchise marketability. Schulz himself did not want to brand his *Peanuts* work as evangelical, a point franchise executives are quick to remember, and the pageant-versus-proclamation delineation provides them the editorial compromise they need.

Whether or not the editorial decisions are noticeable for any individual consumer, the products remain meaningful for millions of fans. For some, new products add to lifetime collections, ongoing since Sparky himself was alive and producing new strips each day. When collector extraordinaire Freddi Margolin sold her collection of *Peanuts* products, a collection that was overflowing her Long Island basement, her assortment spread to new homes, and she netted enough in sales to move to Florida and begin taking in rescue dogs—including foster dogs named Lucy Van Pelt, Linus, and Sally Brown.

For others, the joy of *Peanuts* merchandise is borne out in single impulse purchases. When these purchases are of religiously related goods, the power of the religious message shifts away from the editorializing franchise agents to the hands of the consumers. Though somewhat constrained by the production choices, the purchasers of greeting cards at local Christian bookstores are nonetheless prompted by the blank space in the card to write their own message—one that corresponds to the scriptural caption across the fold. The owners of a *Peanuts* nativity mini-figure set are encouraged to allow their children to play with the depiction of the biblical story, even if twice removed as a *Peanuts* pageant. The owners of the manger ornament or high-end crèche are compelled to put it on display, thus making a religious statement about the season visible to friends and family visiting their homes during the season. Some fans take it even further, allowing the beloved characters to speak their religious interests for them through their own unlicensed adaptations. A Montana woman, for example, enlarged the art from a *Peanuts* greeting card to fashion a 3-foot plywood version of Charlie Brown and the gang approaching the Bethlehem manger, joyously displaying the recreation in her family's suburban yard since 2003.[22]

The franchise executives' desire to see this attraction to *Peanuts* passed on to a new generation has resulted not just in new merchandizing but also in new source material, including a new line of comic books through BOOM! Studios and new animated features. When scripting 2011's *Happiness is a Warm Blanket, Charlie Brown*, co-writer Craig Schulz held tightly to his father's work, drawing the dialogue for the animated special directly and almost exclusively from Schulz's original strip. Clinging so tightly to the original words risked crushing its charm, and exacerbated the challenge of filling in the gaps. When the script called for Linus to vehemently preach from the top of Snoopy's doghouse, a small debate ensued over how to word a brief line of religious text; these words were among the very few in the feature not taken from the strips. Writing with Stephan Pastis, Craig wanted to modify the wording of Linus's scriptural reference, while Amy insisted that their father was not one to modify Scriptures but would have instead used the literal quotation. The disagreement was solved by calling *The Gospel According to Peanuts* author Robert Short, who assured the two that the modified language reflected the way many in the church typically repeat John 8:7.[23] Linus thus preaches to the blanket-criticizing gang, each with their own insecurities: "Who among you can cast the first stone?"

Steve Martino, director of the 2015 computer-animated 3-D *Peanuts* feature film adaptation from Fox's Blue Sky Studios, intended to reignite the franchise's draw amongst younger consumers, was chosen by Craig, who wrote the screenplay with his son (with the blessing of the rest of the Schulz children, who have approval authority over new projects but who have invested time in their own pursuits and are not as directly involved in the franchise as Craig and Jeannie), because Martino expressed a sincere respect for Schulz's original work. Making Sparky's former studio in Santa Rosa into what Jeannie described as the film team's "sort of second home," Martino instructed his animators to "find the pen line of Sparky." "We spent well over a year studying how [Sparky] put pencil lines down and how he created that emotion—how the dot of an eye [conveyed] joy or sorrow," the director said, adding in awe, "Really, it's a Picasso drawing."[24]

Martino had successfully worked with Theodor (Dr. Suess) Geisel's widow, Audrey, on the 2008 CGI version of *Horton Hears a Who*, and he impressed the Schulz team as they planned to launch into a new animated realm. Knowing that he had to find a way to maintain the original work while respecting his new canvas, just as Bill Melendez did, Martino assured the heirs to Sparky's world that he would not stray far from its traditions, but would breathe a fresh breath of its own life back into it for its new visit to the screen, complete with "Linus saying something philosophical and very adult coming out of a voice of someone so young."

Whether or not Linus and the rest of the cast continue to explore religious tendencies and personal spiritual truths in their animated or merchandized reflections will depend on such creative and branding affordances, likely made possible only by a continued reflection on

Schulzian fidelity. Franchise executives may not all be able to command a Schulzian spiritual voice apart from what is extant in the strips, but Schulz's work has left more than enough evidence that religious pondering is as much a part of *Peanuts* as footballs or kite-eating trees.

Sparky's original work, reprinted in newspapers around the globe, continues to inspire individuals to reflect on their own spiritual thoughts. For the January 31, 2005, daily reading in the lite-Christian devotional, *Our Daily Bread*, Anne Cetas used the May 1, 1985, *Peanuts* strip, in which Peppermint Patty questions the exchange value of her own good intentions, to illustrate James 4:17—"To him who knows to do good and does not do it, to him it is sin." Similarly, in 2004, Radio Bible Ministries out of Grand Rapids, Michigan, produced a pamphlet entitled "Been Thinking About Snoopy," using Snoopy as a metaphor for thinking about the character of God. The pamphlet ends with a prayer:

> Father, thank You for a man named Charles Schulz who brought us elements of truth amid our smiles. Thank You for being God on Your terms rather than ours. May Your name be hallowed as we wait on You. May Your kingdom be reflected in our patience. May Your will be done in our disappointments. Please, give us this day our daily bread.[25]

As individuals continue to reflect on Charles Schulz's strips, it is all but guaranteed that what Charlie Brown had to say on the topic of religion will continue to echo across cultures. Just as with the church groups in the 1950s, the present and the future of the *Peanuts* franchise lies not only with its formal artists, its gatekeepers, and its caretakers, but also with those everyday people who it has deeply impacted—those that circulate, display, cherish, and consider *Peanuts*' truths. They are the readers that chuckle . . . the viewers that sigh . . . and all the Charlie Browns of the world that simply understand.

"Blessed are those who mourn, for they will be comforted."

"Blessed are the meek, for they will inherit the earth."[26]

ACKNOWLEDGMENTS

"He knows your heart," Sparky had said of his Heavenly Father. Though I claim no great expertise in the divine work of blessings, it is clear to me that this project has been a more wonderful gift than I could have imagined to ask for. For this, and for so many things in my life, I am so deeply thankful. This most personal and prayerful of thanks I mention first so as to not give the impression that it is mere afterthought. It most assuredly is not. If anything, it has been a humbling and motivating ever-present thought.

Here on terra firma, there has been such a wonderful network of support that has made this part of my research life possible. How I could have ever made it through the highs and lows without my family, I cannot fathom to guess. From my parents, Donna and Ken, faithfully reading my drafts along with me, to my sister, Jennifer, hunting with me for just the right phrases (not to mention traveling with me on one last and very exciting archival trip), I owe them so very much. When I returned home during academic breaks, my older brother, Matt, listened as I filled him in on my journeys before I stopped down the road at our ever-supportive Grandma Maxine's house to pick up the clippings from the funny pages that she and her cat Elmer were keeping for me. Whether or not completion of this book will change the routine of purchasing *Peanuts* gifts for me at Christmas remains to be seen, but I have no doubt that the support of my family will endure.

As I mentioned in the Introduction and Author's Note, the family, friends, and associates of Charles Schulz are also to be thanked for their support of this project. Jeannie, Meredith, Monte, Craig, Amy, and Jill, and a wide host of Sparky's broader family and circle of friends, continue to share his generosity long after his passing. Special thanks are also warmly directed toward those at Charles M. Schulz Creative Associates, its creative director, Paige Braddock, and its staff, along with the Charles M. Schulz Museum and Research Center, including its archivist Cesar Gallegos, former archival assistant Gretchen Emmert, and especially former archivist Lisa Monhoff, without whose insights and unwavering assistance my trips to the archives would have certainly been less enjoyable. As I have mentioned many times over the course of this research, I enjoy the privilege of being part of that rare bracket of researchers who get to chuckle out loud while doing scholarly work.

The list of Sparky's friends, collaborators, and associated organizations who aided my work continues well beyond what is listed here, including Lee Mendelson, Evert Brown, Bill Melendez Productions and Sopwith Productions archives, The Schulz Family Trust, Peanuts Worldwide, Universal UClick, McCann Erickson, Hallmark, the Library of Congress, the Ronald Reagan Presidential Library, the Billy Graham Evangelistic Association, Ken Hall, Warner Press, Anderson University, St. Mary's College, the Peanuts Collector's Club, David Liverett, the First Church of God in Minneapolis, and the Sebastopol United Methodist Church. To these individuals and organizations, and to the many, many other individuals that I met and corresponded with, thank you so very much.

I must also heartily thank those who matched the open generosity of Schulz's personal acquaintances by providing the financial and logistical resources needed to conduct this sort of research. Those individuals and organizations include Washington and Lee University, including the supportive leaders in its Williams School and Office of the Provost, the university's Lenfest Grant program, and the university's Summer Research Scholar program, including outstanding summer research intern Katie Price. Additional thanks are due to the University of Phoenix Office of Scholarship Support, Clemson University's Graduate Student Government, Clemson's Office of Online Education, an array of dedicated librarians across the country, and the Santa Rosa Bible Church's Stan and Lori Willis.

In early phases of this project, I was propelled by wonderful support from academic mentors and friends, including Dr. Andy Billings, Dr. Stephanie Barczewski, Dr. Cynthia Haynes, Dr. Victor Vitanza, and certainly Dr. Tom Inge, who helped facilitate my initial introduction to the Schulz family. Along with others, Tom helped remind me of the scholarly viability of this study, a theme that had begun many years earlier with the open support from academic mentors Dr. Lynnda Beavers and Dr. Faith Mullen, for whom I will always be so thoroughly grateful.

Before leaving these pages, I should also say thanks to those inspirations with whom I had very little direct interaction, but who had very real impacts on the drafting phase of this work. To break myself from the labyrinthine dust of the archives as I began my own writing, I began listening to the engaging prose of John Green, whom I had heard speak at VidCon, and the stirring acoustic echoes of pianist Chad Lawson, whom I had heard speak on NPR. Both, and many other creative properties that I binged on between drafts, served as sources of not only much-needed respite but also much-enjoyed refueling. Lawson's Chopin album in particular will continue to haunt me in very powerful ways, especially his serendipitously Schulzian statement, "Space is my favorite note."

Finally, many thanks are due to the University Press of Mississippi and its staff, especially editor Vijay Shah. A leader in popular culture and comics scholarship, their shared vision for this work has allowed it to reach your hands in its current form.

This long list of thanks does not diminish the sincerity with which I use the term. Many other friends, family, and colleagues passed along insights, encouragements, and *Peanuts* collectibles over the years, for which I am truly grateful. The world likewise continues to say thanks to Charles Schulz each year as so very many still read his strips, watch his holiday classics, and place figurines of his beloved characters on their mantels for friends and family to see. To have now contributed even a small entry to the history of such a globally influential and personally meaningful property has not only been an intellectually rewarding challenge, it has also been an honor and a true joy. To all those whose paths have woven in and supported mine along the way, let me say once more, *thank you.*

—SL

APPENDIX I

CODING PROCEDURE

IN ORDER TO GET DETAILED DATA ON THE FREQUENCY AND TYPES OF RELIGIOUS references in the *Peanuts* comic strips and animated specials, they were "coded" (labeled) according to the following process. Each of the 17,897 *Peanuts* newspaper comic strips was individually read and each of the seventy-five animated titles was viewed and then coded for any religious reference. For the purposes of coding, "religious references" are defined as: any recognizable visual or verbal reference (explicit or embedded) to supernatural faith, theology, pneumatology, church practice, or religious iconography. Of course, any attempt to define religion will highlight the fact that the term has rather blurred boundaries. The operationalized definition used in this study is intended to cast an inclusive net, catching not just elements like the recitation of Christian Scriptures and descriptions of church groups singing hymns but also moments where the mystical practices of fortune-telling and Native American spiritual lore are featured. This study's approach is consistent with other major studies relying on religious coding (e.g., Skill et al and Clarke). Coding was also done for further details including which character made the reference and what themes/topics/tropes were included in the reference.

When it was unclear if a strip or animated scene had a religious reference, according to the definition above, a two-step standard was applied to determine if the instance would be coded for religious reference: 1) *Is it possible to interpret the strip/scene areligiously without losing significant meaning?* If no, then the strip/scene is significantly associated with religion and should be coded as such. If yes, it can be read areligiously without harm to the humor or narrative, then 2) *Are there cues within the context of the strip/scene that indicate that the humor, topical inference, or narrative content should be associated with religious thought or action?* If no, then for the purpose of this study the strip/scene was not considered to have a religious reference. If yes, then the strip/scene was coded as containing a religious reference.

This litmus test allows the scholar to use the artifact itself as the test for whether or not unclear elements should be viewed as secular or religiously affiliated. For instance, in the December 17, 1987, strip, a girl in Linus's class tells him her name is Lydia, but it has been changed from Rachel and Rebecca. One could read the strip areligiously, but the combination of three distinct Old Testament names within one strip serves as the tipping point of the joke and justifies a religious reading, so the strip was coded as such. Conversely, in the June 6, 1963, strip, Linus and Lucy squabble over counting one's blessings. While the phrase "count your blessings" is used within religious discourse, it can be interpreted areligiously as a "glass-is-half-full" practice, and there are no verbal or visual cues within the strip to indicate that the reader should interpret the meaning as associated with religious discourse, so it was not coded as a religious reference.

In the event that a strip was part of a narrative series that contained religious reference, and if the strip in question has unclear content that may be considered religious, the adjacent days' strips were allowed to clarify the meaning of the strip. This allowed for the inclusion of the September 13, 1984, strip, in which an actual spiritual ghost appears to be haunting Peppermint Patty's desk. The strip is part of a series, but on this day the haunting persists with no explanation, requiring the reader to have read the previous day's strip to understand why the teacher had turned pale. Also, authorial intent was allowed in one instance to influence an unclear answer to the second of the two-step questions. On March 22, 1959, when Linus builds a sandcastle that is washed away by the water, the answer to the second question of the two-step test was marginally debatable, but Schulz said in an interview that it was a religious reference to Matthew 7, so it was coded as such.

As with the *Los Angeles Times* study by Lindsey and Hereen, there was a class of references that was excluded because they were merely thin uses of words that had only marginally weak ties to religion, such as strips in which Snoopy eats "angel food cake" or those where characters talk about being "moral" or being a "hypocrite." Also, because they have been secularized in contemporary culture, the holidays Easter, Christmas, and Halloween were not coded for religious reference, nor were legendary characters like Santa Claus, the Tooth Fairy, or characters shown only through Halloween costumes, unless the strip or animated scene contained other salient indications of religious or spiritual meaning. Likewise, strips referencing the Great Pumpkin were not included unless they otherwise contained references to religious belief or practice within the strip, such as when Linus would go door-to-door with tracts to share the message of the Great Pumpkin. Though several of the Great Pumpkin strips were included in the 1984 collection of Schulz's theological strips, *And the Beagles and the Bunnies Shall Lie Down Together*, Schulz explained that the Great Pumpkin originated as an idea in which Linus gets confused between the Great Pumpkin and Santa Claus, and many of the strips operate under that secular premise. When other elements in the strip direct a religious interpretation, strips were coded for such. Schulz did take occasion to associate the Great Pumpkin with religious belief—but simply not every strip that contains the Great Pumpkin contains an identifiable association with religious thought or action, just as every Christmas strip does not contain explicit religious content.

APPENDIX II

LIST OF ANIMATED TITLES AND THEIR AWARDS

TITLE	YEAR	NETWORK	RELEASE/PREMIERE DATE	AWARDS/NOMINATIONS
A Charlie Brown Christmas	1965	CBS	December 9, 1965 (Thursday)	Emmy: Outstanding Children's Program (Winner); Special Classification of Individual Achievement—Charles Schulz/ writer (Nominee); Peabody Award for excellence in broadcasting
Charlie Brown's All-Stars	1966	CBS	June 8, 1966 (Wednesday)	Emmy: Outstanding Children's Program (Nominee); Special Classification of Individual Achievements—Charles Schulz/ writer (Nominee)
It's the Great Pumpkin, Charlie Brown	1966	CBS	October 27, 1966 (Thursday)	Emmy: Outstanding Children's Program (Nominee); Special Classification of Individual Achievements—Bill Melendez/ director (Nominee)
You're In Love, Charlie Brown	1967	CBS	June 12, 1967 (Monday)	Emmy: Outstanding Achievement in Children's Programming—Lee Mendelson (Nominee); Special Classifications of Individual Achievements—Charles Schulz/ writer (Nominee); Special Classifications of Individual Achievements—Bill Melendez/ director (Nominee)
He's Your Dog, Charlie Brown	1968	CBS	February 14, 1968 (Wednesday)	Emmy: Outstanding Achievement in Children's Programming—Lee Mendelson/producer (Nominee)
It was a Short Summer, Charlie Brown	1969	CBS	September 27, 1969 (Saturday)	

TITLE	YEAR	NETWORK	RELEASE/PREMIERE DATE	AWARDS/NOMINATIONS
A Boy Named Charlie Brown	1969	Theatrical Release: Cinema Center Films; CBS	Original Theatrical Release December 4, 1969 (Thursday); Broadcast Network Premiere/CBS April 16, 1976 (Friday)	Academy Award: Best Music—Original Song Score/Vince Guaraldi, Rod McKuen, Bill Melendez, Al Shean, and John Scott Trotter (Nominee)
Play it Again, Charlie Brown	1971	CBS	March 28, 1971 (Sunday)	Emmy: Outstanding Achievement in Children's Programming—John Scott Trotter/music director (Nominee)
Snoopy Come Home	1972	Theatrical Release: Cinema Center Films; CBS	Original Theatrical Release July 14, 1972 (Friday); Broadcast Network Premiere/CBS November 5, 1976 (Friday)	Cinema Writers Circle Awards, Spain: Best Children's Film (Winner)
You're Not Elected, Charlie Brown	1972	CBS	October 29, 1972 (Sunday)	Emmy: Outstanding Achievement in Children's Programming—Charles Schulz/writer (Nominee)
There's No Time for Love, Charlie Brown	1973	CBS	March 11, 1973 (Sunday)	
A Charlie Brown Thanksgiving	1973	CBS	November 20, 1973 (Tuesday)	Emmy: Outstanding Individual Achievement in Children's Programming—Charles Schulz/writer (Winner); Outstanding Children's Special (Nominee)
It's a Mystery, Charlie Brown	1974	CBS	February 1, 1974 (Friday)	
It's the Easter Beagle, Charlie Brown	1974	CBS	April 9, 1974 (Tuesday)	Emmy: Outstanding Children's Special (Nominee)
Be My Valentine, Charlie Brown	1975	CBS	January 28, 1975 (Tuesday)	Emmy: Outstanding Children's Special (Nominee)
You're a Good Sport, Charlie Brown	1975	CBS	October 28, 1975 (Tuesday)	Emmy: Outstanding Children's Special (Winner)
It's Arbor Day, Charlie Brown	1976	CBS	March 16, 1976 (Tuesday)	Emmy: Outstanding Children's Special (Nominee)
Race For Your Life, Charlie Brown	1977	Theatrical Release: Paramount; CBS/HBO	Original Theatrical Release June 3, 1977 (Friday); Premium Cable Release/HBO May 12, 1978 (Friday); Broadcast Network Premiere/CBS November 3, 1979 (Saturday)	

It's Your First Kiss, Charlie Brown	1977	CBS	October 24, 1977 (Monday)	
What a Nightmare, Charlie Brown	1978	CBS	February 23, 1978 (Thursday)	
You're the Greatest, Charlie Brown	1979	CBS	March 19, 1979 (Monday)	Emmy: Outstanding Animated Program (Nominee)
She's a Good Skate, Charlie Brown	1980	CBS	February 25, 1980 (Monday)	Emmy: Outstanding Animated Program (Nominee)
Bon Voyage, Charlie Brown (And Don't Come Back!)	1980	Theatrical Release: Paramount; CBS/HBO	Original Theatrical Release June 13, 1980; Premium Cable Release/ HBO June 6, 1981 (Saturday); Broadcast Network Release/CBS May 7, 1985 (Tuesday);	
Life is a Circus, Charlie Brown	1980	CBS	October 24, 1980 (Friday)	Emmy: Outstanding Animated Program (Winner)
It's Magic, Charlie Brown	1981	CBS	April 28, 1981 (Tuesday)	Emmy: Outstanding Animated Program (Nominee)
Someday You'll Find Her, Charlie Brown	1981	CBS	October 30, 1981 (Friday)	Emmy: Outstanding Animated Program (Nominee); Outstanding Individual Achievement in Animated Programming – Phil Roman/director (Nominee)
A Charlie Brown Celebration	1982	CBS	May 24, 1982 (Monday)	Emmy: Outstanding Animated Program (Nominee)
Is This Goodbye, Charlie Brown?	1983	CBS	February 21, 1983 (Monday)	Emmy: Outstanding Animated Program (Nominee)
It's an Adventure, Charlie Brown	1983	CBS	May 16, 1983 (Monday)	
What Have We Learned, Charlie Brown?	1983	CBS	May 30, 1983 (Monday)	Emmy: Outstanding Animated Program (Nominee); Peabody Award for excellence in broadcast-ing
It's Flashbeagle, Charlie Brown	1984	CBS	April 16, 1984 (Monday)	Emmy: Outstanding Animated Program (Nominee)
Snoopy's Getting Married, Charlie Brown	1985	CBS	March 20, 1985 (Wednesday)	Emmy: Outstanding Animated Program (Nominee)
You're a Good Man, Charlie Brown	1985	CBS	November 6, 1985 (Wednesday)	Young Artist Award: Exceptional Young Actors in Animation Series, Specials, or Feature Film—Jeremy Scott Reinbolt (Nominee); Exceptional Young Actress in Animation Series Specials or Feature Film—Tiffany Reinbolt (Nominee)

TITLE	YEAR	NETWORK	RELEASE/PREMIERE DATE	AWARDS/NOMINATIONS
Happy New Year, Charlie Brown	1986	CBS	January 1, 1986 (Wednesday)	Young Artist Award: Exceptional Young Actress in Animation Series Specials or Feature Film—Kristie Baker (Winner); Exceptional Young Actors in Animation Series, Specials, or Feature Film—Chad Allen (Nominee)
Snoopy: The Musical	1988	CBS	January 29, 1988 (Friday)	
It's the Girl in the Red Truck, Charlie Brown	1988	CBS	September 27, 1988 (Tuesday)	
Why, Charlie Brown, Why?	1990	CBS	March 16, 1990 (Friday)	Emmy: Outstanding Animated Program—One Hour or Less (Nominee)
Snoopy's Reunion	1991	CBS	May 1, 1991 (Wednesday)	
It's Spring Training, Charlie Brown	1992*	Nickelodeon	*1992 Production date; First Released Direct-to-Video in January 1996; Cable Network Release/ Nickelodeon February 23, 1998 (Monday)	
It's Christmastime Again, Charlie Brown	1992	CBS	November 27, 1992 (Friday)	Young Artist Award: Outstanding Young Voice-Over in an Animated Series or Special—John Christian Grass (Nominee)
You're in the Superbowl, Charlie Brown	1994	NBC	January 18, 1994 (Tuesday)	
It Was My Best Birthday Ever, Charlie Brown	1997		Direct-to-Video August 5, 1997 (Tuesday)	
It's the Pied Piper, Charlie Brown	2000		Direct-to-Video September 12, 2000 (Tuesday)	
A Charlie Brown Valentine	2002	ABC	February 14, 2002 (Tuesday)	
Charlie Brown's Christmas Tales	2002	ABC	December 8, 2002 (Sunday)	
Lucy Must Be Traded, Charlie Brown	2003	ABC	August 29, 2003 (Friday)	
I Want a Dog for Christmas, Charlie Brown	2003	ABC	December 9, 2003 (Tuesday)	

He's a Bully, Charlie Brown	2006	ABC	November 20, 2006 (Monday)	
Happiness is a Warm Blanket, Charlie Brown	2011	Fox	November 24, 2011 (Thursday); First Released on Video on March 29, 2011	Young Artist Award: Best Performance in a Voice-Over Role Young Actress—Grace Rolek (Winner)
The Peanuts Movie	2015	Theatrical Release: Blue Sky Studios and 20th Century Fox	Original Theatrical Release November 6, 2015	
This is America, Charlie Brown (Miniseries)				Young Artist Award: Best Young Actor—Brandon Stewart/voice-over role; Best Young Actress—Erin Chase/voice-over role; Best Young Actress—Ami Foster/voice-over role; Best Family Animation Production—Lee Mendelson (Nominee); Best Performance by a Young Actress—Danielle Keaton/ voice-over role
---The Mayflower Voyagers	1988	CBS	October 21, 1988 (Friday)	
---The Birth of the Constitution	1988	CBS	October 28, 1988 (Friday)	
---The Wright Brothers at Kitty Hawk	1988	CBS	November 4, 1988 (Friday)	
---The NASA Space Station	1988	CBS	November 11, 1988 (Friday)	
---The Building of the Transcontinental Railroad	1989	CBS	February 10, 1989 (Friday)	
---The Great Inventors	1989	CBS	March 10, 1989 (Friday)	
---The Smithsonian and the Presidency	1989	CBS	April 19, 1989 (Friday)	
---The Music and Heroes of America	1989	CBS	May 23, 1989 (Tuesday)	
The Charlie Brown and Snoopy Show (Saturday Morning Series)				Emmy: Outstanding Animated Program (Nominee); Young Artist Award: Best Family Animation Series or Special (Winner); Outstanding Young Actress—Gini Holtzman/animation voice-over (Winner); Outstanding Young Actor—Jeremy Schoenberg/ animation voice-over

TITLE	YEAR	NETWORK	RELEASE/PREMIERE DATE	AWARDS/NOMINATIONS
---*Snoopy's Cat Fight*	1983	CBS	September 17, 1983 (Saturday)	
---*Snoopy: Team Manager*	1983	CBS	September 24, 1983 (Saturday)	
---*Linus and Lucy*	1983	CBS	October 1, 1983 (Saturday)	
---*Lucy vs. the World*	1983	CBS	October 8, 1983 (Saturday)	
---*Linus' Security Blanket*	1983	CBS	October 15, 1983 (Saturday)	
---*Snoopy: Man's Best Friend*	1983	CBS	October 22, 1983 (Saturday)	
---*Snoopy the Psychiatrist*	1983	CBS	October 29, 1983 (Saturday)	
---*You Can't Win, Charlie Brown*	1983	CBS	November 5, 1983 (Saturday)	
---*The Lost Ballpark*	1983	CBS	November 12, 1983 (Saturday)	
---*Snoopy's Football Career*	1983	CBS	November 19, 1983 (Saturday)	
---*Chaos In the Classroom*	1983	CBS	November 26, 1983 (Saturday)	
---*It's that Team Spirit, Charlie Brown*	1983	CBS	December 3, 1983 (Saturday)	
---*Lucy Loves Schroeder*	1983	CBS	December 10, 1983 (Saturday)	
---*Snoopy and the Giant*	1985	CBS	September 14, 1985 (Saturday)	
---*Snoopy's Brother Spike*	1985	CBS	September 21, 1985 (Saturday)	
---*Snoopy's Robot*	1985	CBS	September 28, 1985 (Saturday)	
---*Peppermint Patty's School Days*	1985	CBS	October 5, 1985 (Saturday)	
---*Sally's Sweet Babboo*	1985	CBS	October 12, 1985 (Saturday)	

NOTES

INTRODUCTION

1. Including *A Journalist's View of America through Peanuts* (Tokyo: Shinchosha, 1993) and *Words and Philosophy May Change Your Life, Snoopy* (Tokyo: Kairyusha, 2006).

2. January 23, 1962.

3. Don Fraser and Derrick Bang, eds. *Security Blankets: How Peanuts Touched Our Lives* (Kansas City: Andrews McMeel Publishing, 2009), 92–94.

4. Ibid., 39.

5. George Gerbner, Larry Gross, Michael Morgan, and Nancy Signorielli, "Living with Television: The Dynamics of the Cultivation Process," in *Perspectives on Media Effects*, eds. Jennings Bryant and Dolf Zillmann (Hillsdale, NJ: Lawrence Erlbaum Associates, 1986), 17–40, see 18.

6. Ibid., 24.

7. Nielsen Company, "More of What We Want: The Cross-Platform Report Q1 2014," June 2014.

8. Leonard Berkowitz, "Words and Symbols as Stimuli to Aggressive Responses," in *Control of Aggression: Implications from Basic Research*, ed. John F. Knutson (Chicago: Aldine-Atherton, 1973), 125.

9. Schulz uses this ". ." two-dot punctuation mark in the vast majority of *Peanuts* strips in order to create a pause in the dialogue's rhythm that is slightly shorter than when he uses a standard three-dot ellipsis. Perhaps we shall call this punctuation mark a "minilipsis."

CHAPTER 1

1. July 7, 1969.

2. Charles M. Schulz, *Peanuts Jubilee: My Life and Art with Charlie Brown and Others* (New York: Holt, Rhinehart and Winston, 1975), 12.

3. Ibid., 24.

4. Rich Marshall and Gary Groth, "Charles Schulz Interview," *Nemo: The Classic Comics Library* 31, no 1 (January 1992): 5–24, see 18.

5. Ibid., 18.

6. Gary Groth, "Schulz at 3 O'Clock in the Morning," *Comics Journal*, no. 200 (December 1997): 3–48, see 20.

7. Frederick G. Shackleton, "Memories of Sparky," in *They Called Him Sparky: Friends' Reminiscences of Charles Schulz*, ed. David Liverett (Anderson, IN: Chinaberry House, 2006), 53–56, see 53.

8. Ibid., 53.

9. Groth, "Schulz at 3 O'Clock in the Morning," 32.

10. Rheta Grimsley Johnson, *Good Grief: The Story of Charles M. Schulz* (New York: Pharos Books, 1989), 125.

11. It later became Anderson University.

12. The school had previously been called Federal School of Illustrating and Cartooning and would advertise under various combinations of its name's keywords.

13. David Michaelis, *Schulz and Peanuts: A Biography* (New York: HarperCollins, 2007), 155.

14. Letter from Charles M. Schulz to Frank Dieffenwierth, April 1, 1946, Frank Dieffenwierth Manuscript Collection, SC2003.002, Charles M. Schulz Museum and Research Center, Santa Rosa, California.

15. Letter from Charles M. Schulz to Frank Dieffenwierth, October 9, 1946, Frank Dieffenwierth Manuscript Collection, SC2003.002, Charles M. Schulz Museum and Research Center, Santa Rosa, California.

16. Schulz, *Peanuts Jubilee*, 24.

17. Johnson, *Good Grief*, 133.

18. Charles M. Schulz, "Peanuts," *Collegiate Challenge*, 1963, in Charles M. Schulz, *My Life with Charlie Brown*, ed. M. Thomas Inge (Jackson: University Press of Mississippi, 2010), 20–25, see 21.

19. One biography reports that Sparky was baptized in a lake nearby his home church (Michaelis, 190), citing a letter from a church member. In the process of researching this text, neither that church member nor any others available from the youth group's core membership could recall a time when Sparky was baptized. "It's funny someone wouldn't remember it," the cited member's wife noted, unsure herself if Sparky underwent the symbolic rite and skeptical of the possibility that he had without anyone still remembering. According to Joyce, Sparky was not baptized, at least not as far as she knew. Sparky did not believe baptism was necessary for salvation, writing in a Church of God doctrinal statement that "the practice of giving a so-called baptism to young children originated in an apostate church" that wrongfully taught the "false doctrines" that infants are totally depraved and that baptism regenerates one from one's sins (*St. Paul Dispatch*, July 9, 1949, 5). As Sparky never mentioned any baptism event to his children, his widow, Jeannie, or in public interviews, including his statement of faith for Billy Graham's *Decision* newsletter, it is likely that Charles Schulz did not take part in a public baptism service through the Church of God.

20. Charles M. Schulz, "Knowing You Are Not Alone," *Decision*, September 1963, 8–9, see 8.

21. Ruth Forbes, "Memories of Sparky," in *They Called Him Sparky*, 70–72, see 71.

22. Letter from Charles M. Schulz to Fred, Doris, and Martin Lynn Forbes, January 4, 1949, in *They Called Him Sparky*, 59–62, see 62.

23. Letter from Charles M. Schulz to Frank Dieffenwierth, July 17, 1948, Frank Dieffenwierth Manuscript Collection, SC2003.002, Charles M. Schulz Museum and Research Center, Santa Rosa, California.

24. Willmar Thorkelson, "Cartoonist Turns Over Tenth of 'Peanuts' to the Church," *Minneapolis Star*, March 18, 1955, 29, 39, see 39.

25. Marshall and Groth, "Charles Schulz Interview," 18.

26. Schulz, "Peanuts," *Collegiate Challenge*, 21.

27. After pressing Sparky for details, one journalist reported that the cartoonist's tithe was 10 percent of his income, after taxes (Thorkelson, 1955).

28. This would be one of three Charles Browns that Sparky interacted with outside the strips. The first was a high school friend; the second was a colleague at Art Instruction.

29. Schulz, *Peanuts Jubilee*, 32.

30. Charles M. Schulz and R. Smith Kiliper, *Charlie Brown, Snoopy and Me* (Garden City, NY: Doubleday & Company, 1980), 31.

31. Letter from Charles M. Schulz to Ken Hall, October 29, 1958, in *They Called Him Sparky*, 88–89.

32. Michaelis, *Schulz and Peanuts*, 205–214.

33. At birth he was given the name Charles Monroe Schulz, Jr., but went by his nickname "Monte" his whole life, later changing his name on his driver's license to simplify matters.

34. 3737 Thirty-eighth Avenue South.

35. The Merriam Park Church of God stayed at 330 North Prior until 1961. In 1963, a dance school began using the building as the church group moved to a new location.

36. Clifford Thor, "Memories of Sparky," in *They Called Him Sparky*, 35–36, see 35.

37. Schulz, "Knowing You Are Not Alone," 8.

38. *Everyman*, "Happiness is a Warm Puppy," television interview of Charles M. Schulz by Peter France, BBC1, 1977.

39. Thor, "Memories of Sparky," 35.

40. Charles M. Schulz, audio recording of Fred and Doris Shackleton concert, St. Paul, Minnesota, July 17, 1949.

41. Joyce (Schulz) Doty, personal correspondence, April 16, 2014.

42. Elaine Ramsperger, personal interview, September 8, 2014.

43. Dolores Edes, personal interview, October 30, 2014.

44. Avis Kriebel, "The Little Church at 38th and 38th," in *They Called Him Sparky*, 41–43, see 41.

45. Kenneth Hall, "Memories of Sparky," in *They Called Him Sparky*, 95–110, see 96.

46. Kenneth F. Hall, "It Scares Me: Says the Inventor of Peanuts For He has Thirty Million Fans," *Upward*, February 1, 1959, 14–19, see 19.

47. *Young Pillars* also enjoyed some syndication in mainstream newspapers. In 1964, the *Chicago Tribune* ran *Young Pillars* panels in their Sunday magazine's regular faith article written by Reverend Harold Blake Walker.

48. Schulz, "Peanuts," *Collegiate Challenge*, 21, 24.

49. Luke 18:29b–30

50. Letter from Charles M. Schulz to Ken Hall, October 29, 1958, in *They Called Him Sparky*, 88–89, see 89.

CHAPTER 2

1. Leaf Roberts, "A Faithful Witness: Outreaching Love," *Sebastopol United Methodist Church*, 2012.

2. Worried that the church would fold in Sparky's absence, one member even left the congregation. Much to Sparky's pleasure, as he would write to a friend many years later, the church would still be found faithful long after his departure. In 1961, barely three years after the Schulzes left, the little church outgrew their self-made building and bought a new home for themselves at 3149 Thirty-fifth Avenue South.

3. Letter from Charles M. Schulz to Kenny Hall, March 16, 1959, in *They Called Him Sparky*, 89–90, see 90.

4. John W. V. Smith, *A Brief History of the Church of God Reformation Movement*, rev. ed. (Anderson, IN: Warner Press, 1957), 156.

5. Letter from the General Board of Education of the Methodist Church to Charles Schulz, May 12, 1958, Charles M. Schulz Museum and Research Center, Santa Rosa, California.

6. May 5, 1958.

7. November 12, 1959.

8. August 1, 1959.

9. Schulz, "Knowing You Are Not Alone," 9.

10. Ibid.

11. Ibid.

12. October 9, 1956.

13. In 1950, Schulz acquired two books by Schweitzer, *The Quest of the Historical Jesus* and *The Mystery of the Kingdom of God*. He then referenced Schweitzer in three strips (April 26, 1960; December 15, 1963; and July 13, 1996) and in 1992's television special, *It's Christmastime Again, Charlie Brown*.

14. Certain requests were turned down. Those with overt political ties, such as a request for use in a United Nations publication, were often politely rejected. Other requests at times violated syndicate agreements and had to be refused, such as a request to use a strip on personal greeting cards, which would violate an in-progress agreement with *Hallmark Greeting Cards*.

15. Schulz used various paper sizes for his originals. Dailies, for example, were at times drawn on heavy stock that was 6.5 inches x 27.75 inches, with Sundays on 16.75 inches x

23.75 inches, but over the next fifty years, the paper size fluctuated by several inches in both height and width. When originals were not available for approved request, signed proofs of similar size were often sent.

16. Hugh Morrow, "The Success of an Utter Failure," *Saturday Evening Post*, January 12, 1957, 34–35, 70–72, in *Charles M. Schulz: Conversations*, 3–14, see 6.

17. "The Gospel According to Peanuts," KPIX, San Francisco, February 17, 1966, Television.

18. March 22, 1959.

19. "The Gospel According to Peanuts," KPIX, San Francisco.

20. December 20, 1959.

21. January 29, 1960.

22. January 22, 1961.

23. December 23, 1962. Some newspapers did not run the large title panels when the paper wanted to arrange the strip in a more space-saving fashion. Readers of these newspapers would miss a host of interesting art that Schulz would draw over the years in these so-called "throwaway panels."

24. Schulz repeated this gag with Peppermint Patty on September 16, 1987.

25. Kenneth Wilson, "A Visit with Charles Schulz," *Christian Herald*, September 1967, 14–15, 59–66, 79, 81, in *Charles M. Schulz: Conversations*, 28–44, see 35.

26. John Leland, "Faith and the Funny Pages," *New York Times*, August 27, 2006. Italics added.

27. Johnson, *Good Grief*, 129.

28. Publishers voluntarily established the Comics Code Authority. Amongst other edicts, the code declared to comic book authors that "ridicule or attack on any religious or racial group is never permissible." The last remaining publisher withdrew from the Comics Authority in 2011 and each now follows its own internal codes of publishing. For more on the Comics Code Authority, see Amy Kiste Nyberg's *Seal of Approval: The History of the Comics Code* (Jackson: University Press of Mississippi, 1998).

29. "Comics: Good Grief," *Time*, April 9, 1965, 80–84, see 84.

30. Schulz, *Peanuts Jubilee*, 175–76.

31. Letter from Al Morrison to Charles Schulz, November 4, 1963, Charles M. Schulz Museum and Research Center, Santa Rosa, California.

32. Groth, "Schulz at 3 O'Clock in the Morning," 42.

33. Ibid., 43.

34. Ibid., 44.

35. Letter from Charles M. Schulz to the editor of *Vital Christianity*, in *They Called Him Sparky*, 90.

36. Among other topics, Wesley's own writings included volumes on the New and Old Testaments, prayer, poetry, hymns, medicine, and even electroshock therapy.

37. "The Gospel According to Peanuts," KPIX, San Francisco.

38. The 1960 *Doctrines and Discipline of the Methodist Church* manual (Nashville, TN: Methodist Publishing House) pronounced that the denomination "rejoices in the fact that it is a part of the one church of our Lord and shares in a common task" with other believers (6).

39. Groth, "Schulz at 3 O'Clock in the Morning," 20.

40. Ibid., 21.

41. *The Interpreter's Bible*, vol. 1. (New York: Abingdon Press, 1952), xvii.

42. Patricia Swanson, personal interview, June 14, 2014.

43. Ramona Swanson, personal interview, June 1, 2014.

44. Avis Kriebel, personal interview, June 2, 2014.

45. Gerald Jonas, "The 'Peanuts' Man Talks About Children," *Family Circle*, May 1968, 20–28, 80–82, see 80, 82.

46. Charles E. Brown, *The Hope of His Coming* (Anderson, IN: Gospel Trumpet Company, 1927), 9–10.

47. Paul Schoch, personal interview, October 25, 2011.

48. Pete Coleman, personal interview, October 25, 2011.

49. Wilson, "A Visit with Charles Schulz," 43.

50. Years later, Schulz would try to distance himself from the *Decision* piece, saying that he was just writing what he thought the magazine wanted. That statement more likely reflects his thoughts years after the piece was published, when he became increasingly uncomfortable with evangelical Christian terminology, instead of those at the time he wrote the article. Not only had he already given the ultimatum to *Better Homes & Gardens* that they must run his writing his way or not at all, but he also went on to approve the *Decision* reprint for Ken Hall, and he published an article using much of the text from *Decision* in an article for Campus Crusade for Christ's periodical, *Collegiate Challenge*.

51. Schulz, "Knowing You Are Not Alone," 9.

52. Letter from Charles M. Schulz to Ken Hall, c. August 26, 1963, in *They Called Him Sparky*, 93.

53. Johnson, *Good Grief*, 126.

54. Jon Borgzinner, "A Leaf, a Lemon Drop, a Cartoon is Born," *Life*, March 17, 1967, 78B–80, see 78B.

55. Letter from Charles M. Schulz to Ruth and Marvin Forbes, August 28, 1963, in *They Called Him Sparky*, 81–82, see 81.

56. Letter from Charles M. Schulz to Ken Hall, July 8, 1963, in *They Called Him Sparky*, 92.

57. Jonas, "The 'Peanuts' Man Talks About Children," 80.

58. Mary Harrington Hall, "A Conversation with Charles Schulz: or the Psychology of Simplicity," *Psychology Today*, January 1968, 19–21, 66–69, in *Charles M. Schulz: Conversations*, 45-62, see 58.

59. Charles M. Schulz and Kenneth F. Hall, *Two by Fours*. 1965. (New Canaan, CT: Keats, 1973), 42–44.

CHAPTER 3

1. Samuel P. Nelson, "Religion in the Workplace and the Problem of the First Amendment," in *Religion, Politics, and American Identity*, eds. David S. Gutterman and Andrew R. Murphy (New York: Lexington Books, 2006), 177–98.

2. See Thomas F. Gieryn, George M. Bevins, and Stephen C. Zehr, "Professionalization of American Scientists: Public Science in the Creation/Evolution Trials," *American Sociological Review* 50, no. 3 (1985): 392–409; Harry Elmer Barnes, "The Role of Religion in a Secular Age," *Scientific Monthly* 28, no. 5 (1929): 430–45.

3. See Mark G. Toulouse, "The Muddled Middle: Protestantism's Encounter with Homosexuality since the 1960s," in *Sex, Religion, Media*, ed. Dane S. Claussen (Lanham, MD: Rowman & Littlefield, 2002), 43–64.

4. Stephen J. Lind, "Christmas in the 1960s: A Charlie Brown Christmas, Religion, and the Conventions of the Television Genre," *Journal of Religion and Popular Culture* 26, no. 1 (2014).

5. Michele Rosenthal, "Turn it Off!: TV Criticism in the Christian Century Magazine," in *Practicing Religion in the Age of the Media*, eds. Stewart M. Hoover and Lynn Schofield Clark (New York: Columbia University Press, 2002), 138–62.

6. Michael Curtin, "Newton Minow," in *The Encyclopedia of Television*, ed. Horace Newcomb (London: Routledge, 1997).

7. Fred W. Friendly, *Due to Circumstances Beyond Our Control . . .* (New York: Random House, 1967), 168.

8. *Dennis the Menace*, 3:12, "The Fifteen-Foot Christmas Tree," CBS, December 24, 1961, Television.

9. Lind, "Christmas in the 1960s."

10. Peter Cole, Frankie Frankeny, and Leslie Jonath, *Christmas Trees: Fun and Festive Ideas* (San Francisco: Chronicle Books, 2002), 23.

11. Cassandra A. Fortin, "It's Beginning to Look a Lot Like Christmas (1958)," *Baltimore Sun*, October 26, 2008.

12. *Green Acres*, 2:13, "An Old-Fashioned Christmas," CBS, December 21, 1966, Television.

13. *The Lucy Show*, 4:13, "Lucy the Choirmaster," CBS, December 13, 1965, Television.

14. National Christmas Tree Association, "History of Christmas Trees," 2005.

15. Lee Mendelson, *A Charlie Brown Christmas: The Making of a Tradition* (New York: HarperCollins, 2005), 40.

16. "The Saga of Charlie Brown," *Variety*, December 22, 1965, 43.

17. Edward M. Yager, *Ronald Reagan's Journey: Democrat to Republican* (Lanham, MD: Rowman & Littlefield, 2006).

18. David Willat, personal interview, September 24, 2014.

19. See Derrick Bang, *Vince Guaraldi at the Piano* (Jefferson, NC: McFarland & Company, 2012).

20. The initial broadcast of the program did not credit the children in the Episcopal choir for their work, an error attributed to the rush of the production schedule. The oversight was then repeated with subsequent rereleases. In some public commentary, the music would be wrongfully attributed to the sixth-grade class of Mendelson's son, Glenn.

21. Lind, "Christmas in the 1960s."

22. *The Lucy Show*, 4:13, "Lucy the Choirmaster."

23. Charles M. Schulz, "Address to the National Cartoonists Society Annual Convention," La Jolla, California, May 14, 1994, in *My Life with Charlie Brown*, 126–139, see 137; Chuck

Barney, "Holiday Classics Here for New Generation," *Free Lance-Star*, November 30, 2000, 6–7, see 7.

24. Lee Mendelson and Charles M. Schulz, *Charlie Brown and Charlie Schulz* (New York: New American Library, 1971), 156.

25. Bob Foster, "Screenings," *San Mateo Times*, October 21, 1965), 29.

26. Luke 2:8–14. In the special, Linus recites from the King James Version translation. Schulz would primarily use the Revised Standard and King James translations throughout his work.

27. "Security is a Good Show," *Time*, December 10, 1965, 95.

28. Lawrence Laurent, "Loser in Peanuts Finally a Winner," *Washington Post*, December 11, 1965, E18.

29. Cynthia Lowry, "Charlie Brown is Better Left Alone," *Kentucky New Era*, December 10, 1965, 6.

30. Billie Thorington, personal interview, June 25, 2014.

31. Terrence O'Flaherty, "Christmas in Sebastopol," *San Francisco Chronicle*, December 9, 1965.

32. Richard K. Doan, "CBS Plans Second Charlie Brown Special," *New York Herald Tribune*, December 15, 1965, 21.

CHAPTER 4

1. Hall, "A Conversation with Charles Schulz: or the Psychology of Simplicity," 61.

2. Television program viewership is typically reported in "ratings" and "shares" based on viewer surveys and automatic reporting devices in select homes. A "45 in the ratings" would indicate that 45 percent of all households owning a television had someone in the household watching the program. A "45 share" would indicate that 45 percent of all televisions that were turned on during the program were tuned-in to the program.

3. Lee Mendelson, *It's the Great Pumpkin, Charlie Brown: The Making of a Television Classic* (New York: HarperCollins, 2006), 4.

4. Ibid., 17.

5. William Saunders, "All Saints and All Souls," *Arlington Catholic Herald*, 2003.

6. Jack Santino, "Halloween: The Fantasy and Folklore of All Hallows," *Library of American Folklife Center*, September 1982.

7. "Halloween: Pranks & Pumpkins are Traditional," *Life*, November 3, 1941, 69.

8. Mendelson, *It's the Great Pumpkin, Charlie Brown*, 52, 56.

9. Lawrence Laurent, "Laurent Suggests," *Washington Post*, October 27, 1966, H12.

10. Lawrence Laurent, "TV 'Peanuts' is a Delight," *Washington Post*, October 29, 1966, reprinted from October 28 late edition, 28.

11. Clay Gowran, "Charlie Brown & Co. Bewitching on TV," *Chicago Tribune*, October 28, 1966, B8.

12. "Search for Self," seminar pamphlet, *University of Georgia Student Religious Council*, February 7–11, 1960.

13. Alvin Plantinga, "Reason and Belief in God," in *Faith and Rationality: Reason and Belief in God*, eds. Alvin Plantinga and Nicholas Wolterstorff (Notre Dame: University of Notre Dame Press, 1983), 17–93.

14. Edward B. Fiske, "Liturgies Embracing More Pop Art Forms," *New York Times*, May 15, 1967, 1, 48, see 48.

15. "The Gospel According to Peanuts," KPIX, San Francisco.

16. Schulz, *Peanuts Jubilee*, 99.

17. Robert L. Short, *The Gospel According to Peanuts* (Louisville: Westminster John Knox Press, 1964), 10–11.

18. Lewis Nichols, "In and Out of Books," *New York Times Book Review*, March 12, 1967, 8.

19. *The Gospel According to Peanuts* would eventually be rereleased in 2000, with its half-century run totaling over 10 million copies sold. Short also wrote two sequels with John Knox Press: *Short Meditations on the Bible and Peanuts* (1990) and *The Parables of Peanuts* (2002). Similar in approach to Short, but with less market success, Maurice Berquist likewise uses *Peanuts* strips, with Schulz's direct permission, in a 1981 book, *The Doctor is In* (Anderson, IN: Warner Press). Berquist's book is crafted as a letter to Charlie Brown about God's kingdom, using *Peanuts* strips as starting points for sharing words of evangelical encouragement. Others have written similar books on other properties, such as James Kemp's *The Gospel According to Dr. Seuss* (Valley Forge, PA: Judson Press, 2004) and Benjamin Hoff's *The Tao of Pooh* (New York: Penguin Books, 1982)..

20. Letter from Charles Schulz to Robert Short, January 25, 1965.

21. Ordained rabbi and clinical psychologist Abraham Twerski got along well with Sparky and utilizes his work in four general audience books published by St. Martin's, including 1988's *When Do the Good Things Start?*, a book of foundational personal counseling, and 1990's *Waking Up Just in Time*, a book using the Alcoholics Anonymous twelve-step program as more broadly applicable tool for self-improvement. Using a personalized approach to spirituality, Twerski takes *Peanuts* strips and character descriptions to demonstrate his own principles in a vivid and accessible way for readers. Twerski's did the same in 1996's *I Didn't Ask to Be in This Family* and 1999's *That's Not a Fault . . . It's a Character Trait.*

22. Abraham J. Twerski, "Attaining Happiness: Q and A," *Torah Café*, March 2, 2011, Web, accessed September 22, 2014.

23. Ken Martin, "Have It Your Own Way, Charles Schulz!" *Nova*, 1972 62–65, see 64.

24. "The Gospel According to Peanuts," KPIX, San Francisco.

25. Frank Pauer, "A Conversation with Charles Schulz," *Dayton Daily News and Journal Herald Magazine*, May 3, 1987, 1–4, 13, in *Charles M. Schulz: Conversations*, 143–52, see 147.

26. Groth, "Schulz at 3 O'Clock in the Morning," 38.

27. Short, *The Gospel According to Peanuts*, 69.

28. Dardedar, "Re: Religious Cartoons," *phpBB*, May 8, 2009, Web, accessed February 26, 2014.

29. Jeff Swenson, "'The Great Pumpkin' is a Cartoon for Atheists," *Freethunk!* October 13, 2010, Web, accessed February 26, 2014.

30. November 5, 1977.

31. Letter from Charles M. Schulz to Marvin Forbes, October 3, 1957, in *They Called Him Sparky*, 79–80, see 79.

32. Charles Schulz, "Guest Editorial," *Lookout*, October 19, 1958.

33. "Happiness is to Dance with Snoopy and Talk with his Creator," *Youth* 19, no. 6 (March 24, 1968), 10.

34. Wilson, "A Visit with Charles Schulz," 34.

35. Groth, "Schulz at 3 O'Clock in the Morning," 42.

36. Wilson, "A Visit with Charles Schulz," 33.

37. Eugene Griessman, "Atlanta Weekly Interview: Charles Schulz," *Atlanta Weekly*, November 15, 1981, in *Charles M. Schulz: Conversations*, 111–20, see 115.

38. "The Gospel According to Peanuts," KPIX, San Francisco.

39. Schulz, *Peanuts Jubilee*, 158.

40. Ibid., 99.

41. Groth, "Schulz at 3 O'Clock in the Morning," 21.

42. Letter from Charles Schulz to Marvin Forbes, September 29, 1966, in *They Called Him Sparky*, 82–83, see 82.

43. "Citation conferring the degree of doctor of humane letters on Charles Monroe Schulz," Saint Mary's College of California, June 11, 1966.

44. Charles M. Schulz, commencement address, St. Mary's College of California, Moraga, California, June 11, 1966, in *My Life with Charlie Brown*, 26–31, see 30–31.

CHAPTER 5

1. August 21, August 28, and September 4, 1960.

2. Barnaby Conrad, "You're a Good Man, Charlie Schulz," *New York Times Magazine*, April 16, 1967, 32–35, 42, 44, 46, 49, 52, 54, in *Charles M. Schulz: Conversations*, 15–27, see 16.

3. Schulz and Kiliper, *Charlie Brown, Snoopy and Me*, 115.

4. Jim Phelan, "Penthouse Interview: Charles M. Schulz," *Penthouse*, October 1971, 26, 29, 30, 33, see 30.

5. "Happiness is to Dance with Snoopy and Talk with his Creator," 14.

6. Belgian, Bulgarian, Braille, Catalan, Chinese, Czech, Danish, Dutch, English, Filipino, Finnish, French, German, Greek, Hebrew, Hungarian, Icelandic, Italian, Japanese, Korean, Latin, Norwegian, Polish, Portuguese, Russian, Slavic, Spanish, Swedish, Thai, Turkish, Welsh (list compiled by the Peanuts Collector's Club, with additions by the Charles M. Schulz Museum and Research Center).

7. Schulz and Kiliper, *Charlie Brown, Snoopy and Me*, 115.

8. Letter from Charles M. Schulz to Roger Palmquist, May 22, 1958.

9. A suburban mother and teacher, Harriet Glickman, had written to Schulz in 1968 hoping that the introduction of African American characters into the *Peanuts* cast might contribute something toward national healing and racial progress in the wake of the death of Martin Luther King, Jr. Schulz wrote back, worrying that he would look like he was merely patronizing a demographic. Glickman discussed the issue with her African

American friends and assured Schulz that he was in a position for his efforts to be received well. When Sparky introduced Franklin, Glickman's predictions were soundly confirmed accurate, and Sparky sent her the original artwork. Over the years, Sparky would struggle to give Franklin a prominent role, not believing that he could speak with an authentic voice for an African American character.

10. December 17, 1961.

11. Charles M. Schulz, *Around the World in 45 Years*. (Kansas City, MO: Andrews and McMeel, 1994), 19.

12. June 5, 1959.

13. June 18, 1959.

14. In *People v. Belous* (1969), the California Supreme Court struck down the state's Penal Code 274, deciding that it was vague and uncertain. The code had allowed abortion only in the situation where it was necessary to save the life of the mother. In 1972, the California Supreme Court would then invalidate most of the state's 1967 Therapeutic Abortion Act, which partially restricted abortions, for similar reasons of vague language.

15. Schulz, *Peanuts Jubilee*, 175.

16. Meredith (Schulz) Hodges, personal interview, June 4, 2014.

17. Scott McCloud, *Understanding Comics: The Invisible Art* (New York: HarperPerennial, 1993), 66.

18. The Latin word "enthymeme" is fittingly derivative of the Greek "en" (within) and "thymos" (the considering and affective mind).

19. Aristotle, *On Rhetoric*, trans. George A. Kennedy, 1st ed. (New York: Oxford University Press, 1991), I.2.8; 1356b.

20. Lloyd Bitzer, "Aristotle's Enthymeme Revisited," *Quarterly Journal of Speech*, no. 45 (1959): 399–408, see 407.

21. For example, if a speaker were to say, "Socrates is a man, therefore he must be mortal," it would ring true with an audience because they would supply the missing premise that "all men are mortal."

22. Phelan, "Penthouse Interview: Charles M. Schulz," 33.

23. Susan Wittstock, "Fifty Years of Peanuts," *onCampus* 30, no. 3 (September 14, 2000), Web, accessed November 11, 2012.

24. Pauer, "A Conversation with Charles Schulz," 152.

25. Phelan, "Penthouse Interview: Charles M. Schulz," 29.

26. See Appendix I for details on the coding process.

27. In 1951, it is Violet who mis-holds the football for Charlie Brown. Lucy takes over the following year. In 1956, Schroeder holds the ball, and Charlie Brown succeeds in kicking it.

28. Stephen J. Lind, "Reading Peanuts: The Secular and the Sacred," *ImageTexT: Interdisciplinary Comics Studies* 4, no. 2 (2008).

29. September 11, 1991.

30. August 10, 1976.

31. June 18, 1999.

32. Coffee Grounds later became the home of music and street ministry group Agape Force before being split into separate parcels.

33. Elaine Ramsperger, personal interview, September 8, 2014.

34. Monte Schulz, "Regarding Schulz and Peanuts," *Comics Journal*, no. 290 (2008): 27–78, see 60.

35. Michaelis, *Schulz and Peanuts*, 451–76.

36. Schulz, "Regarding Schulz and Peanuts," 56.

37. Letter from Charles M. Schulz to Tracey Claudius, "My Bold Plan," c. 1971.

38. "Good Grief, $150 Million!" *Newsweek*, December 27, 1971, 40–44, see 44.

39. Stan Isaacs, "Charles Schulz: Comic Strips Aren't Art," *Newsday*, August 28, 1977, 15–17, 36, 38, in *Charles M. Schulz: Conversations*, 86–97, see 93; Martin, "Have It Your Own Way, Charles Schulz!" 65; Groth, "Schulz at 3 O'Clock in the Morning," 20.

40. Letter from Charles M. Schulz to Marvin Forbes, September 14, 1973, in *They Called Him Sparky*, 83–84, see 83.

41. Letter from Charles M. Schulz to Roger Palmquist, January 31, 1974.

42. Jean Schulz, personal correspondence, November 29, 2014.

43. Robert Short, "Jesus Laughed!" *30 Good Minutes*, Chicago Sunday Evening Club, October 28, 2001.

44. Eco's poignant essay was originally published in Italian in 1963 as the introduction to the first volume of *Peanuts* translated into Italian, titled *Arriva Charlie Brown!* In this essay, the philosopher praises the cartoonist, writing, "Schulz is a poet. More so than many others." It was later reprinted in English in Eco's *Apocalypse Postponed*, ed. Robert Lumley (Bloomington: Indiana University Press, 1994), 36–44, see 36, 40.

45. Umberto Eco, personal correspondence, September 9, 2014.

46. Groth, "Schulz at 3 O'Clock in the Morning," 37.

47. Wilson, "A Visit with Charles Schulz," 43.

48. May 10, 1988.

49. The *Los Angeles Times* study's methods are similar to those of this study. As in this study, the researchers eliminated thin colloquialisms from their coding results. While some strips may be interpreted differently by the two studies, seeming to make a statistical comparison between them difficult, the difference between Schulz and his peers is still dramatically demonstrated even if the *Los Angeles Times* study was based on a more conservative definition of religious reference. This is true for two reasons. First, even if the difference between the averages were drastically cut, even in half, in order to account for difference in interpretation, *Peanuts* would still outpace its peers' religious references by nearly four times. Second, it is more likely that the difference is much higher than seven times, given that the reported results of the *Los Angeles Times* study actually include *Peanuts*. Were those to be removed for a more statistically accurate comparison, the number of references in *Peanuts* may jump to as much as twelve times more than its peers.

50. Donald B. Lindsey and John Hereen, "Where the Sacred Meets the Profane: Religion in the Comics Pages," *Review of Religious Research* 34, no. 1 (September 1992): 63–77.

51. In 2009, Thomas Nelson published *I Did It His Way*, a collection of religiously themed *B.C.* strips from artist Johnny Hart. Hart drew robust criticism for his 2001 Easter strip in which a menorah slowly fades, panel by panel, until all that remains is a cross at the center. For any syndicate, a comic like *B.C.* would be a prized commodity, given that

it had reached 2,600 subscribers worldwide, matching the level of record-setting success of Schulz's *Peanuts* (a strip that Hart's *B.C.* emulated in many other aesthetic and thematic ways). Standing behind Hart, the syndicate did not pull the strip from newspapers, instead issuing a statement that the strip was a recognition of two important religious holidays. Hart himself spoke out, strongly rejecting claims of anti-Semitism or offensive proselytizing, saying that he had intended to honor both sacred symbols, the menorah and the cross, pointing out their relationship to one another, and lamenting the quickness of some to criticize any statement of faith in the comics.

52. *Archie's One Way* (New York: Archie Enterprises, 1973); *Archie's Something Else* (New York: Archie Enterprises, 1975).

53. Examples include Dennis Hengeveld's *Reverend Fun* and Reverend Zorowski's *Church Mice*.

54. Groth, "Schulz at 3 O'Clock in the Morning," 38.

55. "Happiness is to Dance with Snoopy and Talk with his Creator," 9–10.

56. Leonard Greenspoon, "The Bible in the Funny Papers," *Bible Review* 7, no. 5 (October 1991): 30–41; Leonard Greenspoon, "The New Testament in the Comics," *Bible Review* 9, no. 6 (December 1993): 40–45.

57. September 27, 1964.

58. April 30, 1965.

59. September 17, 1967.

60. Sparky used this embedded verse again on February 4, 1978, putting quotation marks around the text on April 14, 1970, and March 5, 1998, and having Marcie read the verse in class on April 13, 1984.

61. Charles M. Schulz, "But a Comic Strip Has to Grow," *Saturday Review*, April 12, 1969, in *My Life with Charlie Brown*, 164–69, see 165.

62. July 15, 1994.

63. January 2, 1971.

64. July 10, 1976.

65. August 8, 1980.

66. May 31, 1996.

67. *The Gulistan*, Chapter I.XII.

68. February 10, 1964.

69. December 23, 1970.

70. February 4, 1975.

71. May 30, 1991.

72. Groth, "Schulz at 3 O'Clock in the Morning," 38.

73. Ibid.

74. "Happiness is to Dance with Snoopy and Talk with his Creator," 11.

75. September 12, 1993.

76. August 1, 1960.

77. February 17, 1974.

78. Hall, "A Conversation with Charles Schulz: or the Psychology of Simplicity," 62.

79. Schulz, "Regarding Schulz and Peanuts," 30.

80. Wilson, "A Visit with Charles Schulz," 33.

CHAPTER 6

1. August 14, 1960.

2. Mendelson and Schulz, *Charlie Brown and Charlie Schulz*, 177–78.

3. Gary R. Edgerton, *The Columbia History of American Television* (New York: Columbia University Press, 2009), 247.

4. Jack Gould, "C.B.S. is Dropping Its Theater Films," *New York Times*, January 10, 1972, 47; Sally Bedell Smith, "Paley's Latest Feat: His Return," *New York Times*, September 11, 1986, D7.

5. Mendelson and Schulz, *Charlie Brown and Charlie Schulz*, 177–78.

6. Vincent Canby, "Screen: Good Old Charlie Brown Finds a Home," *New York Times*, December 5, 1969, 50.

7. Gene Shalit, "Good Grief! It's 'A Boy Named Charlie Brown,'" *Look*, January 27, 1970, 68.

8. Charles M. Schulz, "Charles Schulz and Peanuts," *Cartoonist Profiles*, no. 12, December 1971, in *My Life with Charlie Brown*, 32–36, see 33.

9. Ibid., 33.

10. Judith Martin, "Peanuts: 'It's Not Funny,'" *Washington Post*, June 30, 1970, D7.

11. Evert Brown, personal interview, August 31, 2014.

12. A "Jew's harp," also known as a mouth harp, Ozark harp, jaw harp, juice harp, or jewes trump, is a curved metal frame and reed that is placed between the teeth and plucked, with the reverberating note being changed by the performer changing the shape of his or her mouth.

13. Evert Brown, personal correspondence, August 29, 2014.

14. See Appendix II for list of programs, airdates, and awards.

15. See Appendix I for details on how the specials were coded for different religious references.

16. Charles Solomon, *The Art and Making of Peanuts Animation* (San Francisco: Chronicle Books, 2012), 31.

17. Sparky too had spent a little time sketching churches in Europe. On a 1987 trip to visit Jeannie's daughter studying in England, Sparky visited the Church of St. Augustine of Canterbury in Upton Lovell, Wiltshire and sketched the seventeenth-century church with a marker on a messenger bag at hand.

18. "Phil Roman," interview by Jennifer Howard, *Academy of Television Arts and Sciences Foundation*, June 25, 2002, Web, accessed September 28, 2014.

19. Leonard Maltin, "An Interview with Charles M. Schulz," *Charlie Brown: A Boy for All Seasons* (New York: Museum of Broadcasting, 1984), 19–23, in *Charles M. Schulz: Conversations*, 121–27, see 126.

20. "Bill Melendez," interview by Jennifer Howard, *Academy of Television Arts and Sciences Foundation*, June 23, 2001, Web, accessed September 28, 2014.

21. Michael Barrier, "Charles M. Schulz," *MichaelBarrier.com*, 1988/2003, Web, accessed March 23, 2014.

22. In 1971, on a rare occasion during an atypical year in his personal life, Schulz did not view the final product of *Play It Again, Charlie Brown* even after it went to air.

23. Lee Mendelson, personal correspondence, June 25, 2012.

24. Though Sally mistakenly hears the "calling birds" lyrics as "calming birds," eighteenth-century lyrics refer to the birds as "colly birds," a dialectal reference to black birds. Schulz uses this term in his December 25, 1978, strip.

25. *A Charlie Brown Celebration* (1982).

26. *It's a Mystery, Charlie Brown* (1974). The phrasing is an interpretation of Genesis 3:19, found in a burial rites passage from the Anglican Book of Common Prayer.

27. Stan Isaacs, "Charles Schulz: Comic Strips Aren't Art," in *Charles M. Schulz: Conversations*, 97.

28. *The Charlie Brown and Snoopy Show*, "Linus' Security Blanket," October 15, 1983.

29. Todd V. Lewis, "Religious Rhetoric and the Comic Frame in The Simpsons," *Journal of Media and Religion* 1, no. 3 (2002): 153–65, see 153.

30. *Lucy Must Be Traded, Charlie Brown* (2003).

31. *The Simpsons*, 24:18, "Pulpit Friction." Fox, April 28, 2013, Television.

32. *The Simpsons*, 13:6, "She of Little Faith," Fox, December 16, 2001, Television.

33. Cynthia Gorney, "The *Peanuts* Progenitor," *Washington Post*, October 2, 1985, D1–D3, see D2.

34. Mark Joseph, "Mark Joseph Interviews Charles Schultz," *The Bully! Pulpit*, 1997.

35. Mark Miller, "It's Tough to Be a Little Kid," *Newsweek*, January 1, 2000, 25.

36. Lind, "Christmas in the 1960s."

37. Thomas Skill, James D. Robinson, John S. Lyons, and David Larson, "The Portrayal of Religion and Spirituality on Fictional Network Television," *Review of Religious Research* 35, no. 3 (1994): 251–67, see 265.

38. Scott H. Clarke, "Created in Whose Image? Religious Characters on Network Television," *Journal of Media and Religion* 4, no. 3 (2005): 137–53, see 143.

39. Chaim Perelman and L. Olbrechts-Tyteca, *The New Rhetoric*, trans. John Wilkinson and Purcell Weaver (Notre Dame: University of Notre Dame Press, 1969/2000), 116–17.

40. Leonard Berkowitz and Karen Heimer Rogers, "A Priming Effect Analysis of Media Influences," in *Perspectives on Media Effects*, eds. Jennings Bryant and Dolf Zillmann (Hillsdale, NJ: Lawrence Erlbaum Associates, 1986), 57–81.

41. Marshall and Groth, "Charles Schulz Interview," 17.

42. Skill, Robinson, Lyons, and Larson, "The Portrayal of Religion and Spirituality on Fictional Network Television."

43. In 2012, the beloved children's television and book series *The Berenstain Bears* tackled the challenge in *The Berenstain Bears and the Easter Story* by Jan and Mike Berenstain. In their storybook, they used the context of an Easter pageant to discuss Christ's triumphal entry, death, and resurrection at Easter, using a formula similar to what Schulz used in *A Charlie Brown Christmas*. The Berenstains have produced other religious books, including the 2012 *The Berenstain Bears Holy Bible, NIrV* (Grand Rapids: Zondervan).

44. Charles M. Schulz, Bible marginalia, Mark 14:36.

45. Ibid., Luke 10:41.

46. Schulz, "Peanuts," *Collegiate Challenge*, 24.

47. Charles M. Schulz, "What Do You Do with a Dog That Doesn't Talk?" *TV Guide*, February 23, 1980, 22–26, see 23, 26.

48. Ibid., 22.

CHAPTER 7

1. "Toasts of the President and Queen Elizabeth II of the United Kingdom at a Dinner Honoring the Queen in San Francisco, California: March 3, 1983," *Ronald Reagan Presidential Library and Museum*, October 6, 2009, Web, accessed November 29, 2014.

2. Milton Friedman and Rose D. Friedman, *Two Lucky People: Memoirs* (Chicago: University of Chicago Press, 1998), 569.

3. Letter from Charles M. Schulz to Mrs. Ronald (Nancy) Reagan, March 7, 1983.

4. Lee Mendelson, personal correspondence, November 29, 2014.

5. Because of the ambitious nature of their work, including finishing other *Peanuts* animation titles at the same time, the studio had to hire many freelancers to complete the work on *This is America, Charlie Brown*, adding extra responsibility for the director who had to more frequently spot-check the work to make sure the drawings of Sparky's unique characters stayed on model.

6. Jean Schulz, personal interview, December 1, 2014.

7. Bell was voiced by master voice actor Frank Welker. Welker's extensive voice acting career includes the villain leader Megatron in the *Transformers* animated series, the young Kermit the Frog in Jim Henson's *The Muppet Babies*, the monkey Abu in Disney's *Aladdin*, and Jim Davis's comic strip cat Garfield after the original voice actor for the animated programs, Lorenzo Music, passed away. In *This is America, Charlie Brown*, Welker also provided the voices for Theodore Roosevelt, Abraham Lincoln, Thomas Edison, Wilbur Wright, and Squanto. He returned to voice the mayor in 2000's *It's the Pied Piper, Charlie Brown*.

8. Michael Cavna, "'A Charlie Brown Thanksgiving': On Charles Schulz's Birthday, Here are 7 Things You Don't Know About Tonight's Holiday 'Peanuts' Specials," *Washington Post*, November 26, 2014.

9. In certain reprints of the episode, the contrast and saturation make the cross difficult to see. The only other labeled Bible, marked "Holy Bible," appears in the eighteen-minute 2002 television special *Charlie Brown's Christmas Tales* when Linus and Lucy are arguing over whether the Bible requires that he buy her a Christmas present. "You can't bluff an old theologian," he tells her.

10. Lincoln did use the phrase in his final delivered speech, widely considered one of the greatest in American history.

11. Tony Kennedy and Jeremy Gerard, "'Peanuts' Revised After Objections," *St. Petersburg Times*, October 18, 1988.

12. August 1, 1968.

13. July 10, 1970.

14. June 6, 1993.

15. Groth, "Schulz at 3 O'Clock in the Morning," 33.

16. Schulz, "Regarding Schulz and Peanuts," 69.

17. Groth, "Schulz at 3 O'Clock in the Morning," 35.

18. Martie Zad, "Tiny Tots' Tapes Offer a Variety of Animals," *Washington Post*, July 9, 1995, FC5.

19. Retroflix Reviews, "Cartoon Review: This is America, Charlie Brown 'The Mayflower Voyagers,'" November 13, 2010, Web, accessed November 31, 2014.

20. Charles M. Schulz, *The Charlie Brown Dictionary*, vol. 2 (New York: World Publishing, 1973), 82.

21. Charles M. Schulz, *The Charlie Brown Dictionary*, vol. 3 (New York: World Publishing, 1973), 161.

22. Decades after the release of *This is America, Charlie Brown*, an Arkansas school district would come under fire after one parent complained to the Arkansas Society of Free Thinkers (ASFT) when that parent heard that a public school would be taking a group of second graders to see a stage adaptation of *A Charlie Brown Christmas*, complete with recitation from the Gospel of Luke, at a local church. The school district argued that there were no constitutional violations at play and did not cancel the field trip. When the ASFT continued to protest, the church canceled the special matinee performance in order to save the school from further backlash, and instead invited any interested parents to bring their children to the regularly scheduled public performance (Johnson, 2012).

23. Wilson, "A Visit with Charles Schulz," 40.

24. David W. Moore, "Two of Three Americans Feel Religion Can Answer Most of Today's Problems," *Gallup*, March 29, 2000.

A quarter of century later, those numbers would remain high, with 79 percent of adult Americans self-identifying as having a personal religious affiliation, 73 percent self-identifying as Christian (PEW Forum on Religion & Public Life, 2012).

25. Jill Schulz, personal interview, July 12, 2013.

26. Thorkelson, "Cartoonist Turns Over Tenth of 'Peanuts' to the Church," 29.

27. Ibid., 39.

28. April 3, 1968.

29. Mary Ellen (Kinsey) Rudee, who was also given voice credit on the program, performed the rest of the routine.

30. Amy (Schulz) Johnson, personal interview, October 11–12, 2013.

31. Alan Haacke, "Amy Schulz Skates with Peanuts Gang and Glides to New Life," *Deseret News*, November 17, 1979, P7.

32. Brad Lowder, personal interview, December 30, 2013.

33. *Everyman*, "Happiness is a Warm Puppy."

34. Ibid.

35. *Doctrine and Covenants*, 1:30.

36. Wilson, "A Visit with Charles Schulz," 33.

37. Marty Jones, "A Chat with Charles Schulz," *Aspiring Cartoonist*, no. 2 (1994): 2–5, in *Charles M. Schulz: Conversations*, 153–58, see 154.

Sparky commemorated the event in the October 4, 1970, Peppermint Patty strip. He later recalled giving Amy the flowers on her fifteenth, not fourteenth birthday, a difference that neither Amy's memories nor her diaries could reconcile. Given that he had to write his strips ten weeks in advance, Sparky would have likely written the October 4 strip almost exactly on Amy's fourteenth birthday, August 5, 1970. Perhaps he spoiled his surprise for her one year early in the strip, but it is more likely that he simply remembered the event one birthday later than it was.

38. Jill Schulz, personal interview, July 12, 2013.

39. According to Mormonism's sacred text, the *Doctrine and Covenants* (a series of revelations given to their prophets, such as Joseph Smith), the Melchizedek Priesthood refers to those blessed to officiate in matters of the LDS church, a power and authority restored to the church after the Apostles Peter, James, and John were said to have literally visited Joseph Smith. The notion of a high priesthood after the order of Melchizedek has its roots in the New Testament, with the writer to the Hebrews speaking of Christ as such a priest. Schulz, however, did not see this as an indication that further revelation would come in restoration of such a literal priesthood. He noted in his Bible at the relevant passage in Hebrews chapter 7 that "to the ancients, this kind of fanciful writing meant more than to us." His trusted *The Interpreter's Bible* volume on Hebrews argued that the reference to Melchizedek was solely an argumentative move to justify calling Christ a priest at all, a priesthood that early Jewish converts would be highly resistant to accept.

40. Amy Schulz, personal interview, November 25, 2014.

41. October 31, 1982.

42. Letter from Charles M. Schulz to Amy Schulz, May 11, 1982.

43. Letter from Charles M. Schulz to Amy Schulz, March 22, 1982.

44. Letter from Charles M. Schulz to Amy Schulz, March 31, 1982.

45. Letter from Charles M. Schulz to Amy Schulz, November 25, 1981.

46. Letter from Charles M. Schulz to Amy Schulz, October 14, 1981.

47. Letter from Charles M. Schulz to Amy Schulz, October 9, 1981.

48. Letter from Charles M. Schulz to Amy Schulz, February 1, 1982.

49. Letter from Charles M. Schulz to Amy Schulz, December 29, 1981.

50. Letter from Charles M. Schulz to Amy Schulz, June 8, 1982.

51. Letter from Charles M. Schulz to Amy Schulz, November 25, 1981.

52. Letter from Charles M. Schulz to Amy Schulz, November 13, 1981.

53. Meredith (Schulz) Hodges, personal interview, June 3, 2014.

CHAPTER 8

1. April 9, 1985.

2. July 8, 1977.

3. December 12, 1983.

4. August 9, 1983.

5. August 9, 1994.

6. Published in hardcover by Holt, Rinehart and Winston, 1971.

7. Conrad, "You're a Good Man, Charlie Schulz," 15.

8. In 2010, Monte purchased the financially struggling conference, running it successfully with the significant assistance of his girlfriend Nicole Starczak.

9. Schulz, "Regarding Schulz and Peanuts," 59.

10. Lesley M. M. Blume, "Barnaby Conrad: Author, Matador, Bon Vivant, and Thorn in Hemingway's Side," *Paris Review*, March 4, 2013.

11. April 21, 1961.

12. Letter from Theodor Geisel to Charles M. Schulz, May 8, 1961, Charles M. Schulz Museum and Research Center, Santa Rosa, California.

13. Billie Jean King, "Billie Jean King in Conversation at the Charles M. Schulz Museum and Research Center," interview with Karen Johnson, Charles M. Schulz Museum and Research Center, January 15, 2012.

14. Marshall and Groth, "Charles Schulz Interview," 18.

15. Michael Robertson, "Could the Father of 'Peanuts' Ever Retire?" *San Francisco Chronicle*, May 21, 1985, 22.

16. Schulz, *Peanuts Jubilee*, 100.

17. Mark Farinas, "Exactly What Kind of Christian Was Charles Schultz?" *Two Thousand Man*, December 23, 2005, Web, accessed April 11, 2006.

18. Isaacs, "Charles Schulz: Comic Strips Aren't Art," 93.

19. Griessman, "Atlanta Weekly Interview: Charles Schulz," 116.

20. Zachary Kroger, "Atheist," *YouTube*, July 29, 2006, Web, accessed September 29, 2014.

21. Virginia Heffernan, "God and Man on YouTube," *New York Times*, November 4, 2007.

22. Letter from Charles Schulz to Frank Dieffenwierth, July 17, 1948, Frank Dieffenwierth Manuscript Collection, SC2003.002, Charles M. Schulz Museum and Research Center, Santa Rosa, California.

23. Wilson, "A Visit with Charles Schulz," 40.

24. Ibid., 40–41.

25. *Everyman*, "Happiness is a Warm Puppy."

26. Gary Lombardi, "Sparky University, Unit 5: Sparky & Spirituality," Charles M. Schulz Museum and Research Center, August 21, 2008.

27. *The Interpreter's Bible*, vol. 7, 563.

28. Schulz, "Peanuts," *Collegiate Challenge*, 24.

29. Short, "Jesus Laughed!"

30. Griessman, "Atlanta Weekly Interview: Charles Schulz," 116.

31. Jonas, "The 'Peanuts' Man Talks About Children," 28.

32. Griessman, "Atlanta Weekly Interview: Charles Schulz," 116.

33. Letter from Charles M. Schulz to Amy Schulz, March 22, 1982.

34. Letter from Charles M. Schulz to Amy Schulz, March 31, 1982.

35. Joanne Greenberg, personal interview, May 22, 2014.

36. Schulz's answers to questions confirmed that he thought of atheists as a separate group of which he was not a part. "Your quotation of scripture could offend atheists," Groth had joked to him in 1997. "Oh who cares?" Schulz quipped back. "We're going to offend somebody. But at least I know what I'm taking about there" (36).

37. Don Melichar, "A Leap of Faith: The New Right and Secular Humanism," *English Journal* 72, no. 6 (October 1983): 55–58.

38. Christopher P. Tourney, *God's Own Scientists: Creationists in a Secular World* (New Brunswick, NJ: Rutgers University Press, 1994). See also Leo Pfeffer, "How Religious is Secular Humanism?" *Humanist*, September/October 1988, 13–18, 50.

39. Johnson, *Good Grief*, 137.

40. Thorkelson, "Cartoonist Turns Over Tenth of 'Peanuts' to the Church," 39.

41. Craig Schulz, personal correspondence, June 3, 2014.

42. "Cartoonist Charles Schulz to Head Capital Campaign for National D-Day Memorial," *PR Newswire*, October 16, 1997.

43. R. Eugene Sterner, "A Personal Tribute to Sparky," in *They Called Him Sparky*, 24–29, see 28.

44. Robert H. Reardon, "Remembering Charles Schulz," in *They Called Him Sparky*, 12–21, see 19–20.

45. Bernetta Nelson, personal interview, June 2, 2014.

46. Walt Ortman, personal interview, June 2, 2014.

47. Letter from Charles Schulz to Marvin Hartman, June 17, 1982, Charles M. Schulz Museum and Research Center, Santa Rosa, California.

48. Madelyn Hartman, "Sparky Draws Marvin," in *They Called Him Sparky*, 37–40, see 37.

49. May 22, 1985.

50. Letter from Charles Schulz to Marvin Hartman, September 12, 1985, Charles M. Schulz Museum and Research Center, Santa Rosa, California.

51. H. A. Williams, *True Wilderness*. 1965. (London: Continuum, 2002), 166.

52. Ibid., 167.

53. Brian Kolodiejchuk, ed., *Mother Teresa: Come be My Light* (New York: Random House, 2007), 198.

54. On February 24, 1986, Lucy bowed with hands folded by her bed and said, "And I pray that I might be a better person . . . and that I will get even better . . and better, and better, and better, and . . that's enough!"

55. Hall, "A Conversation with Charles Schulz: or the Psychology of Simplicity," 60.

56. *Everyman*, "Happiness is a Warm Puppy."

57. Kenneth F. Hall, personal interview, July 8, 2013.

58. Groth, "Schulz at 3 O'Clock in the Morning," 21.

59. Mark 12:28–31.

60. With this note, he included these references: Judges (Matthew 7, John 12:44, Romans 2:1, Luke 6:37, Psalm 24); Keepers (Genesis 4); Neighbors (Luke 10); Servants (Luke 22:24).

CHAPTER 9

1. Stephanie Revelli, personal interview, June 15, 2014.

2. Joan Secchia, personal interview, May 12, 2014.

3. Groth, "Schulz at 3 O'Clock in the Morning," 19.

4. Letter from Charles M. Schulz to Frank Dieffenwierth, July 10, 1949, Frank Dieffenwierth Manuscript Collection, SC2003.002, Charles M. Schulz Museum and Research Center, Santa Rosa, California.

5. Groth, "Schulz at 3 O'Clock in the Morning," 46.

6. Sandi Patty, personal interview, November 12, 2013.

7. July 24, 1995.

8. September 6, 1995.

9. December 18–19, 1985; reprised in 1992's *It's Christmastime Again, Charlie Brown.*

10. Eileen Ogintz, "'Peanuts'-eye View of Cancer," *Chicago Tribune*, March 16, 1990.

11. Becky Reardon, personal interview, October 17, 2013.

12. Jean Schulz, "Why, Charlie Brown, Why?" *Jean Schulz's Blog, Charles M. Schulz Museum and Research Center*, February 27, 2013, Web, accessed September 29, 2014.

13. Letter from Charles M. Schulz to Amy Schulz, April 7, 1982.

14. Santa Rosa Memorial Hospital, *Lamplighter*, Fall 1981, 3.

15. Nick Gazin, "Nick Gazin's Comic Book Love-In #28," *Vice*, August 10, 2011, Web, accessed September 29, 2014.

16. Letter from Charles M. Schulz to Amy Schulz, August 27, 1981.

17. Schulz, "What Do You Do with a Dog That Doesn't Talk?" 24.

18. Sharon Waxman, "Charlie Blue: The Fragile Child Lurking Inside the Cartoonist," *Washington Post*, October 22, 1996, D1–D2, see D2.

19. Groth, "Schulz at 3 O'Clock in the Morning," 33.

20. Hall, "A Conversation with Charles Schulz: or the Psychology of Simplicity," 60.

21. Schulz, "But a Comic Strip Has to Grow," 165.

22. Charles M. Schulz, "Peanuts—How It All Began," *Liberty*, Winter 1973, 14–16, in *My Life with Charlie Brown*, 85–87, see 87.

23. March 14, May 15, and May 29, 1995.

24. Monte Schulz, personal correspondence, September 27, 2012.

25. Schulz, "But a Comic Strip Has to Grow," 168.

26. Schulz, "What Do You Do with a Dog That Doesn't Talk?" 26.

27. Al Roker, "Cartoonist Charles Schulz," *Today Show*, NBC, January 3, 2000, Television.

28. Gary Lombardi, personal interview, October 28, 2011.

29. Groth, "Schulz at 3 O'Clock in the Morning," 19.

30. Ibid.

31. James 5:17.

32. May 14, 1973.

33. *Everyman*, "Happiness is a Warm Puppy."

34. Ibid.

35. May 18, 1986; reprised for 2003's *Lucy Must Be Traded, Charlie Brown.*

36. January 8, 1981.

37. Psalm 35:1.

38. February 12, 1966.

39. Marvin Forbes, "The Valleys of Life," c. 1982.

40. Charles Bartley, "A Celebration of Life in Loving Memory of Charles Monroe Schulz," public memorial, Santa Rosa, California, February 21, 2000.

41. Amy (Schulz) Johnson, personal interview, June 15, 2000.

42. Forbes, "The Valleys of Life."

43. Andy Meisler, "Don't Grow Up," *New Choices*, June 1995, 56–59, in *My Life with Charlie Brown*, 60–66, see 65.

44. Letter from Family Christian bookstore to Jeannie Schulz and family, February 17, 2000, Charles M. Schulz Museum and Research Center, Santa Rosa, California.

45. Letter from Jean Schulz to Family Christian bookstore, March 2000, Charles M. Schulz Museum and Research Center, Santa Rosa, California.

46. The portrait of Jesus was a print of Warner Sallman's popular "Head of Christ," marketed and distributed by publisher Kriebel & Bates, two employees of the Church of God's Gospel Trumpet Company in the 1940s.

47. Renamed the Wells Fargo Center for the Arts in 2005.

48. One year later, another of Amy's children would stand in as the surrogate at a Mormon baptism service for Charles Schulz. February 12 was a Monday, a family day for the LDS church, and thus the temple was closed. At 5:30 a.m. on February 13 they held the service. LDS doctrine teaches that baptism is essential for salvation and that proxy baptism allows the dead who are living in the spirit world the ability to accept or reject the act done on their behalf in order to proceed in their own afterlife process of becoming like God. Representing Sparky's work at the ceremony was *Drabble* cartoonist Kevin Fagan.

49. At the 1990 public memorial for Muppets creator Jim Henson, cast members with puppets in hand took the stage and also performed "Just One Person." The number had originally been written for 1975's *Snoopy: The Musical*, which was only a moderate success. In 1977, Bernadette Peters and Robin the Frog (Jerry Nelson) covered the song on *The Muppet Show*. At Henson's memorial, Kermit the Frog was not on stage for the number. He had been performed by Henson.

50. At the memorial service, Father Lombardi revised the wording to make it more accessible: "When we know not how to pray, the good Lord intercedes for us with sighs too deep for words."

EPILOGUE

1. "Sparky put on the Christmas Ice Show for fifteen or so years," Jeannie said, "and when we decided to stop that event the family felt it would be important that the Arena continue to have community events."

2. Schulz himself never fully owned the rights to his characters; the obligatory relinquishing of rights to the syndicate was customary in cartooning.

3. Chavon Sutton, "Good Grief: Peanuts Gang Rights Sold for $175 million," *CNN Money*, April 27, 2010.

4. Barrier, "Charles M. Schulz."

5. Ibid.

6. Paige Braddock, personal interview, November 1, 2011.

7. Charles M. Schulz Creative Associates, *Peanuts Quick-Reference Art Guide* (Santa Rosa, CA, 2009).

8. Paige Braddock, personal interview.

9. Ibid.

10. Team member, Charles M. Schulz Creative Associates, personal interview, November 1, 2011.

11. "Media Information on Christian Retail," *CBA* (formerly called Christian Booksellers Association), 2011, Web, accessed November 24, 2012.

12. Anne L. Borden, "Making Money, Saving Souls: Christian Bookstores and the Commodification of Christianity," in *Religion, Media, and the Marketplace*, ed. Lynn Schofield Clark, 67–89, see 68 (Piscataway, NJ: Rutgers University Press, 2007).

13. "About CBA," *CBA* (formerly Christian Booksellers Association), 2011, Web, accessed November 24, 2012.

14. The passage in Nehemiah tells of the Old Testament priest Ezra reading the Law of Moses to the Israelites who wept when hearing it; the governor Nehemiah then instructed the people that the day is "holy to our Lord. Do not grieve, for the joy of the Lord is your strength." In verse 12, the people went away to eat and drink and "to celebrate with great joy because they now understood the words that had been made known to them."

15. Charles M. Schulz Creative Associates, *Peanuts Quick-Reference Art Guide*.

16. Paige Braddock, personal interview.

17. Ibid.

18. Elisabetta Porcu, "Popular Culture in Japan: Buddhist Temples, Icons, and Branding," *Journal of Religion and Popular Culture* 26, no. 2 (2014): 157–72.

19. E.g., September 18, 1977.

20. Team member, Charles M. Schulz Creative Associates, personal interview, November 1, 2011.

21. Peggy Wrightsman-Parolin, personal correspondence, November 13, 2012.

22. The response to unauthorized use of copyrighted *Peanuts* material has shifted over the years, estimated in 1989 to be a $1 million per year cost to stop instances like a group of Hare Krishnas who allegedly had a warehouse full of bootleg *Peanuts* products. In 2012, the Peanuts.com site of Peanuts Worldwide suggested that action against copyright violation would be directed uniquely at content that used the characters "in an unfavorable fashion."

23. John 8:7 (KJV): "So when they continued asking him, he lifted up himself, and said unto them, He that is without sin among you, let him first cast a stone at her."

24. Michael Cavna, "You're A Good Plan, Charlie Brown: A Peek into the Meticulous Vision Behind 2015's 'Peanuts' Feature Film," *Washington Post*, April 7, 2014.

25. "Been Thinking About Snoopy," *RBC (Radio Bible Class) Ministries*, Grand Rapids, Michigan, August 2004.

26. Matthew 5:4–5.

BIBLIOGRAPHY

"About CBA." *CBA* (formerly Christian Booksellers Association), 2011. Web, accessed November 24, 2012.

Aristotle. *On Rhetoric*. Trans. George A. Kennedy. 1st ed. New York: Oxford University Press, 1991.

Barnes, Harry Elmer. "The Role of Religion in a Secular Age." *Scientific Monthly* 28, no. 5 (1929): 430–45.

Barney, Chuck. "Holiday Classics Here for New Generation." *Free Lance-Star*, November 30, 2000, 6–7.

Barrier, Michael. "Charles M. Schulz." *MichaelBarrier.com*, 1988/2003. Web, accessed March 23, 2014.

"Been Thinking About Snoopy." *RBC (Radio Bible Class) Ministries*. Grand Rapids, Michigan, August 2004.

Berkowitz, Leonard. "Words and Symbols as Stimuli to Aggressive Responses." In *Control of Aggression: Implications from Basic Research*, ed. John F. Knutson. Chicago: Aldine-Atherton, 1973.

Berkowitz, Leonard, and Karen Heimer Rogers. "A Priming Effect Analysis of Media Influences." In *Perspectives on Media Effects*, eds. Jennings Bryant and Dolf Zillmann, 57–81. Hillsdale, NJ: Lawrence Erlbaum Associates, 1986.

"Bill Melendez." Interview by Jennifer Howard. *Academy of Television Arts and Sciences Foundation*, June 23, 2001. Web, accessed September 28, 2014.

Bitzer, Lloyd. "Aristotle's Enthymeme Revisited." *Quarterly Journal of Speech*, no. 45 (1959): 399–408.

Blume, Lesley M. M. "Barnaby Conrad: Author, Matador, Bon Vivant, and Thorn in Hemingway's Side." *Paris Review*, March 4, 2013.

Borden, Anne L. "Making Money, Saving Souls: Christian Bookstores and the Commodification of Christianity." In *Religion, Media, and the Marketplace*, ed. Lynn Schofield Clark, 67–89. Piscataway, NJ: Rutgers University Press, 2007.

Brown, Charles E. *The Hope of His Coming*. Anderson, IN: Gospel Trumpet Company, 1927.

Canby, Vincent. "Screen: Good Old Charlie Brown Finds a Home." *New York Times*, December 5, 1969, 50.

"Cartoonist Charles Schulz to Head Capital Campaign for National D-Day Memorial." *PR Newswire*, October 16, 1997.

Cavna, Michael. "You're A Good Plan, Charlie Brown: A Peek into the Meticulous Vision Behind 2015's 'Peanuts' Feature Film." *Washington Post*, April 7, 2014.

Charles M. Schulz Creative Associates. *Peanuts Quick-Reference Art Guide*. Santa Rosa, CA, 2009.

Clarke, Scott H. "Created in Whose Image? Religious Characters on Network Television." *Journal of Media and Religion* 4, no. 3 (2005): 137–53.

Cole, Peter, Frankie Frankeny, and Leslie Jonath. *Christmas Trees: Fun and Festive Ideas*. San Francisco: Chronicle Books, 2002.

"Comics: Good Grief." *Time*, April 9, 1965, 80–84.

Conrad, Barnaby. "You're a Good Man, Charlie Schulz." *New York Times Magazine*, April 16, 1967, 32–35, 42, 44, 46, 49, 52, 54. In *Charles M. Schulz: Conversations*, ed. M. Thomas Inge, 15–27.

Curtin, Michael. "Newton Minow." In *The Encyclopedia of Television*, ed. Horace Newcomb. London: Routledge, 1997.

Dardedar. "Re: Religious Cartoons." *phpBB*, May 8, 2009. Web, accessed February 26, 2014.

Doan, Richard K. "CBS Plans Second Charlie Brown Special." *New York Herald Tribune*, December 15, 1965, 21.

Eco, Umberto. *Apocalypse Postponed*, ed. Robert Lumley. Bloomington: Indiana University Press, 1994.

Edgerton, Gary R. *The Columbia History of American Television*. New York: Columbia University Press, 2009.

Everyman. "Happiness is a Warm Puppy." Television interview of Charles M. Schulz by Peter France. BBC1, 1977.

Farinas, Mark. "Exactly What Kind of Christian Was Charles Schultz?" *Two Thousand Man*, December 23, 2005. Web, accessed April 11, 2006.

Fiske, Edward B. "Liturgies Embracing More Pop Art Forms." *New York Times*, May 15, 1967, 1, 48.

Fortin, Cassandra A. "It's beginning to look a lot like Christmas (1958)." *Baltimore Sun*, October 26, 2008.

Foster, Bob. "Screenings." *San Mateo Times*, October 21, 1965.

Fraser, Don, and Derrick Bang, eds. *Security Blankets: How Peanuts Touched Our Lives*. Kansas City: Andrews McMeel Publishing, 2009.

Friedman, Milton, and Rose D. Friedman. *Two Lucky People: Memoirs*. Chicago: University of Chicago Press, 1998.

Friendly, Fred W. *Due to Circumstances Beyond Our Control* . . . New York: Random House, 1967.

Gerbner, George, Larry Gross, Michael Morgan, and Nancy Signorielli. "Living with Television: The Dynamics of the Cultivation Process." In *Perspectives on Media Effects*, eds. Jennings Bryant and Dolf Zillmann, 17–40. Hillsdale, NJ: Lawrence Erlbaum Associates, 1986.

Gieryn, Thomas F., George M. Bevins, and Stephen C. Zehr. "Professionalization of American Scientists: Public Science in the Creation/Evolution Trials." *American Sociological Review* 50, no. 3 (1985): 392–409.

"Good Grief, $150 Million!" *Newsweek*, December 27, 1971, 40–44.

Gorney, Cynthia. "The *Peanuts* Progenitor." *Washington Post*, October 2, 1985, D1–D3.

Gould, Jack. "C.B.S. is Dropping Its Theater Films." *New York Times*, January 10, 1972.

Gowran, Clay. "Charlie Brown & Co. Bewitching on TV." *Chicago Tribune*, October 28, 1966, B8.

Greenspoon, Leonard. "The Bible in the Funny Papers" *Bible Review* 7, no. 5 (October 1991): 30–41.

———. "The New Testament in the Comics." *Bible Review* 9, no. 6 (December 1993): 40–45.

Griessman, Eugene. "Atlanta Weekly Interview: Charles Schulz." *Atlanta Weekly*, November 15, 1981. In *Charles M. Schulz: Conversations*, ed. M. Thomas Inge, 111–20.

Groth, Gary. "Schulz at 3 O'Clock in the Morning." *Comics Journal*, no. 200 (December 1997): 3–48.

Haacke, Alan. "Amy Schulz Skates with Peanuts Gang and Glides to New Life." *Deseret News*, November 17, 1979, P7.

Hall, Kenneth F. "It Scares Me: Says the Inventor of Peanuts For He has Thirty Million Fans." *Upward*, February 1, 1959, 14–19.

Hall, Mary Harrington. "A Conversation with Charles Schulz: or the Psychology of Simplicity." *Psychology Today*, January 1968, 19–21, 66–69. In *Charles M. Schulz: Conversations*, ed. M. Thomas Inge, 45–62.

"Halloween: Pranks & Pumpkins are Traditional." *Life*, November 3, 1941, 69.

"Happiness is to Dance with Snoopy and Talk with his Creator." *Youth* 19, no. 6. United Church Press, March 24, 1968.

Heffernan, Virginia. "God and Man on YouTube." *New York Times*, November 4, 2007.

The Interpreter's Bible. New York: Abingdon Press, 1952.

Inge, M. Thomas, ed., *Charles M. Schulz: Conversations*. (Jackson: University Press of Mississippi, 2000).

Isaacs, Stan. "Charles Schulz: Comic Strips Aren't Art." *Newsday*, August 28, 1977, 15–17, 36, 38. In *Charles M. Schulz: Conversations*, ed. M. Thomas Inge, 86–97.

Johnson, Rheta Grimsley. *Good Grief: The Story of Charles M. Schulz*. New York: Pharos Books, 1989.

Jonas, Gerald. "The 'Peanuts' Man Talks About Children." *Family Circle*, May 1968, 20–28, 80–82.

Jones, Marty. "A Chat with Charles Schulz." *Aspiring Cartoonist*, no. 2 (1994): 2–5. In *Charles M. Schulz: Conversations*, ed. M. Thomas Inge, 153–58.

Joseph, Mark. "Mark Joseph Interviews Charles Schultz." *The Bully! Pulpit*, 1997.

King, Billie Jean. "Billie Jean King in Conversation at the Charles M. Schulz Museum and Research Center." Interview with Karen Johnson. Charles M. Schulz Museum and Research Center, January 15, 2012.

Kolodiejchuk, Brian, ed. *Mother Teresa: Come be My Light*. New York: Random House, 2007.

Kroger, Zachary. "Atheist." *YouTube*, July 29, 2006. Web, accessed September 29, 2014.

Laurent, Lawrence. "Laurent Suggests." *Washington Post*, October 27, 1966, H12.
———. "Loser in Peanuts Finally a Winner." *Washington Post*, December 11, 1965, E18.
———. "TV 'Peanuts' is a Delight." *Washington Post*, October 29, 1966, reprinted from October 28 late edition, 28.
Lewis, Todd V. "Religious Rhetoric and the Comic Frame in The Simpsons." *Journal of Media and Religion* 1, no. 3 (2002): 153–65.
Lind, Stephen J. "Christmas in the 1960s: A Charlie Brown Christmas, Religion, and the Conventions of the Television Genre." *Journal of Religion and Popular Culture* 26, no. 1 (2014).
———. "Reading Peanuts: The Secular and the Sacred." *ImageTexT: Interdisciplinary Comics Studies* 4, no. 2 (2008).
Lindsey, Donald B., and John Hereen. "Where the Sacred Meets the Profane: Religion in the Comics Pages." *Review of Religious Research* 34, no. 1 (September 1992): 63–77.
Liverett, David, ed. *They Called Him Sparky: Friends' Reminiscences of Charles Schulz.* Anderson, IN: Chinaberry House, 2006.
Lowry, Cynthia. "Charlie Brown is Better Left Alone." *Kentucky New Era*, December 10, 1965, 6.
Maltin, Leonard. "An Interview with Charles M. Schulz." In *Charlie Brown: A Boy for All Seasons*, 19–23. New York: Museum of Broadcasting, 1984. In *Charles M. Schulz: Conversations*, ed. M. Thomas Inge, 121–27.
Marshall, Rick, and Gary Groth. "Charles Schulz Interview." *Nemo: The Classic Comics Library* 31, no. 1 (January 1992): 5–24.
Martin, Judith. "Peanuts: 'It's Not Funny.'" *Washington Post*, June 30, 1970, D7.
Martin, Ken. "Have It Your Own Way, Charles Schulz!" *Nova*, 1972, 62–65.
McCloud, Scott. *Understanding Comics: The Invisible Art.* New York: Harper Perennial, 1993.
McGuire, Scott. "The Peanuts Animation and Video Page." *FiveCentsPlease.org*, February 23, 2012. Web, accessed March 31, 2012.
"Media Information on Christian Retail." *CBA* (formerly called Christian Booksellers Association), 2011. Web, accessed November 24, 2012.
Meisler, Andy. "Don't Grow Up." *New Choices*, June 1995, 56–59. In Charles M. Schulz, *My Life with Charlie Brown*, ed. M. Thomas Inge, 60–66.
Melichar, Don. "A Leap of Faith: The New Right and Secular Humanism." *English Journal* 72, no. 6 (October 1983): 55–58.
Mendelson, Lee. *A Charlie Brown Christmas: The Making of a Tradition.* New York: HarperCollins, 2005.
———. *It's the Great Pumpkin, Charlie Brown: The Making of a Television Classic.* New York: HarperCollins, 2006.
Mendelson, Lee, and Charles M. Schulz. *Charlie Brown and Charlie Schulz.* New York: New American Library, 1971.
Michaelis, David. *Schulz and Peanuts: A Biography.* New York: HarperCollins, 2007.
Miller, Mark. "It's Tough to Be a Little Kid." *Newsweek*, January 1, 2000, 25.
Moore, David W. "Two of Three Americans Feel Religion Can Answer Most of Today's Problems." *Gallup*, March 29, 2000.

Morrow, Hugh. "The Success of an Utter Failure." *Saturday Evening Post*, January 12, 1957, 34–35, 70–72. In *Charles M. Schulz: Conversations*, ed. M. Thomas Inge, 3–14.

National Christmas Tree Association. "History of Christmas Trees." 2005.

Nelson, Samuel P. "Religion in the Workplace and the Problem of the First Amendment." In *Religion, Politics, and American Identity*, eds. David S. Gutterman and Andrew R. Murphy, 177–98. New York: Lexington Books, 2006.

Nichols, Lewis. "In and Out of Books." *New York Times Book Review*, March 12, 1967, 8.

Nyeberg, Amy Kiste. *Seal of Approval: The History of the Comics Code Authority*. Jackson: University Press of Mississippi, 1998.

Nielsen Company. "More of What We Want: The Cross-Platform Report Q1 2014." June 2014.

O'Flaherty, Terrence. "Christmas in Sebastopol." *San Francisco Chronicle*, December 9, 1965.

Ogintz, Eileen. "'Peanuts'-eye View of Cancer." *Chicago Tribune*, March 16, 1990.

Pauer, Frank. "A Conversation with Charles Schulz." *Dayton Daily News and Journal Herald Magazine*, May 3, 1987, 1–4, 13. In *Charles M. Schulz: Conversations*, ed. M. Thomas Inge, 143–52.

Perelman, Chaim, and L. Olbrechts-Tyteca. *The New Rhetoric*. Trans. John Wilkinson and Purcell Weaver. Notre Dame: University of Notre Dame Press, 1969/2000.

Pfeffer, Leo. "How Religious is Secular Humanism?" *Humanist*, September/October 1988, 13–18, 50.

Phelan, Jim. "Penthouse Interview: Charles M. Schulz." *Penthouse*, October 1971, 26, 29, 30, 33.

"Phil Roman." Interview by Jennifer Howard. *Academy of Television Arts and Sciences Foundation*, June 25, 2002. Web, accessed September 28, 2014.

Plantinga, Alvin. "Reason and Belief in God." In *Faith and Rationality: Reason and Belief in God*, eds. Alvin Plantinga and Nicholas Wolterstorff, 17–93. Notre Dame: University of Notre Dame Press, 1983.

Porcu, Elisabetta. "Popular Culture in Japan: Buddhist Temples, Icons, and Branding." *Journal of Religion and Popular Culture* 26, no. 2 (2014): 157–72.

Retroflix Reviews. "Cartoon Review: This is America, Charlie Brown 'The Mayflower Voyagers.'" November 13, 2010. Web, accessed November 31, 2014.

Roberts, Leaf. "A Faithful Witness: Outreaching Love." *Sebastopol United Methodist Church*. 2012.

Robertson, Michael. "Could the Father of 'Peanuts' Ever Retire?" *San Francisco Chronicle*, May 21, 1985, 22.

Roker, Al. "Cartoonist Charles Schulz." *Today Show*. NBC, January 3, 2000. Television.

Rosenthal, Michele. "Turn it Off!: TV Criticism in the Christian Century Magazine." In *Practicing Religion in the Age of the Media*, eds. Stewart M. Hoover and Lynn Schofield Clark, 138–62. New York: Columbia University Press, 2002.

"The Saga of Charlie Brown." *Variety*, December 22, 1965.

Santa Rosa Memorial Hospital. *Lamplighter*, Fall 1981.

Santino, Jack. "Halloween: The Fantasy and Folklore of All Hallows." *Library of American Folklife Center*, September 1982.

Saunders, William. "All Saints and All Souls." *Arlington Catholic Herald*, 2003.

Schulz, Charles M. "Address to the National Cartoonists Society Annual Convention." La Jolla, California, May 14, 1994. In Charles M. Schulz, *My Life with Charlie Brown*, ed. M. Thomas Inge, 126–39.

———. *Around the World in 45 Years*. Kansas City, MO: Andrews and McMeel, 1994.

———. "But a Comic Strip Has to Grow." *Saturday Review*, April 12, 1969. In Charles M. Schulz, *My Life with Charlie Brown*, ed. M. Thomas Inge, 164–69.

———. "Charles Schulz and Peanuts." *Cartoonist Profiles*, no. 12, December 1971. In Charles M. Schulz, *My Life with Charlie Brown*, ed. M. Thomas Inge, 32–36.

———. *The Charlie Brown Dictionary*. New York: World Publishing, 1973.

———. "Knowing You Are Not Alone." *Decision*, September 1963, 8–9.

———. "Peanuts." *Collegiate Challenge*. In Charles M. Schulz, *My Life with Charlie Brown*, ed. M. Thomas Inge, 20–25.

———. "Peanuts—How It All Began." *Liberty*, Winter 1973, 14–16. In Charles M. Schulz, *My Life with Charlie Brown*, ed. M. Thomas Inge, 85–87.

———. *Peanuts Jubilee: My Life and Art with Charlie Brown and Others*. New York: Holt, Rhinehart and Winston, 1975.

———. "What Do You Do with a Dog That Doesn't Talk?" *TV Guide*, February 23, 1980, 22–26.

Schulz, Charles M., and Kenneth F. Hall. *Two by Fours*. Anderson, IN: Warner Press, 1965.

Schulz, Charles M., and M. Thomas Inge, ed. *My Life with Charlie Brown*. Jackson: University Press of Mississippi, 2010.

Schulz, Charles M., and R. Smith Kiliper. *Charlie Brown, Snoopy and Me*. Garden City, NY: Doubleday & Company, 1980.

Schulz, Jean. "Why, Charlie Brown, Why?" *Jean Schulz's Blog, Charles M. Schulz Museum and Research Center*, February 27, 2013. Web, accessed September 29, 2014.

Schulz, Monte. "Regarding Schulz and Peanuts." *Comics Journal*, no. 290 (2008): 27–78.

"Search for Self" seminar pamphlet. *University of Georgia Student Religious Council*, February 7–11, 1960.

"Security is a Good Show." *Time*, December 10, 1965, 95.

Shalit, Gene. "Good Grief! It's 'A Boy Named Charlie Brown.'" *Look*, January 27, 1970, 68.

Short, Robert L. *The Gospel According to Peanuts*. Louisville: Westminster John Knox Press, 1964.

Skill, Thomas, James D. Robinson, John S. Lyons, and David Larson. "The Portrayal of Religion and Spirituality on Fictional Network Television." *Review of Religious Research* 35, no. 3 (1994): 251–67.

Smith, John W. V. *A Brief History of the Church of God Reformation Movement*. rev. ed. Anderson, IN: Warner Press, 1957.

Smith, Sally Bedell. "Paley's Latest Feat: His Return." *New York Times*, September 11, 1986, D7.

Solomon, Charles. *The Art and Making of Peanuts Animation*. San Francisco: Chronicle Books, 2012.

Sutton, Chavon. "Good Grief: Peanuts Gang Rights Sold for $175 Million." *CNN Money*, April 27, 2010.

Swenson, Jeff. "'The Great Pumpkin' is a Cartoon for Atheists," *Freethunk!* October 13, 2010. Web, accessed February 26, 2014.

Thorkelson, Willmar. "Cartoonist Turns Over Tenth of 'Peanuts' to the Church." *Minneapolis Star*, March 18, 1955, 29, 39.

"Toasts of the President and Queen Elizabeth II of the United Kingdom at a Dinner Honoring the Queen in San Francisco, California: March 3, 1983." *Ronald Reagan Presidential Library and Museum*, October 6, 2009. Web, accessed November 29, 2014.

Toulouse, Mark G. "The Muddled Middle: Protestantism's Encounter with Homosexuality Since the 1960s." In *Sex, Religion, Media*, ed. Dane S. Claussen, 43–64. Lanham, MD: Rowman & Littlefield, 2002.

Tourney, Christopher P. *God's Own Scientists: Creationists in a Secular World*. New Brunswick, NJ: Rutgers University Press, 1994.

Twerski, Abraham J. "Attaining Happiness: Q and A." *Torah Café*, March 2, 2011.

Waxman, Sharon. "Charlie Blue: The Fragile Child Lurking Inside the Cartoonist." *Washington Post*, October 22, 1996, D1–D2.

Williams, H. A. *True Wilderness*. 1965. London: Continuum, 2002.

Wilson, Kenneth. "A Visit with Charles Schulz." *Christian Herald*, September 1967, 14–15, 59–66, 79, 81. In *Charles M. Schulz: Conversations*, ed. M. Thomas Inge, 28–44.

Wittstock, Susan. "Fifty Years of Peanuts." *onCampus* 30, no. 3 (September 14, 2000). Web, accessed November 11, 2012.

Yager, Edward M. *Ronald Reagan's Journey: Democrat to Republican*. Lanham, MD: Rowman & Littlefield, 2006.

Zad, Martie. "Tiny Tots' Tapes Offer a Variety of Animals." *Washington Post*, July 9, 1995, FC5.

INDEX